NEOLIBERAL PARLIAMENTARISM

TOM McDOWELL

NEOLIBERAL PARLIAMENTARISM

The Decline of Parliament at the Ontario Legislature

UNIVERSITY OF TORONTO PRESS
Toronto Buffalo London

Toronto Buffalo London
utorontopress.com

ISBN 978-1-4875-2809-6 (cloth)
ISBN 978-1-4875-2811-9 (EPUB)
ISBN 978-1-4875-2810-2 (PDF)

Library and Archives Canada Cataloguing in Publication

Title: Neoliberal parliamentarism : the decline of parliament at the Ontario Legislature / Tom McDowell.

Names: McDowell, Tom, 1980– author.

Description: Includes bibliographical references and index.

Identifiers: Canadiana (print) 20210224436 | Canadiana (ebook) 20210224533 | ISBN 9781487528096 (cloth) | ISBN 9781487528119 (EPUB) | ISBN 9781487528102 (PDF)

Subjects: LCSH: Ontario. Legislative Assembly. | LCSH: Neoliberalism – Political aspects – Ontario. | LCSH: Ontario – Politics and government – 20th century. | LCSH: Ontario – Politics and government – 21st century.

Classification: LCC JL273.M33 2021 | DDC 328.713 – dc23

University of Toronto Press acknowledges the financial assistance to its publishing program of the Canada Council for the Arts and the Ontario Arts Council, an agency of the Government of Ontario.

Canada Council for the Arts
Conseil des Arts du Canada

Funded by the Government of Canada
Financé par le gouvernement du Canada
Canada

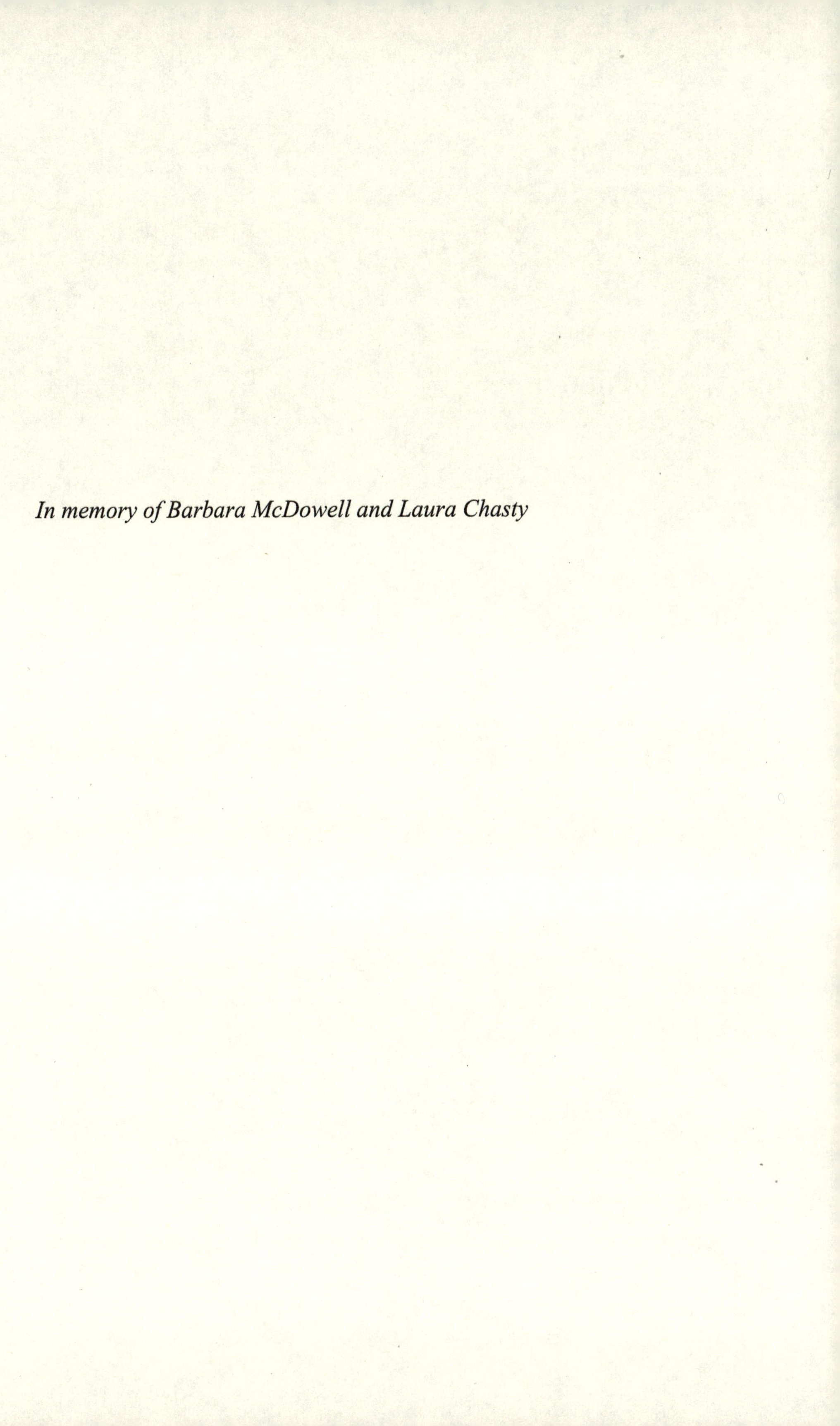

In memory of Barbara McDowell and Laura Chasty

Contents

Tables

Preface

The idea for this book was conceived during my term in 2006–7 as a member of the non-partisan Ontario Legislature Internship Programme (OLIP). Since 1975, OLIP, which is financed and administered by the Ontario Legislative Assembly, has provided recent university graduates with the opportunity to experience the internal workings of the machinery of government by immersing themselves in the daily work of the legislature. Interns are assigned to work with members of provincial Parliament (MPPs) on both the government and the opposition sides of the House, and they are granted the opportunity to observe important, usually in-camera, events, such as House Leaders' and caucus meetings.

Private conversations I had with both MPPs and long-tenured legislative staffers revealed a lingering sense that there had once existed a golden age of parliamentary governance, which had long since passed and was unlikely to ever return. What surprised me the most about this opinion was how widely shared it was and how deeply resigned many were to this inevitability. Even though some of these individuals were affiliated with the governing party, there existed a prevalent sense that the concentration of power in the executive and the decline of Parliament was a process that they – or anyone, for that matter – were powerless to stop.

When I began researching the history of Parliament in Ontario, it became apparent that there were few comprehensive analyses of the evolution of legislative procedure over a period of sufficient length to capture it in such a way that patterns of behaviour could be meaningfully established. Given that parliamentary procedure is determined by a mixture of written rules and unwritten precedents, it can take decades to understand the full impact of reforms.

My objective was to begin to address this gap in the literature – in part, by conducting a comprehensive study of the evolution of parliamentary procedure at the Ontario Legislature. Not only did I know the institution well, but, given its location and its exposure to some of the restrictive procedural strategies that had been applied in other jurisdictions to secure the implementation of state-restructuring reforms, it also served as an excellent case model.

I made the conscious decision early in the research process to rely upon the available historical documentation as the foundation for this research project, rather than interviews with former MPPs and staffers. While elite interviews can be elucidating, they depend upon actors accurately recalling both the circumstances and the rationalizations for decisions that have long passed, thereby introducing the potential for revisionist interpretations of events.

As I worked through the legislative records, certain clear patterns began to emerge. Most of the major reforms to parliamentary procedure at Queen's Park were clustered around the passage of key pieces of neoliberal-restructuring legislation. While governments during the 1980s used this process to break parliamentary stasis and to overcome opposition resistance to neoliberal reforms, by the 1990s, the use of restrictions on the legislature had become increasingly commonplace, part of a broader strategy to bypass democratic opposition to highly contentious austerity measures.

This is not a phenomenon that has been unique to Ontario. Significant ruptures in parliamentary procedure have occurred elsewhere: governments representing parties of both left and right allegiances have attempted to overcome the often slow and deliberate nature of parliamentary procedure by smashing precedent that has evolved over hundreds of years. In the early 1980s, for example, the Social Credit Bennett government made extensive use of closure and other restrictions on the British Columbia Legislative Assembly to secure the implementation of a package of highly controversial austerity reforms (McDowell 2020).

In the mid- to late 1990s, the Labour government in New Zealand rammed a variety of sweeping, neoliberal restructuring measures through Parliament with unparalleled speed. Roger Douglas, the former finance minister responsible for developing these reforms, described his government's institutional strategy this way: "It is uncertainty, not speed, that endangers the success of structural reform programs." To this end, he wrote, "Speed is an essential ingredient in keeping uncertainty down to the lowest possible level" (Roger Douglas, quoted in Marcetic 2017, n.p.).

Similar sentiments were echoed by current Alberta Premier Jason Kenney, who told the press in the lead-up to the 2019 general election that, if elected, his government would move quickly to implement structural reforms to the state apparatus. Revealing that he took inspiration from Douglas, Kenney noted that "the first and most important lesson is that you move quickly . . . you move with speed because speed creates its own momentum." Since governments too often get caught up in "endless process," rapidly moving legislation through institutions "makes it harder for the opponents of reform to obstruct it" (Jason Kenney, quoted in Bellefontaine 2018).

There is, in other words, something fundamentally different about the strategies and approaches to legislative governance in this era that remains poorly understood. As this book discusses, a process has emerged in Ontario that I have called *neoliberal parliamentarism*. It involves the systematic effort to manipulate the rules of Parliament to insulate reforms from legislative scrutiny in support of a broader ideological agenda, and it can be traced all the way back to the early 1980s. This process was most clearly expressed under the premiership of Mike Harris, whose government made major reforms to Parliament to secure the institution of a radical, state-wide administration-restructuring program at breakneck speed.

These procedural reforms, although commonly designed to be temporary and to implement controversial measures on the grounds that they are necessary to address economic or fiscal crises, often become established as precedents and customary elements of parliamentary culture. In other words, these procedural ruptures, designed to implement controversial neoliberal measures, leave long-term scars on the legislature, charting the course for future governments to follow the blueprints that these ruptures have established.

The practical realities of governing in the increasingly contentious political environment under neoliberalism have been accompanied by what Brown (2015) has termed a "neoliberal political rationality," which diminishes the role of democratic institutions. Increasingly, governments have adopted an anti-parliamentary rhetoric that views legislative institutions as impediments to cultivating a market-based, competitive order (47). As the neoliberal state has been reformed to respond primarily to the demands of global competition and to create ideal conditions for free market exchange, parliament has become caught up in a broader systemic and epistemological transition.

This approach was advanced most coherently by seminal neoliberal thinker Friedrich Hayek, who, as is shown in chapter 3, thought that parliamentary sovereignty was the essential problem with modern liberalism. Hayek believed that sovereign parliamentary assemblies held a "mental bias," which made them systemically prone to rent-seeking from special interest groups, leading to the perpetual expansion of the state into social spheres that were best left to the spontaneous nature of market relations (Hayek 1982, 1:143)

In this way, the neoliberal approach to legislative governance has inverted the idea of responsible government. The executive has been increasingly framed as a legitimate "check" on the irrational impulses of the legislature, which is prone to profligate spending and state expansionism. In such a situation, parliament interferes with the executive's ability to respond nimbly to changing market conditions and to cultivate competitive advantage. Allowing time for formalized debate and scrutiny is contradictory to these objectives, appearing as "political" activities that interfere with the rational governance of the market sphere. Instead, the executive's role is to serve as a vehicle for the pursuit of a market order, curtailing the inefficient and autocratic tendencies of a sovereign legislative assembly and cultivating the conditions necessary for the competitive mechanism to function most effectively.

This Hayekian influence is particularly clear in the anti-parliamentary discourse of modern right-wing politicians, and, as is discussed in detail in chapters 8 and 10, it has been used to justify the brazen abuse of parliamentary procedure. This trend has intensified in recent years under the Doug Ford government, which has embraced the international, right-wing, populist trend to portray legislative institutions as an impediment to the pursuit of rational policy approaches (McDowell 2021).

The neoliberalization of parliamentary governance also impacted the actions of the more centrist governments of Bill Davis, Bob Rae, and Dalton McGuinty, whose appeals to economic and fiscal crises to rationalize applying restrictions on the legislature emerged from a similar logic, which prioritized economic rationalism over democratic process and parliamentary scrutiny. Governments from all three parties commonly cited the need to respond to the demands of market competition and the fiscal crisis of the state to justify placing restrictions on the legislature. It has been on these grounds – that economic and fiscal circumstances dictated immediate action – that most of the major parliamentary precedents in Ontario's modern history have been established.

The objective of this book is neither to dismiss existing literature on the decline-of-parliament thesis nor to offer a universal law for changes to procedure in recent decades. Rather, its purpose is to propose an alternative interpretation of history, one that views the structural forces surrounding parliament as essential to its operation. It proceeds from the standpoint that parliament should be studied as a social relation, situated in a particular historical time and place, and subject to influences from broader structural forces. That is, parliament is not a neutral institution; its rules are shaped not only by centuries of historical precedent but also by the social and political forces that condition the ideas and actions of its members.

The book offers a chronological narrative of the evolution of parliamentary procedure at the Ontario Legislature from 1981 to 2021. I attempted to capture the nuance of historical circumstances as they unfolded, largely allowing the actors to describe events and their implications as they understood them at the time.

The circumstances that led up to some of the most significant ruptures in parliamentary procedure demonstrate the complexities and contradictions that governments confronted when attempting to implement neoliberal policies and manage the affairs of the House against the headwinds of forceful resistance from the opposition parties. They also foreshadowed a shift in strategic approach towards more formalized restrictions on the legislature during the 1990s and beyond.

My main point is to show that although there may not have ever been a golden age at Queen's Park, the contradictions of the neoliberal era have required a different, more restrictive form of parliamentary governance – one that has had a permanent impact on the capacity of the legislature to hold the executive to account.

Acknowledgments

Given that this book has been several years in development, numerous people are deserving of recognition for their contributions. The foundational ideas for this project were nurtured during my PhD in the Policy Studies program at Ryerson University, where I benefited tremendously from the guidance of my supervisor, Bryan Evans. Through numerous conversations, Bryan helped to shape the book's central argument and focus, and his expertise in political economy and Ontario politics were critical in helping to formulate its central thesis.

I also owe considerable thanks to two members of my dissertation committee, John Shields and Colin Mooers for their helpful suggestions. My external supervisor, Graham White, also made numerous expert suggestions about the history of legislative procedure in Ontario.

More broadly, I owe immense gratitude to Don Jackson, professor emeritus at Algoma University, who introduced me to many of the ideas used in this study. Don's continued friendship has been indispensable to my intellectual and personal development.

Terry Ross, my Canadian politics professor from my time as an undergraduate student at Algoma, is to be credited for teaching me most of what I know about the internal machinations of Canadian political institutions.

My years as an assistant professor at Algoma University, from 2007 to 2011, gave me the time and space to read and reflect extensively. Algoma University is a special place with a Special Mission, and it was my privilege to both attend as a student and work as a professor.

I owe considerable gratitude to the Ontario Legislature Internship Programme (OLIP), which in 2006 provided me with the unique opportunity to experience the internal machinery of the legislative process. It was here that, under the guidance of former OLIP director Henry Jacek, many of the questions and observations that formed the basis of this book were developed.

Although I benefited from my interactions with many legislative staffers as well as current and former members of provincial Parliament from all three major parties, special recognition is owed to Gilles Bisson: it was in part his passion for the legislature and willingness to share his vast institutional knowledge that inspired my interest in the parliamentary process.

Few people played a more pivotal role in the development of this book than Dan Quinlan at University of Toronto Press, who exercised exemplary patience with this first-time book author as we navigated the review process. I would also like to extend thanks to my two anonymous reviewers and the anonymous editorial board member, all of whom offered excellent recommendations on earlier iterations of the manuscript. I was most fortunate to have such knowledgeable reviewers, and their critiques contributed immensely to the final product. Stephanie Stone and Alison Jones provided indispensable editing assistance.

I am fortunate to have a loving and supportive family. I would like to thank Paul and Sharol Bachmeier; Angela, Denise, Ed, and Scott Chasty; and Sarah and Mark Rawlingson for their love and support over the years. Gord and Cathy McDowell deserve special mention for their help bringing this project to fruition.

I am forever indebted to the late Laura and Margaret Chasty and Barbara and Margaret McDowell for the roles they played in my upbringing.

NEOLIBERAL PARLIAMENTARISM

1 Parliamentary Governance in the Age of Neoliberalism

Introduction

As recently as a few decades ago, the idea of mass demonstrations on the streets of major European and North American cities to protest the use of parliamentary procedures would hardly have been conceivable. Parliament had long been considered peripheral to the policy-making process and was broadly viewed within the academic literature as a "dead letter" (Brodie 2018, 77). Yet, in recent years, both the United Kingdom and Canada have seen sizeable public gatherings, with individuals protesting their respective governments' use of the ancient parliamentary practice of prorogation. This and other misuses of process in legislatures around the world have led to an emerging view that parliament has entered an era of crisis.

Although recent analyses have suggested that parliament may actually be in a renaissance (Brodie 2018), the preponderance of the literature agrees that political power has shifted upward, away from parliament, and towards the executive branch. Savoie (1999, 635) contends that this shift to the centre has been accompanied by the emergence of "court government," in which primary, political decision-making authority is located in the hands of the prime minister or premier and the partisan staffers who support them. Valuable work has been done to interrogate the concentration of power in the hands of first ministers, but comparatively little has been written to explain *how* this upward shift of political power has played itself out in parliament. The literature also lacks a coherent explanation as to *why* this pattern has become prevalent in recent years.

In this book, I argue that the answers to these questions are to be found in part in the complex relationship between parliament and the broader social forces that surround it. That is, the practical challenges presented by the demand for governments to implement neoliberal public policy has necessitated a streamlined political apparatus that can rapidly and resolutely actualize controversial public policy. I argue that a process, which I refer to as *neoliberal parliamentarism*, has emerged, in which parliamentary procedures and practices have been gradually reformed to accommodate politically contested retrenchment policies by limiting the capacity of a legislature to scrutinize the actions of the executive branch. When viewed over the entire neoliberal period, it is evident that parliamentary reform has functioned both as a critical instrument in the process of neoliberal restructuring and as a vehicle for a shift in what Nicos Poulantzas called the "balance of forces" in society (Poulantzas 2008, 43).

Parliamentary process is organized according to the *Standing Orders*, which structure the procedural rules that each legislature uses to govern its affairs, as well as by a series of unwritten customs, norms, and understandings passed down over the centuries. This system of unwritten precedents relies on the sense of shared responsibility among parliamentarians that all actors are united by a covenant of reverence and respect for the equal and fair application of the rules of parliament and for the historical integrity of the institution itself. Once norms have been broken, they establish new precedents, which allow future governments to use these same approaches. This kind of norm-breaking has facilitated and legitimized the passage of politically contested neoliberal policy initiatives.

One of the fundamental problems for the realization of neoliberal policy in practice has been that its theoretical origins fail to offer a blueprint for how to coherently respond when its ideas confront widespread popular resistance (Biebricher 2019). Political implementation in societies with sovereign legislatures is a problem that most neoliberal authors have confronted, though few have provided a satisfactory solution. This led seminal neoliberal thinkers such as James Buchanan (1988) and Friedrich Hayek (1982, 1988) to embrace a logic of neoliberal constitutionalism that would deprive parliament of its role as the site of sovereign power, while placing real authority in the hands of institutions dedicated to the extension of a market order. In practice, this has provided an intellectual diagram, consistent with neoliberal thought, that legitimates the use of the executive power to adapt to the changing realities of a world governed by the zero-sum logic of market competition. As this book shows, economic and fiscal crises were repeatedly invoked as justifications for the curtailment of the legislative power and the smashing of centuries of parliamentary precedent on the grounds that economic rationalism demanded it. Although the reforms pursued in recent years have occurred in the context of a sovereign legislature, the legitimate implementation of contentious neoliberal policy reforms has demanded an increasingly centralized state apparatus with the ability to transcend institutional resistance.

Efforts at implementing austerity policies designed to shrink the welfare state have long encountered political resistance. Retrenchment, Paul Pierson claimed, involved "a delicate effort to transform programmatic change into an electorally attractive proposition, or at least to minimize the political costs" associated with implementing policies that tended to undermine the economic interests of a significant segment of the population (Pierson 1994, 8). The politics of neoliberalism, then, have made for "a distinctive and difficult enterprise" for governments attempting to undertake this shift from Keynesianism to neoliberalism, requiring various solutions to implement policies that are rejected by sizeable segments of the population (1).

This book offers two central explanations for the decline of parliament in the age of neoliberalism. First, the *Realpolitik* of neoliberalism has required a reformed parliamentary apparatus, which can overcome legislative opposition to the implementation of its most controversial policies. The existence of parliamentary resistance to neoliberal reforms has presented governments with a choice: they either work through the often time-consuming and arduous process of allowing legislators the opportunity to deliberate, air their grievances, and rigidly scrutinize legislation; or they can act pre-emptively, applying seldom-used parliamentary rules and processes to end debate.

In choosing the latter course, governments have left significant imprints on the practice of parliamentary governance, permanently reforming its procedures. Periods of seismic, path-breaking shifts in parliamentary traditions, such as the ones explored in this book, leave in place precedents that other governments use to speed the passage of their own legislative initiatives. As these precedents are applied more extensively, they become entrenched in the sinews of the institution and used for a variety of issues. In Ontario, all three major parties dating back to the early 1980s contributed to the decline of the legislature while in government, suggesting a continuity to this process that crossed party and ideological lines. One of the most significant findings from the Ontario Legislature is that nearly every major procedural precedent in recent decades was established to facilitate the passage of neoliberal initiatives. Parliamentary reform was an essential ingredient to the implementation of neoliberalism, overcoming institutional resistance.

Second, neoliberal political theory emerged from the standpoint that the supremacy of parliament constitutes a dangerous encroachment upon individual liberty. This position is associated with neoliberalism's most influential thinker, Friedrich Hayek, who argued that mid-twentieth-century liberalism had been corrupted by its embrace of a form of rationalism that granted parliament the authority to make decisions on behalf of the broader community. Sovereign legislatures were incentivized to privilege rent-seeking political minorities, whose votes politicians required for re-election, thus giving rise to the perpetual expansion of the welfare state. In this way, Hayek and many of his neoliberal contemporaries came to view the legislature as an instrument of exploitation and inefficiency. They believed that the constitutional order ought to be reformed to deprive parliament of its position as the ultimate source of political authority. This portrayal of parliament as a forum for special interest groups to pillage the state treasury, while undermining the actual needs of the majority, expressed through the market mechanism, has increasingly been embraced in practice as a rationale for the concentration of power in the executive, and it has provided an intellectual framework for the rise of a right-wing, anti-parliamentary populism in recent years. Anti-democratic actions have thus been advanced by governments as a way to protect the majority from the irrational impulses of an unrestrained legislature, using the executive authority to ensure the state's priorities bent towards a policy of economic rationalism. In this way neoliberalism has flipped the logic of democratic representation on its head, advancing the idea that the executive is required to act as a check on the legislature in order to protect markets from political coercion.

There have been few comprehensive analyses of parliament on the left. The neo-Marxist literature has long argued that parliament in capitalist society functions as an empty shell serving the interests of capital; it is "mostly comprised of men who cannot see the system in this guise, who attribute the deficiencies in it which they perceive as separate and specific 'problems,' remediable within its confines" (Miliband 2009, 54). However, in the neoliberal era, parliament has represented one of the few legitimate, institutional channels through which neoliberal reforms can be challenged, deliberated, and even amended. Consequently, the struggle over parliamentary procedure has been a critical battlefield upon which the class conflict has been waged throughout the neoliberal period.

The conflict between the executive and the legislative branches functions as a reflection of broader social conflict, articulated in parliamentary institutions as a struggle over the *time* necessary to implement controversial austerity measures. The shift towards what Bryan Evans and Greg Albo (2011, 7) have termed "permanent austerity" has demanded a legislature that is able to implement contentious reforms in short order, at any given time, and with a minimum of interference from oppositional political forces.

Parliamentary reform at the Legislative Assembly of Ontario, commonly referred to as Queen's Park, has occurred in a series of stops and starts, largely pushed over the edge by opposition obstruction, which has snarled proceedings, requiring weary parliamentarians to work night shifts in the House. Through the normalization of the use of procedural reforms to suit its needs at a particular time, and the gradual erosion of what Steven Levitsky and Daniel Ziblatt (2018, 106) call "forbearance," the executive has become considerably more powerful at the expense of the legislative branch as power has drifted towards the centre of the political apparatus. Parliamentary assemblies have been reconfigured in ways that limit their capacity to carry out their constitutional responsibility as a counterforce to the excesses of the authority of the executive branch. What the literature lacks, and this book hopes to offer some insight towards, is an analysis of both the concrete processes used to secure the implementation of public policy through oft-ignored parliamentary institutions and the ways in which the process of neoliberalization has reshaped those institutions.

Neoliberalism and the State

First, it is important to establish a working definition of neoliberalism and understand how its ascendancy has evolved over several decades. This is not an easy task, however, because the term has been used broadly, to describe a variety of phenomena. I take a broad definition of neoliberalism, describing it as a political philosophy that views the state's primary role as the extension of market-based forms of governance over all aspects of human life (Bruff 2014). It reflects a new stage of capitalism, one that rejects the "grand bargain" between capital and labour, which characterized the Keynesian, welfare-state era through a mixed economy, and reasserts the accumulation of capital and the transfer of wealth and power to private enterprise as the primary ends of state activity. Neoliberalism has reoriented the state's role towards privileging the interests of private enterprise to "strengthen their hegemony" and to remake social and political institutions in the image of the market (Duménil and Lévy 2011, 1).

Over the last several decades, the neoliberal project has succeeded in establishing itself as culturally and politically hegemonic. Antonio Gramsci claimed that hegemony was the process through which a dominant class embedded its authority by making its power appear as though it were naturally occurring or consistent with common sense understandings of the world (Gramsci 1971). Hegemony occurred when members of a ruling bloc became conscious of their common interests and sought to extend their world view to the subordinate classes in society. Every society had its "religious moment," which occurred when the dominant group had established "complete hegemony" and its ideas had come to appear as though they were self-evident truths (ibid., 697).

The neoliberal orthodoxy emerged in response to what its thinkers believed was a foundational crisis of the variety of liberalism that emerged during the nineteenth and twentieth centuries (Biebricher 2019). Neoliberal intellectuals claimed that a gradual shift in liberal thought towards constructivist rationalism had undermined the foundations of liberty by placing arbitrary authority in the hands of a sovereign parliament, which had a "mental bias" to privilege rent-seeking interest groups (Hayek, 1982, I, 143). They believed that granting arbitrary authority to any individual or group of individuals was a bad idea because no one could have the necessary knowledge to plan the life of another. Legislatures should be constrained by constitutions that required them to adhere to evolved or traditional knowledge, transmitted most reliably through the market mechanism.

Following the thought of the eighteenth-century Scottish moralists, the neoliberals argued that knowledge was most reliably acquired through spontaneous processes. They sought to reform liberalism, advocating for an approach to government that would affirm the free market as the primary source of knowledge and the foundation for political rule. Their philosophy, specifically that of Friedrich Hayek, advanced a radical program that involved reforming constitutional government by stripping Parliament of its sovereignty. Buchanan (1988), for instance, advocated for constitutional amendments that would require legislatures to pass balanced budgets, thus tying the hands of legislators to allocate resources. The legislature should be constrained within an agreed-upon set of principles that were guided by the spontaneity of the market.

The excesses of the welfare state, which the neoliberals believed to be at the heart of the problem with modern society, represented the limits of rationalism and parliamentarism, interfering in the marketplace and interrupting the capacity of abstract, unbridled competition to yield conclusions about how the world ought to be governed.

Although the rejection of parliamentary sovereignty was once considered a radical element of the neoliberal project, it is consistent with the broader denial of rationalism and human design that is at the heart of its theory of knowledge. Chapter 3 shows that the neoliberal orthodoxy amounts to a rejection of the nineteenth-century democratic reforms to the structure of liberalism. That perspective sought to return the state to a position in which the legislature played a limited role, one that was more characteristic of an eighteenth-century conception of legislative institutions in which the legislature was not sovereign. Parliamentary sovereignty granted the legislature arbitrary authority to engage in the social planning and welfare statism that it understood as having a destructive impact on modern society.

Despite their rejection of rational design and the supremacy of parliament, early neoliberal thinkers nevertheless envisioned a positive role for the state in developing the conditions necessary for the market (Biebricher 2019). They recognized that it would not be possible to establish ideal conditions for market competition without the use of an active state to cultivate an environment consistent with implementing that competition. The neoliberalization process was not merely about reforming policy practices but also about establishing the conditions necessary to embed the principle of market competition in the fabric of institutions by reforming customary practice.

However, the complexion neoliberalism takes depends considerably upon the characteristics of the social institution it seeks to reform. Jamie Peck has argued that neoliberalism has only ever existed in "impure" forms because its vision of a pure, free, market-led society is more ideological than attainable, meaning that its application has often been chiefly concerned with adapting to, and reorganizing, power structures in accordance with its principles (Peck 2010, 7). In this way, neoliberalism has often emerged in "messy hybrids," with each experiment existing as its own form of "reconstruction," reflecting a key "conjunctural episode or moment in the contradictory evolution of neoliberal practice" (6). While neoliberalism's "burden" is that it can never hope to remake the world in its utopian image, it has nonetheless proven "resilient" and able to take on chameleon forms according to where and when it appears (7).

This variegated nature has enabled neoliberalism to overcome political resistance in order to transform the character of various social and political institutional forms. We know a great deal, for instance, about the impacts of neoliberalization on the public administration. Beginning in the 1980s, the emergence of the New Public Management (NPM) philosophy fundamentally altered the structure of public administration, reorienting it to outcomes-based, corporate-sector practices. NPM valued market-driven virtues such as efficiency, competition, ownership, and output; it led to the adoption of "managerialist private sector practices," such as "strategic planning, re-engineering, customer service, quality assurance" (Dixon, Kouzmin, and Korac-Kakabadse 1998, 164). This process resulted in the establishment of more rigid, public-sector managerial structures with the capability to establish accountability and compliance with the virtues of fiscal prudence and efficiency.

The rise of "common sense managerialism" (Evans 2005) emphasized a clear accountability model with a focus on results over process. This shift towards private-sector management practices included seeking to reduce non-management public-sector salaries, increasing labour discipline, and resisting union demands for improved employment security). Demand for reform was further driven by "global forces," which placed "relentless pressures on governments to manage their public households in ways that enable their economies to be competitive" (Aucoin and Heintzman 2000, 45).

The process of actualizing this shift in public-sector philosophy and institutional culture, however, required overcoming "path dependency" within the public administration itself (Djelic and Quack 2007, 161). *Path dependency* is a commonly used concept in the social sciences, and it refers to "historical sequences in which contingent events set institutional patterns with deterministic properties into motion" (161–2). During the neoliberalization of the public sector, one of the most significant hurdles that governments needed to overcome was the cultural devotion of many senior public servants to the Keynesian orthodoxy that had shaped most of their careers. The Keynesian era "legitimated state intervention," granting the historically passive public service considerable latitude in state planning (Evans 2005, 25). Though the political class set the agenda, the nuances of policymaking were often left to the public sector to organize, design, and implement.

The neoliberal era demanded a different kind of politics, which were to be steered from the *centre* of the political apparatus. Cabinet ministers devoted to neoliberal orthodoxy were "no longer prepared to play the role of policy amateur as their predecessors were"; the result was that they faded into the background because bureaucrats did much of the important planning work (Evans 2005, 39–40). The end of this post-war Keynesian consensus created "an environment where the fundamental assumptions and principles of a generation were questioned and challenged," leading to the establishment of clear hierarchies to enforce and supervise neoliberal, restructuring processes that were not always embraced by public servants (40).

Achieving these objectives in practice, however, required "a concentration of decision-making capability at the centre of the state" (Evans 2005, 36). For Pusey, senior public-sector leaders were the "switchmen of history" because "when they change their minds the destiny of nations takes a different course" (1991, 2). The way to overcome the existence of post-war Keynesian constructionists in the public service was to place individuals, loyal to the neoliberal project and willing to enforce the principles of NPM, in senior management positions. Over time, the idea of economic rationalism became embedded as conventional practice within the public service.

In Ontario, this transformation took place in the mid-1990s, when the government of Mike Harris, pursuing an aggressive, neoliberal agenda, sought to undertake the restructuring of the province's public sector, with the objective of reducing the size of the government (Evans 2005). The Harris government attempted to "enlist the state and its leadership in implementing neoliberal restructuring in Ontario," recognizing that the kind of change it envisioned demanded the cooperation of the public administration (ibid., 26). Where such cooperation could not be taken for granted, it brought forward legislation that gave the Executive Council, commonly referred to as the *Cabinet*, considerable latitude to fill in the details of the restructuring processes through regulation.

The neoliberalization of the public administration underscores two important points. First, the thesis presented by the neo-Marxist school, that neoliberalism has required a centralized state apparatus to secure its reforms, discussed in more detail in chapter 4, has been borne out in practice through structural reforms to the public administration that were controlled and directed from the centre. Second, it begs the question: if neoliberalization has remade the public administration in its own image, can the same be said of the legislative branch? Has neoliberalism, wittingly or unwittingly, led to the reimagination of legislative procedure to overcome resistance within the political branch of the state and to secure the implementation of controversial, neoliberal, restructuring policies? Given that the literature has largely ignored the role of the political apparatus in the neoliberalization process, this book attempts to address this void in part by interrogating the relationship between the transition to neoliberalism in Ontario and the evolution of parliamentary process from 1981 to 2021.

2 Neoliberal Parliamentarism and the Ontario Legislature

The Role of Parliament in the Westminster System

In the Westminster tradition, the written rules of parliamentary governance are established by the House itself through the Standing Orders. These act as a rule book for Parliament, determining how much time will be devoted to certain issues, who may speak and when, how debates and votes will be conducted, and how decisions will be made. The Standing Orders at Queen's Park are reviewable by a majority vote in the legislature and can be changed at the whim of the Assembly at any time.

The procedures of the Westminster parliamentary system are established upon an unwritten system of conventions passed down through the centuries (Russell 2009). As such, they have developed largely on the basis of precedent, making it possible, in recent years, for long-obsolete parliamentary procedures to be resurrected on a regular basis as governments have sought to expedite the passage of their legislation through parliament. In most cases, the use of these provisions has been opposed to the spirit of these mechanisms, which were designed to enable the executive to actualize legislation in emergency circumstances, such as where agreement with the opposition was not possible or in the event of a national emergency. The contemporary use of conventions such as closure for partisan political reasons and as a regularly occurring part of parliamentary business, however, is contrary to their intent.

The history of the British parliamentary tradition is, in many ways, a study of the continually evolving relationship between parliament and the Crown. From its feudal origins to its contemporary, representative-democratic form, the structure of parliament has been the subject of a central debate about the degree of power that the Crown must cede to ensure the legitimate functioning of government, while providing sufficient limitations on the power of the executive. In the nineteenth century, the development of responsible government was designed to make parliament, as the central representative body of the electorate, the "sovereign," or primary, source of political authority.

The notion of parliamentary sovereignty implies that there are no limits on the authority of parliament, with the exception of the courts, which interpret the constitutionality of the laws passed by the legislature. Parliamentary sovereignty includes the authority to pass laws that cannot be vetoed or repealed by executive action alone. To have its ideas actualized as policy, a government must first receive the assent of a majority of the legislature. Parliament serves as a forum for political leadership, a competition of ideas between elections, a forum for publicly deliberating and contesting the issues and ideas of a given age, a means of legitimating and actualizing the law, and a forum in which the government is held to account.

Parliament is also the only means through which a government can be removed from office, by way of a vote of non-confidence. While this concept of parliamentary supremacy lies at the root of the modern Westminster system, reform through the centuries has been balanced by the desire to give the executive sufficient power to break deadlock in parliament that might interfere with its ability to effectively govern the affairs of the nation. Thus, there remain several procedural mechanisms in the British parliamentary tradition that allow a government to move parliamentary debate forward in the event of a stalemate between it and the opposition. These procedures, many of which originated hundreds of years ago, have come under considerable scrutiny in recent years, as executives have become far more brazen in their use of these mechanisms to restrict parliamentary debate.

Walter Bagehot described parliamentary government as being primarily characterized by the fusion between the legislative and executive branches in the same institutional body. The crucial link between them is expressed in the legislature through Cabinet, which he described as "a board of control chosen by the legislature," which is entrusted to govern the nation (Bagehot 1873, 49). Kaare Strom (2000, 264) claims that parliament can be understood as a "form of constitutional democracy in which executive authority emerges from, and is responsible to, the legislative authority." Cabinet takes responsibility for the administrative and policy-making functions of the state, but must seek the approval of the legislature for its decisions to take the force of the law.

Paul G. Thomas claimed that parliamentarians must take on the "dual role" of both "supporting strong responsive government by enabling the efficient passage of government business, yet at the same time they are expected to hold the first minister and the cabinet accountable" (Thomas 2010, 160). He argued that there exists an "inevitable tension" between these two roles: the executive confronts pressures to pass legislation in accordance with its agenda, while at the same time giving parliament the opportunity to subject it to scrutiny. This tension lies at the very "heart of the process" because governments mediate the conflict between their "need to have legislation passed in a reasonable period of time and the right of elected representatives to understand, discuss, and change proposed laws" (162). The extent to which any parliament can be said to fulfil its obligation to represent the democratic interests of the body politic at large relies entirely upon the maintenance of this equilibrium between the executive and legislative branches. While the parliamentary majority must tolerate and acknowledge the right of the executive to govern, at the same time the executive must also respect the right and responsibility of private members to oppose and hold it to account as well as to fulfil their duty to represent the public interest.

The executive-legislative relationship is further defined by the fact that the executive controls the organization of the affairs of parliament. Not only do most bills originate from the executive, but the government also controls the organization of House business, such as what bills will be introduced, when they will be introduced, the issues the House will debate, how much time is allocated for debate, and how many days the House sits. Government business is understood to take precedence, with certain days set aside for opposition business. This means that the executive has the right to both have its agenda considered by the House and establish the rules about when and for how long those issues will be debated.

The mediation of the conflict between the executive and legislative branches over the use of parliamentary *time* has become arguably the most critical battleground for power in legislative politics. Since time is "in short supply in absolute terms," there is constant pressure to move legislation forward to ensure that it becomes law as quickly as possible (Döring 1995, 223). This political pressure is particularly acute when highly unpopular or contentious legislation that has the potential to negatively impact a government's electoral standing is brought forward, as has often been the case in the age of neoliberalism.

The opposition, then, plays an important role in modern parliamentary democracies, performing the function of scrutinizing executive behaviour and holding it accountable. Ludger Helms (2008, 6) believed that "there can be no real democracy without opposition" since the scrutiny and deliberation of the executive branch was a critical element of democratic accountability. He contended that the opposition's "right to publicly and legitimately oppose the policies and actions of the government of the day" has been central to the exercise of parliamentary democracy (Helms 2004, 22).

It is important to distinguish between ordinary efforts to extend debate or public consideration of an issue and *obstruction*, which occurs when members behave in ways that are consistent with the rules of the legislature but do so in such a way that misuses their intent, designed to deliberately delay or prevent parliamentary decisions from being rendered (Bücker 1989). While obstruction may or may not have a malicious intent, its effect is to hinder the government from executing its legislative agenda. Examples include the extension of debate through filibustering ad nauseam and the frequent use of votes on division, motions to adjourn, points of order, and petitions to delay the proceedings of the House.

Obstructionist approaches have a long standing in the parliamentary tradition. At Westminster in the United Kingdom, the problem of parliamentary obstruction can be traced all the way back to the eighteenth century. Obstruction was considered of "slender significance" until the rise of what became known as *Parnellism* in the late nineteenth century (Rutherford 1914, 166). Geddes W. Rutherford described how Parnellism was named after Charles Stewart Parnell, a former Irish member of Parliament (MP) who employed parliamentary obstruction on a variety of government initiatives to bring attention to Ireland's political concerns. Though obstruction had previously been mostly a transient event, the rise of the "age of Parnellism" saw an increase in the use of conscious obstruction as an opposition tactic to influence policy reform (174).

The executive has two principal remedies available to it to overcome obstruction. The first is *closure*, which allows a government to bring an end to debate that, in its opinion, has exceeded the length necessary to provide adequate scrutiny. Closure is the whip hand that the executive retains to ensure that it can proceed with its legislation despite the protestations of the opposition. Second, the government has at its disposal the capacity to bring forward *motions of time allocation*, often referred to as *guillotine* motions, to place strict time limits on debate of proposed legislation at its various stages (Rutherford 1914, 176). Though time allocation in the Westminster tradition can be traced back to the nineteenth century, it was never used at the Ontario Legislature before the 1980s.

The right of the opposition to hold up proceedings, then, is a critically important tactic and one that is commonly used to hold a government to account and to advance the political objectives of the minority. It is also, however, subject to misuse, and, at its most extreme, it can call into question the capacity of the executive to govern at all, leaving parliament in a state of paralysis. The critical question, as Chris Charlton (1997, 21) posited, is, "When does legitimate opposition become obstruction?" Put differently, where does the opposition's right to delay House proceedings end and the right of the executive to implement its agenda begin?

The problem, as Rutherford noted, is "as perplexing as it is serious" because the legislature "is verily between the devil and the deep blue sea" (Rutherford 1914, 179). The right of the legislature to delay proceedings is essential because it offers members the opportunity to signal their displeasure with legislation to which they are opposed, drawing attention to causes that might otherwise be ignored or marginalized. Just as Parnell was able to use his ability to obstruct the government's agenda to achieve long-sought reforms for Ireland, opposition members today are able to wield the leverage provided to them by their ability to delay proceedings as an important counterforce to the executive.

At the same time, no legislature could function if the opposition were to be allowed to continually obstruct the proceedings of the House, making it impossible to pass legislation. In such scenarios, the use of closure or the guillotine is necessary to ensure that the elected government can execute its duties and implement its agenda.

The ideal is to find an equilibrium that allows the opposition to both fully deliberate matters before the House and scrutinize the government, while at the same time ensuring that the executive can actualize its platform. The argument put forward in this book is that, in recent years, the pendulum has swung considerably in the direction of the executive at Queen's Park, moving this equilibrium out of balance and leading to an increasingly dominant executive.

The Rise of Court Government in Canada

It has become a commonly held view that parliamentary democracy has entered a period of terminal decline as power has become concentrated at the centre of the political apparatus. Denis Smith's (1979) seminal paper, "President and Parliament," which claimed that the prime minister's control over both the executive and the legislative branches in the Canadian constitutional scheme gave him or her more power than most leaders in presidential systems, spawned a rich body of literature studying the exercise of political power in Canada. J.R. Mallory (1979, 26) claimed that as the state's responsibilities have expanded, "the insatiable requirements of governments to assuage the rising demands of the public for new legislation has meant a gradual increase in the amount of parliamentary time which governments require to get their business through." The result has been to turn Parliament into "a legislative sausagemachine," passing legislation more quickly than it can properly debate or scrutinize it (ibid.). While some scholars have argued that power in Canada has long been highly centralized relative to countries elsewhere in the Commonwealth (Malloy 2004; Franks 1999), a near-consensus has emerged that political power has shifted towards the centre of government.

Given that the executive branch functions as the nucleus of political power in Canada, much of the research that has been published on the concentration of authority at the centre has been devoted to a study of power dynamics within the executive itself. Donald Savoie has argued that politics today can best be characterized as "court government," in which political power and decision-making authority rest "in the hands of the prime minister and a small group of carefully selected courtiers rather than with the prime minister acting in concert with his elected cabinet colleagues" (Savoie 1999, 637). In court government, the Cabinet, Parliament, and the bureaucracy are subordinated to the first minister and his or her courtiers, who exercise extensive decision-making authority over the activities of government. This new approach to governance is due, in part, to the rigid party discipline and leader-centric governments that have come to characterize modern Canadian politics (Savoie 1999).

Peter Aucoin (1986) argued that while there was considerable evidence that power was shifting towards the centre, the personality of the prime minister played an important role in how this process manifested itself. He noted that both Pierre Trudeau and Brian Mulroney, for instance, had profoundly different leadership styles. While Trudeau's leadership style led him to implement an executive system based upon rational management, Mulroney's was largely structured upon a system of brokerage politics. Aucoin wrote,

> The major determinants of such change are invariably political, and not administrative in character, and derive from the leadership paradigms of chief executive officers – their philosophy of government, management style and political objectives. (Aucoin 1986, 5)

Aucoin's chief point was that such calculations are made for political advantage; they are not, in and of themselves, part of an organic, administrative shift of power towards the centre.

In a similar vein, H.D. Munroe claimed that human agency functions as a central determinant of the concentration of power in the Prime Minister's Office (PMO). Despite the very real existence of centralizing forces since the early 1970s, "the exercise of prime ministerial power is significantly shaped by personal style" (Munroe 2011, 531). Munroe contended that the charismatic characteristics of certain first ministers give them greater influence within Cabinet than leaders with weaker personal attributes. He offered a detailed sketch of Pierre Trudeau's ability to control his Cabinet during the October Crisis of 1970, arguing that it was his skilled personal attributes that allowed him to maintain the obedience of Cabinet members while taking such a radical step as enacting the War Measures Act. Furthermore, Munroe's study demonstrated that Pierre Trudeau remained committed to a "rational management" approach to governance, even at a time when centralizing pressures were at their most extreme (2011, 533).

C.E.S. Franks argued that Canada's weak federal structure and the diverse cultural, political, and economic complexion of its various provinces, has necessitated a more deliberative, executive-driven relationship between the federal government and the provinces than might be the case in a more cohesive union. This has led to a relationship that is more reliant upon negotiation among first ministers, both constitutionally and on key policy matters, than would be ideal. This reliance upon executive federalism has shaped a policy regime that often ignores legislatures on such matters, thus undermining the democratic accountability of both levels of government to its citizens (Franks 1995).

Since the dialectic between the executive and parliament is symbiotic, the impact of the concentration of political power at the centre has been to weaken the capacity of Canada's Parliament to hold the executive accountable. This has led to the emergence of a prevailing view among researchers and practitioners that parliamentary democracy has been in a state of decline for several decades. Peter Milliken, the longest-serving Speaker in the history of the House of Commons, argued that the reforms to Parliament have eroded its role to such an extent that it has lost its relevance. "Parliament can hardly be weakened any more than it already is" under the Stephen Harper government, which attempted to "control every aspect of House business" (Milliken, quoted in Harris 2014, 430). MP Brent Rathgeber resigned from the Conservative caucus in 2013 over what he described as an intolerable level of control "by unelected staffers about half my age" in the PMO. He argued that MPs must "take a stand" and declare that "we are not going to read these talking points that are written by PMO staffers" (Rathgeber, quoted in Campion-Smith and MacCharles 2013).

Former federal Liberal leader Michael Ignatieff argued that parliamentary democracy had become a "hollowed out" forum, undermined by "the prime minister's capacity to dictate House business, put together omnibus bills and ram them through, while imposing party discipline, [which] has concentrated executive authority at the expense of the legislature" (Ignatieff, quoted in Ibbitson 2013). Peter Aucoin, Lori Turnbull, and Mark D. Jarvis (2011) claimed that Parliament had become gradually less effective at holding the executive to account. The power concentrated in the executive allowed first ministers to wield extraordinary authority over the legislative branch, and the intensification of this trend in recent decades had led to a further weakening of Canada's system of parliamentary democracy.

For Smith, "the golden age of legislatures is past because the executive is now expected to deal with more and increasingly complex demands from individuals and groups." Thus, legislatures may "communicate constituents' concerns, but they are in no position to satisfy them" (D. Smith 2013, 21). He suggested that before the arrival of modernity and complex society, it might have been possible to have meaningful parliamentary supervision of the executive branch, but the problems of the twentieth and twenty-first centuries demanded the kind of decisive action that only the executive could take.

Similar criticisms have been levied against the Ontario Legislature in recent years. Tracey Raney, Sasha Tregebov, and Gregory Inwood (2013, 12) argue that extensive turnover in the post-1985 period meant that newer members, unfamiliar with the Legislature's "clubby style," introduced a more partisan approach to politics. They contend that this change in the legislature's general atmosphere had impacted the role of legislators in the following way:

> The increasingly nasty mood in the legislature coincided with reassertions of executive dominance. Less moderation and more stridency meant governments felt more justified in pushing their agenda at the expense of more collegial relations. Individual MPPs were unwilling to object this, as each had a chance of grasping the golden ring of a cabinet post. The professionalization of politics increased the stakes and the rewards for success, and compromise became an increasingly dirty word among increasingly ideological partisans. Hence, the executive was driven to tighten the rules to enact its agenda, backed by a more disputatious winner-take-all set of relations within the legislature. (Raney, Tregebov, and Inwood 2013, 13)

The intensification of partisanship not only pervaded the legislature; relations among House Leaders also became characterized by a lack of cooperation and hard-line negotiations. Unable to find consensus among the three parties, governments began to change the rules so that they could pass their legislation without opposition support. The consequence of this new partisan atmosphere, then, was to ultimately "harden the lines between government and opposition and diminish the role of the legislature in the public policy process" (Raney, Tregebov, and Inwood 2013, 13). Chris Charlton (1997) argued that while an obstructionist culture within the opposition in Ontario ultimately forced governments to enact reforms to overcome obstruction, this culture did not fully take hold until the early years of the Rae government, when the Progressive Conservatives refused to cooperate with virtually any aspect of the New Democratic Party (NDP) agenda.

Numerous reasons have been provided for the decline of the legislature in Ontario. David Cameron, Celine Mulhern, and Graham White (2003) argued that the effect of the Harris government reducing the number of seats from 130 to 103 was "a downsizing of democracy" since members of provincial Parliament (MPPs) were forced to represent more constituents, while still attending to their parliamentary responsibilities. The authors also argued that a heightening of party discipline in recent years had resulted in too much power being concentrated in the leaders' offices. Evans (2008) claimed that the introduction of a competitive dynamic to the Legislative Assembly after the end of the forty-three-year Progressive Conservative dynasty altered the collegiality among the three parties that had characterized the earlier period.

Other explanations for what Peter Russell and Lorne Sossin (2009) call "parliamentary democracy in crisis" include: the introduction of television in the legislature (Savoie 1999; Raney, Tregebov, and Inwood 2013), the increased need for competitiveness in a period of globalized capitalism (Savoie 2010; Elgie and Stapleton 2006), a heightening of party discipline (Malloy 2004), increased partisanship, the end of evening sittings, and an erosion of respect and collegiality among parliamentarians (Raney, Tregebov, and Inwood 2013).

Other scholars, however, have maintained that the executive dominance thesis may be "overdrawn" (Bakvis 2001, 76). Herman Bakvis contended that leader-centric structures of party loyalty have been a part of the Canadian democratic process since the days of John A. Macdonald. He argued that, at the federal level, Jean Chrétien's approach was to give Cabinet members more responsibility so as to clear the Cabinet agenda of superfluous items and give his ministers autonomy and free reign in important portfolios such as transportation and foreign affairs (Bakvis 2001). Therefore, an analysis suggesting that court government is a new phenomenon ignores the extent to which first ministers have exercised authority in the past. Furthermore, he argued,

> one has to be careful in accepting the supposition that ministers have simply dropped out of the picture, or that all power automatically flows upward. It is possible to argue that even if cabinet as a forum for decision-making has become less relevant, much of the power has shifted down to individual ministers and departments. (Bakvis 2001, 66)

Similarly, Paul G. Thomas claimed that the idea that the prime minister has become a "friendly dictator" or descriptions of Cabinet as a "focus group" for the prime minister are overstated. While "labels" such as these "represent good rhetoric," they make for "poor analysis." Rather, he argued, there are actually "more constraints on the exercise of prime-ministerial power than is popularly assumed" (Thomas 2004, 80). However, he claimed that as the policy environment has become more complex and multi-dimensional, governments have increasingly engaged in horizontal or coordinative relationships with other jurisdictions, resulting in a variety of "centrifugal forces" that undermine the authority of the first minister (85).

Policy issues today are "increasingly cross-cutting" and, consequently, "do not fit neatly into traditional ministerial boxes" (Thomas 2004, 84). The expansion of private-sector partnerships has also added to the complexity and decentralization of the policy-making process. Though Cabinet has come to serve largely as a body to help first ministers achieve their political objectives, "the constitutional principle of individual ministerial responsibility and the tyranny of the clock oblige the prime minister to share authority and power with other cabinet members" (85).

Jonathan Malloy (2004) contended that while the role of Parliament has been minimized in recent years as party discipline has intensified, executive relationships have long favoured the first minister. He raised the example of Paul Martin's Cabinet revolt, which resulted in Jean Chrétien's resignation as prime minister, as demonstrating the fact that Cabinet remains a counterforce to the power of the first minister. Patrick Weller (2003) argued that the assumption that Cabinet is irrelevant is based upon a methodological flaw: scholars who support the theory of court government do so on the basis of an analysis of prime ministers; they should focus on Cabinet itself rather than drawing reductionist conclusions on the basis of the changing role of the prime minister. Taking this approach, he argued, one cannot help but come away with the view that Cabinet remains a vital part of the policy-making process. While the overall trajectory of government policy is becoming concentrated at the centre of government, "ministers exert authority within their portfolios and there is no consistent trend to suggest that prime ministers determine everything; they are influential in those areas where they care to act, as they always were" (ibid., 720). For Weller, until a normative methodological approach is established, it is overly simplistic to declare Cabinet dead.

Departing from the decline-of-parliament thesis, Thomas argues that "legislatures are not as powerless and irrelevant as the prevailing stereotype suggests" (2010, 154). Although he acknowledges that legislatures do confront challenges, they are not in "absolute decline," but rather in the throes of what he calls "institutional adaptation challenges" (160). That is, parliament has been slow to adapt to the changing political and social environment in which they operate. Ian Brodie (2018) goes so far as to claim that parliament may well be in its halcyon days. He makes the case that the federal Parliament today affords more opportunities to the opposition to influence the parliamentary agenda than at any previous time in Canada's history.

The History of Procedure at the Ontario Legislature

Although this book focuses on the decline of Parliament at Queen's Park in recent decades, parliamentary governance in Ontario has rarely represented an "ideal type" of democracy (Pilon 2017, 106). As late as the 1960s, the Ontario Legislature was "still governed by the mid-nineteenth century rules it adopted in 1867" as the executive continued to exercise remarkable control over the affairs of the legislature, even by Westminster standards (Schindeler 1969, 143).

There have been instances of opposition obstruction during the legislature's history, including an example in the early twentieth century, when the opposition used "every conceivable variety of the filibuster technique, including long excerpts from Alice in Wonderland," to prompt the sitting premier of the day, Ernest Drury, to call an early election; however, throughout its history, the Ontario Legislature has often been pitifully weak in the face of a dominant executive (151).

The government's control over House procedure was particularly evident during the premiership of "the patriarch," Leslie Frost (MacDonald 1998, 298). By the 1950s, the opposition parties at Queen's Park were "both decimated and fragmented" (Bryden 1975, 248). From 1951 to 1955, for example, there were only ten opposition members out of ninety seats in the legislature, while from 1955 to 1959 there were only eleven (Bryden 1975). Former NDP leader Donald MacDonald (1998, 320) claimed that, during the 1950s, the legislature functioned effectively as "an appendage to the premier's office, beholden to the government for its every need." Additionally, parliamentary debate was almost exclusively concerned with government business.

> It was as though there were two sets of rules – one for him and one for the rest of the House. If he wished to intervene, he simply rose and took over. This was accepted by his own members, including those in the cabinet, and was tolerated by the Speaker. Periodically, there were protests from opposition members, but even they lived with his breach of parliamentary procedures, partly because they were powerless to stop it, and partly out of gratitude that what they had to say was worthy of attention from the premier. (MacDonald 1998, 300)

For Graham White, the expansion of the scope of government during the Frost era "combined with extended periods of one-rule to produce an overwhelming dominance of the executive over the legislature" (1980, 358). Throughout this period, oral and written questions were not permitted in the legislature, meaning that there was little opportunity to make the executive answerable for its behaviour. Estimates were subject to "perfunctory attention and the public accounts were never reviewed, the public accounts committee being a huge body that hardly ever met" (Bryden 1975, 248). Members received only a desk in the chamber and 20 to 25 per cent of the cost of a stenographer while the House was in session (Bryden 1975).

The primary mechanism for holding the executive to account was established through a series of standing committees. However, these committees were dominated by members of the governing party and were "so large and poorly organized as to be quite unwieldy"; consequently, they were largely ineffective at scrutinizing executive actions (Bryden 1975, 248). Committees also performed the function of allowing members to acquire information, given that they did not have research staff at their disposal. Kenneth Bryden has argued that these committees were tolerated by Premier Frost as a means of keeping government backbench members "out of his own hair" (ibid.). Attempts to establish special agencies to design a form of accountability were ultimately unsuccessful (Bryden 1975).

It was not until the 1960s that "a slow and undramatic but real improvement in the relative position of the legislature" began to occur. These changes were largely the result of "constant pressure for change from numerically enlarged oppositions on a not unreceptive Premier John Robarts" (Bryden 1975, 249). The size of standing committees was reduced to allow more manageable processes, and committees began to meet more often to scrutinize government legislation, which was sent to them with regularity. Time was set aside for daily Oral Questions, where the government could be held accountable in the legislature. Although no processes were put in place during the 1960s to scrutinize delegated legislation (discussed later in this chapter), the John Robarts government did establish a Public Accounts Committee, which allowed members to ask questions about economic matters. Additionally, the Committee of Supply came to take on a much more prominent role in legislative proceedings, absorbing more than half the total sitting time of the House (Bryden 1975).

This "modest regeneration" reached its zenith in 1969 with the establishment of a parliamentary committee to review the role of the legislature and, with it, a new set of Standing Orders, which formalized many of the gains made during the previous decade (Bryden 1975, 249). The new Standing Orders gave official recognition to a forty-five-minute, daily Question Period. At the same time, however, the government placed time limits on the Committee of Supply – to ninety sittings, or 225 hours (Bryden 1975).

In the early 1970s, shortly after winning his first mandate as premier, and in response to the fact that his party's backbench members had become "rife with frustration at the impotent lot of a government private member in an executive dominated chamber," Bill Davis announced the establishment of a commission to review more substantive changes to the legislature (White 1979, 117). The Ontario Commission on the Legislature, which was chaired by Progressive Conservative Party strategist and intellectual Dalton Camp, made several suggestions, the most significant of which was to take steps to allow more influence for MPPs.

One of the commission's central findings was that a representative deficit existed in most constituencies. Among the steps it recommended was to provide MPPs with their own office and staff at the legislature, as well as in their constituencies, thus making them full-time rather than part-time legislators. The Camp Commission proposed that sufficient funds be provided to the opposition parties to offer a more empowered counterforce to the executive. It also urged the government to increase the size of the legislature, thereby reducing the number of constituents that each MPP was responsible for, and suggested that the government allocate more staff for the House Leaders, the Clerk's Office, and the Legislative Library, all of which would work on behalf of MPPs (White 1980).

Other recommendations included the appointment of independent agencies accountable to the legislature and the establishment of a parliamentary committee to study the need for further changes. The all-party committee eventually agreed to make changes to the Standing Orders to allow private members' bills to come to second reading, unless blocked by twenty members standing in their places or by a petition of one-third of the members of the legislature. However, when the first private member's bill was brought for second reading under this new provision, Premier Bill Davis sent out a press release, announcing that it would be allowed to proceed no further, as if to reinforce the notion that it was the executive, not Parliament, that held *actual* authority (Lyon 1984).

It was not until the Progressive Conservative dynasty had been reduced to a minority government in the 1975 general election that the opposition truly managed to throw off the yoke of the dominant executive. The challenges of a minority government "made it absolutely essential" that the Davis government begin to "treat the opposition with greater respect, and for the NDP and the Liberals to accept some responsibility for the operation of the House." This reality was further acknowledged through the establishment of an informal House Leaders' Committee, which became the chief vehicle through which the House schedule was established during the two minority Parliaments at the end of the 1970s. The House Leaders, Bob Welch for the Progressive Conservatives, Ian Deans for the NDP, and Jim Breithaupt for the Liberals, "quickly developed a strong respect and liking for one another," thereby creating "an atmosphere of genuine cooperation and consultation." The House Leaders' Committee cultivated a "more efficient and acceptable management of House business" and led to the development of "a more mature attitude towards the legislature" (White 1979, 121).

The advent of the House Leaders' Committee granted a degree of influence to the opposition, which could use its right to hold up the proceedings of the legislature to leverage concessions from the government. For example, it might agree to stand down on a signature government initiative in exchange for increasing the amount of time allocated to debate on another issue of public concern. The establishment of the committee reduced the amount of "needless bickering and confrontation in the House" over routine matters that were more easily resolved through open channels of communication among the three major parties, leading to a "healthier atmosphere in the House." The committee "acquired substantial power" and came to serve as the primary way in which House scheduling was established during the 30th and 31st minority Parliaments (White 1979, 121).

To summarize, the existence of a strong executive throughout much of Ontario's history was the result of a convergence of factors. First, during the Progressive Conservative reign in the 1950s and 1960s, Ontario served as one of the most characteristic examples of one-party-dominant political systems in the Western democracies (Leduc and White 1974). During this period, the pre-eminence of the Tory dynasty over the electoral cycle nurtured a parliamentary culture in which the roles of the government and the opposition became firmly entrenched.

Second, since the government had assumed almost complete control over the proceedings of the legislature, the opposition became ossified in its role as subordinate to the government. In a survey of MPPs taken during the 1970s, Lawrence Leduc and Walter L. White (1974) showed that the Liberals, in particular, had become decidedly deferential to the government, preferring to focus on constituency issues, and placing more emphasis on legislative initiatives that were consistent with this objective, than holding the government to account.

Third, and as an extension of the previous point, White claimed that members of the Ontario Legislature did not "act sufficiently like legislators" and were chiefly concerned with looking after affairs within their own constituencies. A member viewed their primary responsibilities as being "a representative of his constituents, performing services for individuals and groups in his riding," rather than doing work "proposing and criticizing major policies, scrutinizing and evaluating the government's performance, and the like" (White 1979, 118).

What differentiates the era of contemporary reforms under analysis in this study from the Ontario Legislature's pre-1970s configuration is that the present era has been characterized by the conscious and formal reformation of the rules, precedents, and processes of the legislature to expressly prevent the opposition from performing its function to scrutinize the executive. Early executive dominance was conditioned by an institutionalized culture at Queen's Park, which, as White (1979) has noted, was shaped by the fact that many MPPs maintained antiquated ideas of the role of Parliament. Throughout this early period, there were no time limits on debate, meaning that members retained the capacity to delay the proceedings of the Assembly, a right they availed themselves of on occasion (Schindeler 1969).

Procedural reforms from the 1981–2021 period, meanwhile, have resulted in the gradual formalization of procedures, such as time allocation, into the Standing Orders. As governments have increasingly sought to speed the passage of their legislation as a matter of political strategy, they have reformed procedures to enable this to occur. Doing so, however, has had the effect of formalizing and consolidating the executive's dominance over the legislature. Over several decades, governments have eliminated every conceivable method of meaningfully delaying the proceedings of the legislature; consequently, the opposition is no longer able to avail itself of this important leverage in its dialectic with the executive branch.

This concrete reconstitution of the rules and procedures of the legislature over the last few decades has "locked in" the executive's ability to control the affairs of the House, leaving in place a procedural structure that can enable the swift passage of legislation and accommodate political radicalism in the seat of government. Indeed, as chapter ten will show, when the Doug Ford government came to office in 2018 with an ambitious austerity plan, it found that the rules of the legislature had already been organized to enable the rapid implementation of its political agenda.

Why Ontario?

Ontario's unique pattern of historical development offered three critically important variables that made it ideal for an analysis of the evolution of parliamentary governance. First, and most importantly, while many other jurisdictions were undergoing significant neoliberal state reformation programs during the 1970s and 1980s, Ontario largely continued on a Keynesian trajectory until the early 1990s. Ontario's transition to neoliberalism "was tentative and protracted" because successive governments lacked the political will to undertake the massive restructuring project that was required to reform the Ontario state (Evans 2008, ii). The implementation of neoliberalism in Ontario occurred in a series of "fits and starts," beginning in 1969 with reforms to the structure of the executive branch and modest efforts at restraint under the Davis government. It was not until 1995, however, when the Harris government was elected, that meaningful efforts at neoliberal reform were made (ibid.). The period of neoliberalization in Ontario then occurred quickly, as a significant rupture from the Keynesian model.

Another rupture under the Ford government is presently under way, offering a point of comparison between two ideologically aligned governments with aggressive restructuring agendas, separated by two decades. This is an opportunity not only to observe examples of aggressive reform but also to understand how non-right-wing parties have addressed the challenges of governing parliament during contentious political times.

The second variable is that all three major political parties in Ontario – the Liberal Party, the New Democratic Party, and the Progressive Conservative Party – have held power during the period under consideration. This is important because it means that analysis is not obscured by the fact that a single party has held power for the entire period. It is possible to compare their approaches to establish whether and to what extent differences in party affiliation impact attitudes towards parliamentary governance once a party is in office. The third variable is that Ontario's mixture of minority and majority governments allows us to compare approaches under distinct parliamentary configurations.

Neoliberal Parliamentarism

The critical question today, particularly given the emergence of authoritarian-style movements around the world, is whether the process of neoliberalization has contributed to the concentration of political power in the executive and the decline of parliament. To categorize the evolution of this process, I argue that an approach to legislative governance, which is referred to throughout this book as *neoliberal parliamentarism*, has emerged in Ontario. This is a form of parliamentary governance conceived in the early 1980s, and unique to the neoliberal era, in which the rules and precedents of Parliament have been reformed in a systematic manner to secure the actualization of legislation and to insulate decisions from the influence of the legislature or other democratic accountability mechanisms. Neoliberal parliamentarism can be said to exist wherever a legislative body provides the environment for the rapid implementation and consolidation of the principles of the hegemonic system at the expense of accountability and scrutiny.

Although this process has occurred slowly, over a period of decades, it has had the impact of significantly reconstituting the practice of parliamentary governance in Ontario, seeking to streamline proceedings and subverting meaningful institutional counterforces to the executive. It obliterates the need for institutions that risk delaying or tampering with its ability to deliver on its promises to its voters, thus reducing parliamentary process to an institutional inefficiency.

This form of legislative governance has relied primarily upon two strategies: First, it has located fundamental decision-making authority in the executive branch, granting it the power to supervise implementation processes through its use of delegated legislation, which does not require parliamentary approval. Second, it has changed the rules of the legislature to ensure the quick passage of its legislation using mechanisms such as time allocation and omnibus legislation to limit debate.

These shifts in parliamentary procedure at Queen's Park have closely mirrored the patterns of neoliberal policy implementation in Ontario. Bryan Evans and Carlo Fanelli (2018, 150) have argued that Ontario undertook a "slow turn toward neoliberalism" compared to other provinces, experiencing public-sector restraint during the early 1980s under the Davis government that stopped short of many of the more significant structural reforms that occurred elsewhere during that period. It was when the Harris government in the 1990s, however, that "unequivocal neoliberalism" came to Ontario in the form of a highly aggressive, state-restructuring agenda (Coulter 2009, 194). Although the McGuinty and Wynne Liberals, in office from 2003 to 2018, offered "an alternative in tone and style" by adopting a Third Way approach to public policy, this amounted to consolidating and entrenching the aggressive neoliberalism of the Harris era (Evans and Fanelli 2018, 150).

The evolution of neoliberal parliamentarism in Ontario has followed a similarly circuitous path. It began in the early 1980s, when the Davis government introduced time allocation to break a parliamentary stalemate over a public-sector wage freeze enshrined in the Inflation Restraint Act. It then reached a more clearly patterned form during the mid-1990s, as the Harris Tories took an uncompromising approach to implementing their neoliberal restructuring plan. As broader social conflict over cuts to social services was replicated at Queen's Park, the floor of the legislature became one of the few places where oppositional forces could confront the government and require it to answer for its actions. Thus, the assertion of control over the rules and processes of Parliament became a critical tool in the Harris government's approach to implementing policy, allowing it to shield its reforms from democratic influence and carry out its agenda at unprecedented speed.

In their recent book, *How Democracies Die,* Levitsky and Ziblatt (2018) claim that "norm-breaking" has been central to democratic decline. Norms are the unwritten ethical values that lie at the foundation of parliamentary governance, causing political actors to use restraint in their exercise of power. Norm-breaking is simply the practice of departing from conventional standards of behaviour, which are usually part of the common values and social conventions observed by a particular social group but are not necessarily inscribed as formally written rules or laws. In stable political societies, norm-breaking is exceedingly rare because norms are generally understood to reflect the values they purport to stand upon. It is usually during times of crisis, when the logic of an institution comes into conflict with the values of those individuals who function within it, that the edifice holding these understandings in place begins to slowly crumble.

The decline of the legislature in Ontario occurred through the gradual chipping away of many of these norms, emboldening future governments to take up the torch passed to them by their predecessor, lighting their own path to the realization of their political objectives. Of critical importance today is whether we are on the brink of a new frontier of norm-breaking, one that will shatter the old paradigm, or whether this is a process that can be turned back.

Studying Parliament

One of the most significant challenges of conducting an analysis of parliament is that there is a lack of comprehensive studies of legislative process, which leaves a dimly lit path for researchers to follow. A Library of Parliament report on the state of the literature stated plainly that scholars "do not appear to be interested in how rules and procedures create a power structure." This might be the case, the report hypothesized, because influence inevitably works "in conjunction with outside events, behind the formalities of the political process" (Sutherland 2009, 154). In other words, the mediation of influence in parliament is difficult to measure with any degree of precision because of the multiple factors that must be accounted for when attempting to quantify shifts in power relations.

Chris Charlton (1997, 28) claimed that it was possible to "build a quantitative case to prove the existence of obstruction" by averaging the amount of time provided for debate on second reading on legislation before Parliament. In a comparison of the Ontario Legislature with the federal House of Commons, she found that average House time for a bill to become law throughout the 1970s and 1980s was significantly higher in Ottawa than at Queen's Park. She also showed that the 35th Parliament of Ontario, governed by the New Democrats under the premiership of Bob Rae, provided more time for debate on legislation than previous governments. More recently, Niels Goet, Thomas Fleming, and Radoslaw Zubek (2020) used machine-readable data to conduct an automated textual analysis of the evolution of procedure at Westminster from 1811 to 2015. They found that disruptions in the partisan environment were the most reliable indicators of procedural change.

In his recent book on Canada's Parliament, Ian Brodie (2018, 87) offered what he admitted were a series of "crude" indicators for establishing Parliament's effectiveness. He provided several categories for measuring the relationship between the legislative and executive. First, he explored the fate of government legislation, making the case that a comparison of the total number of government bills passed during a given session demonstrates that the government is not simply able to "ram bills through parliament without much effort" (89). Second, he claimed that an analysis of private members' business today in comparison with the past indicates an increase in the attention given to opposition issues and the number of private members' bills passed by the House.

Third is what Brodie called "the battle for time" (Brodie 2018, 89). Time is "the most precious commodity parliament has," and the struggle over control of it comes to characterize much of the executive-legislative relationship (ibid.). He argued that time allocation requires the government to make "difficult tradeoffs" because of the cumbersome process involved in bringing forward and debating time allocation motions. Instead, he suggested a government that intends to maximize the number of bills it moves through the House "will eventually reach a compromise with the opposition parties to allow expedited passage of some of its bills" (92).

Although Brodie is to be credited for offering concrete measurements with which to assess the evolution of the parliamentary process, the categories he establishes are limited in what they can tell us about the executive-legislative dynamic. He acknowledges that "not all government bills are created equal," but he does not account for the type or relevance of the initiative being pursued by the legislation in question (Brodie 2018, 88). Government legislation, particularly today, given the prevalence of omnibus bills, comes in all shapes, sizes, and varieties. Some bills are designed to address matters more limited in scope, while others can make reforms to dozens of statutes. Some bills may be particularly contentious; others may achieve a broader consensus.

If we are to comprehend the power dynamics that lurk behind the executive-legislative dichotomy, we must establish degrees of relations among the variables to determine whether any meaningful patterns emerge that might tell a unifying story. It is not enough to draw a bill-to-bill comparison without understanding the social and political relations that went into them. Governments may choose not to bring a bill forward for second or third reading in a session for any number of reasons. Governments routinely re-table legislation that is substantively similar to bills that died on the Order Paper after prorogation, days or weeks after the new session resumes. This was the case as recently as 2018 in Ontario, when the Wynne government brought the legislature back for a short session to pass a number of bills that it was unable to complete in the previous session.

Power in Parliament is not determined by allowing more private members' bills, or by having more safeguards in place, without any meaningful authority to sanction government action. Rather, it is measured by the capacity of a government to exercise its will, in accordance with its own timeline, and on its own terms. In other words, power in Parliament is determined by the capacity of the government to do what it wants, when it wants. Such an approach seeks to establish plausible relationships between variables to understand how social relations, both inside and outside Parliament, make up its complexion.

The critical question is not whether a parliamentary opposition is provided with certain scheduled opportunities to bring forward legislation that it might see as relevant – although this is an important element of a parliamentary opposition's role. Such concessions amount to only a fraction of the proceedings of the legislature in any given parliament and are peripheral to the primary business of the House. What is most essential is the capacity granted to the opposition to debate, scrutinize, and, at times, modify the most momentous and contested reforms a government brings forward. In other words, analyses of parliament should focus primarily on the trajectory of its accountability function since this is the terrain upon which the power struggle between the legislative and the executive is played out.

As Thomas has argued, executive-legislative relations are difficult to measure because they interact with external variables, occurring "indirectly over time" (2010, 154). In other words, parliamentary relations do not evolve in a straight line, but rather gradually, over a period of years, spanning multiple governments. It can be misleading to point to a single example of opposition resistance as evidence that parliament works if that example is an outlier to a broader structural shift that is taking place. In practice, the strength of opposition resistance has often been a response to the imposition of politically contentious policies and has, in turn, provided the necessary justification for governments to tighten their control over legislative procedure.

Although there were undoubtedly numerous variables that contributed to the decline of Parliament at Queen's Park, this book will focus on the understudied role played by the transition to neoliberalism and the ways in which the demands placed upon the state over the course of this period have impacted the legislative process. The evidence shows that nearly early every major example of norm-breaking at the Ontario Legislature occurred in an effort to thwart parliamentary resistance to a signature piece of neoliberal legislation, on the grounds that it was necessary to address an economic or fiscal crisis. Conversely, nearly every signature piece of neoliberal legislation was subjected to one, some, or all the institutional changes examined in this book. Legislative reform was thus an essential ingredient in the implementation of highly controversial neoliberal restructuring plans in Ontario.

Approach

I develop the story of the Ontario Legislature through quotations from key figures as a means of contextualizing the evidence presented as the actors themselves were experiencing it. The analysis emerges from an exploration of two primary sources. First, it takes an overview of each day of Hansard, from the beginning of the 32nd Parliament in 1981 to the 42nd Parliament under the Ford government in 2021, to explore the evolution of parliamentary procedure. Other background documentation such as government records acquired through the Archives of Ontario, sessional papers, the *Journals of the Legislative Assembly*, newspaper articles, and standing committee transcripts were also consulted. I proceed by exploring the prevalence of the following themes:

- Omnibus legislation
- Time allocation and closure
- Delegated legislation
- Number of sitting days during the parliamentary calendar
- Changes to the legislature's Standing Orders
- Other examples of contempt for the parliamentary process

Second, this book surveys each piece of government legislation brought forward over the period under consideration to provide an overview of the use of delegated legislation. The following sections provide an explanation and brief historical overview of the primary procedures that are analysed throughout this book.

Omnibus Legislation

According to Audrey O'Brien and Marc Bosc (2009, n.p.), *omnibus bills* are legislation that is designed to "amend, repeal or enact several acts, and [is] characterized by the fact that it is made up of a number of related but separate initiatives." Omnibus bills group together numerous legislative initiatives into a single bill, to be considered by the House as a package. Consequently, they often involve a wide variety of unrelated issues (Kirchhoff and Tsuji 2014). Omnibus bills are "neither intrinsically good nor bad" in and of themselves (Dodek 2016, 8). In the past, they were commonly used to enact housekeeping measures, to have several related items considered by the House, in a single bill, for speed and efficiency.

While larger legislative initiatives, similar in form to omnibus bills, are found in the annals of the British and Australian parliamentary traditions, the treatment in the Westminster system of omnibus legislation as single acts of Parliament is unique to Canada (Marleau and Montpetit 2000). The first instance of an omnibus bill can be traced to 1888, when the Ontario government packaged private bills to bring together two separate railways into a single piece of legislation (ibid.). Though an accepted element of House procedure, omnibus bills were previously used only sparingly (Dodek 2016).

Louis Massicotte claimed that there are two central advantages for the executive in using omnibus bills. First, they "save time and shorten legislative proceedings by avoiding the preparation of dozens of distinct bills necessitating as many second reading debates." Second, they "generate embarrassment within opposition parties by diluting highly controversial moves within a complex package." This approach allows the government to then "turn to the public and lament the fact that opposition parties wanted to prevent the adoption of measure so and so, which everybody likes" (Massicotte 2013, 16).

The application of omnibus legislation in recent years, however, has become "democratically problematic" as governments have packaged numerous unrelated items together to circumvent the legislative process as a conscious strategy. Under these circumstances, "omnibus bills make it difficult for parliamentarians to properly scrutinize a bill's content and exercise their function in holding the government to account" because there is little time to properly analyse numerous legislative initiatives under time constraints (Dodek 2016, 9).

Franks contended that, in recent years, omnibus bills "have morphed from short bills dealing with minor items mentioned in the budget speech to enormous omnibus bills that go way beyond what is mentioned in the budget." Consequently, many contemporary omnibus bills "subvert and evade the normal principles of parliamentary review of legislation" (Franks 2010, n.p.).

When parliamentarians are unable to exercise their responsibility to hold the executive to account, "they fail in their representative function and risk making a mockery out of the constitutional right to vote by emptying it of any substance" (Dodek 2016, 10).

With multiple items grouped together, important issues often do not receive adequate consideration, either in debate in the House or at committee stage. Legislative committees typically "invite affected interest groups and informed members of the public to express their views on the legislation under consideration." This public consultation process is particularly critical "when legislation proposes major changes or involves complex technical matters" (Franks 2010). Denis Kirchhoff and Leonard Tsuji (2014) show that the use of omnibus legislation by the federal government to streamline environmental approval processes has undermined the capacity of Indigenous community representatives to participate in scrutinizing legislation that profoundly impacts their communities.

Closure and Time Allocation

Robert Marleau and Camille Montpetit (2000, 558) define *closure* as "a procedural device used to bring debate on a question to a conclusion" by requiring that the question be put to a vote. It was first introduced at Westminster in 1881 as a method of overcoming a parliamentary stalemate that appeared to have no other means of resolution. Its intent was not to give the government the power to impose its agenda on Parliament at will, but rather to provide it with a means of ending a parliamentary deadlock where no other solution appeared plausible (Marleau and Montpetit 2000).

The inability of governments to reach settlements on parliamentary timetables with opposition parties over longer periods of time led to the advent of *time allocation*. A motion to allocate time in the legislature differs from closure in that it does not stipulate that a question must be immediately put, but instead establishes a fixed timetable for its passage, which is then subject to ratification by the Assembly. In substance, however, time allocation has the same effect as closure since it empowers the government to bring an end to a debate (Marleau and Montpetit 2000). This makes it easier for the executive to secure the timely implementation of its agenda since it establishes formal limits on the amount of time that can be spent debating and scrutinizing the executive branch without having to resort to the use of closure.

Delegated Legislation

Delegated legislation grants "to Ministers, departments, boards or other authorities the power to make and apply subordinate legislation described only in general terms in the acts" (O'Brien and Bosc 2009, n.p.). It includes the use of Orders in Council, regulations, and other statutory instruments to give ministers the authority to create rules that have the force of law under the parent legislation passed by the Assembly (ibid.). Orders in Council require the signature of the Governor-in-Council to take force. However, regulations can be made by a delegated authority without a requirement that such approval be granted. Given the similarities of all these instruments, the word *regulation* is often used as a universal term to capture all varieties of delegated legislation. Because these terms are often used interchangeably by the parliamentary actors observed for this project, I adopt this practice of using *regulation* generically, to refer to all delegated legislation, to avoid confusion.

The use of delegated legislation allows the executive "to fill in many of the details" of legislation passed in the House, and it causes members to "surrender most of the power of scrutiny and veto they would have been able to exercise if those details had been included in the parent bill" (Beith 1981, 166). It can provide governments with the flexibility to make difficult or controversial decisions without having to expose themselves to public and parliamentary scrutiny.

Mallory argued that delegated legislation is necessary because "parliament has neither the technical skill nor the time to process the mass of detailed regulation." However, he warned that unless it was carefully monitored, it risked establishing a regime of "bureaucratic tyranny" (1953, 462). While it would be impossible for the executive to conduct the complex and far-reaching responsibilities of a modern government without access to these powers, if they are used too extensively, they risk undermining the capacity of the Assembly to hold the government to account.

Governance through delegated authority provides three obvious benefits to the executive. First, it frees the executive "from the necessity of introducing legislative proposals subject to the full parliamentary process." Second, it "relieves the pressures of time on the floor" of the Assembly, allowing the executive to implement its policies at a speed that is nearly impossible when they are subjected to the rigours of the parliamentary process. Third, it allows for heightened control and supervision over the policy-implementation process and permits the executive to "introduce detailed rules and make swift legislative responses to emergencies" (Bates 1986, 114).

The problem, as Michael Taggart maintained, is not the use of delegated legislation itself, but "that parliaments keep delegating broad, open-ended powers, and not infrequently refuse to resile in the face of parliamentary opposition." As its use has grown in the post-war era, most delegated legislation today "has evaded most, if not all, of those parliamentary safeguards" (Taggart 2005, 624). Matthew Flinders has claimed that delegated legislation is "a model of accountability that was designed to legitimate the development of a minimalist late-Victorian state," but that has come to assume a significant role in the process of public-sector management, serving as the "buckle" between the public administration and parliament (Flinders 2004, 767).

Delegated legislation at the Ontario Legislature is subject to scrutiny through the Standing Committee on Regulations and Private Bills. The committee's mandate is to study regulations "with particular reference to the scope and method of the exercise of delegated legislative power without reference to the merits of the policy or objectives" (Ontario. Legislative Assembly 2020). The committee's primary objective is to rise above partisan bickering to perform the critical task of providing sober assessments of the procedural and administrative processes used to implement legislation. Since 1991, the Standing Committee on Government Agencies, an all-party committee that reviews the appointments and actions of semi-independent agencies and boards, has offered an additional way to provide oversight of the policy-implementation process (Pond 2008).

One of the claims made in this book is that delegated legislation has increasingly served as a critical instrument in the neoliberal restructuring process. Major, highly controversial austerity policies, such as reforms to the province's hospital and education system, as well as the restructuring of its major cities, were achieved largely by way of regulation. During the Harris era, the government granted supervisory committees sweeping powers to override democratically elected local school board and city council representatives to impose fiscal retrenchment. Consequently, during the neoliberal restructuring of Ontario, the expansive use of regulations has been an important point of contention between government and opposition.

Conclusion

The mediation of the equilibrium between the executive and legislative branches forms the essence of the story this book will attempt to tell. What follows traces the contours of this process, relying primarily upon Hansard transcripts, the *Journals of the Legislative Assembly*, and government legislation to offer a narrative about how this process unfolded. One of the advantages of this approach is that it provides the perspectives of the actors involved in the context of the historical moment in which they occurred. This avoids the problem of revisionist approaches to events often found in interviews with public officials. We can also acquire a perspective on how both government and opposition members reacted to rule changes, while bypassing the prejudice that often plagues reinterpretations of historical events by actors who already know how circumstances will play out. This book largely allows the actors to speak for themselves, weaving a narrative about how procedure has changed at Queen's Park. The objective is to gain footing on the largely untrodden ground of the relationship between broader policy trends and observable changes to the functioning of political institutions.

The challenge, however, is that there is little reliable, documentary evidence beyond Hansard transcripts and government legislation that tells the story of the legislature as well as these resources do. A search of Cabinet documents at the Archives of Ontario dating back to 1981 revealed background information on policy-making processes, but had little to say about parliamentary procedure or methods of governance.

The subsequent chapters attempt to lay down another brick in the foundation of our understanding of the decline-of-parliament thesis by providing a historical overview of the weakening of the legislative apparatus in Ontario. Following a theoretical consideration of the role of the state in the age of neoliberalism in chapters 3 and 4, the chapters proceed chronologically, reviewing the tenure of each Ontario Parliament from the beginning of the Davis government's final mandate up to the Ford government's first term in office. It is hoped that taking a journey through the annals of Ontario's parliamentary history will reveal the gradual erosion of the legislature's accountability function and the rationale for this shift in approach to legislative governance.

3 Renovating Liberalism: Rejecting the Sovereignty of Parliament

Introduction

Neoliberalism developed in response to what its early theorists believed was a crisis of welfare-state, liberal capitalism in the mid-twentieth century (Biebricher 2019). Neoliberal thinkers lamented the extent to which the bureaucratic central planning of the Keynesian welfare state had overtaken the principles of free market competition as the primary objective of state activity. Although the political reforms advanced by neoliberal theorists have received less attention than their economic reforms, they believed the continued expansion of the welfare state reflected a problem *within* the political forms of liberalism itself. That is, the ascendency of Keynesianism was taken as a reflection of the failures of modern parliamentary democracies to serve the actual needs and concerns of the majority, whose interests were most effectively reflected through the outcomes of free market transactions. The idea that parliament needed to be reformed so that it could be "depoliticized" and adopt the principles of economic rationalism has deep roots in the neoliberal tradition. Increasingly, public officials have embraced this essential logic in their attitudes towards parliament.

Most neoliberals believed that the rules and procedures of democratic institutions functioned as an impediment to implementing their reforms. Parliamentary sovereignty, which granted an assembly of individuals supreme law-making authority, was for neoliberalism's most renowned thinker, Friedrich Hayek, the root of the problem with modern society. Not only did a sovereign parliament possess the authority to rigidly impose its ideas on the community, but it also exploited the many at the expense of the few by way of an incentive structure that privileged elite special interests.

This chapter contends that one of neoliberalism's chief objectives was to "renovate" liberalism by rolling back the notion of parliamentary sovereignty that lies at the foundation of the modern liberal-democratic state. In so doing, the neoliberals sought a constitutional order closer to the kind envisioned by John Locke in the seventeenth century rather than the form of representative parliamentary democracy that had become prevalent around the world during the nineteenth and twentieth centuries. These reforms, which had led to developments such as responsible government and the expansion of democratic suffrage, were understood by neoliberals such as Hayek to represent the main point of departure, when liberalism had become corrupted by an entirely different epistemological world view.

Old and New Forms of Liberalism

For John Dewey ([1935] 1963, 620), *liberalism* is a political system designed to protect individual natural rights that existed before the formation of concrete social organization, such as life, liberty, and property. There have been principally two historical forms of liberalism. The first, which I shall refer to as "old liberalism," is represented by the logic of John Locke, who claimed that the state's central function should be to secure certain fundamental "natural rights," which governed civil conduct before formal political society was established. Though the liberal state was grounded in a social contract, political, and legal rights were initially extended only to a narrow class of property-owning men.

It was not until early in the nineteenth century that a "new liberalism" came into existence. It emerged from a fundamentally different epistemology, which prioritized rationalism as well as responsible government and democratic rights over the natural law tradition. The idea persisted during this period that it was possible to use human reason to overcome ancient structural inequities. It was under new liberalism that reforms to the electoral system to expand the democratic franchise to all adults and responsible government, were realized.

John Locke and "Old" Liberalism

The "old" form of liberalism is most clearly expressed by Locke, who believed that human behaviour is conditioned by a series of natural laws, which act as a guide for human action. These natural laws are intrinsic characteristics common to individuals across time and space, which incline them to carry out certain behaviours. Natural law confers upon people certain rights, such as to life, liberty, and the pursuit of property. Absolute sovereignty is vested in God, but since human beings are unable to access His will, they are guided in practice by their own reason, applying these natural rights to the realm of the law.

Natural laws identify certain fixed and immutable truths about the nature of the world that are not subject to reform. Individuals use their reason to improve the application of the laws of nature to them, but not to supersede or transcend them. By *reason*, Locke did not mean the "faculty of the understanding which forms trains of thought and deduces proofs," but rather "definite principles of action from which spring all virtues and whatever is necessary for the proper building of morals." Reason helps us to understand how the laws of nature should be administered, but is not so much the "maker of that law as its interpreter" (Locke [1689] 2014, 111).

Beginning from a perspective that viewed the accumulation of property as a natural right, Locke argued that the democratic franchise and political rights ought to extend only to those who were deemed rational enough to belong to civil society by owning property. God, Locke claimed, gave the earth to "the industrious and the rational" to cultivate for their own use and enjoyment, but not for the frivolity of the "quarrelsome and contentious," who did not use their labour to appropriate the land. He claimed that, according to natural law, this latter group of individuals, who, either by choice or by conquest, did not hold property could not possibly belong to civil society since they lacked the reason to do so.

> These men having, as I say, forfeited their lives, and with it their liberties, and lost their estates; and being in the state of slavery, not capable of any property, cannot in that state be considered as any part of civil society; the chief end whereof is the preservation of property. (Locke [1689] 2014, 50)

Locke was thus able to logically justify the exclusion of all members of the "quarrelsome and contentious" from the democratic franchise on the grounds that they were not considered a part of civil society. He also drew a clear distinction between the political and economic functions of the state. Locke saw the establishment of the state as a social contract between free and consenting individuals seeking to preserve property that they had acquired through their own industriousness. The state existed primarily to provide protection for this economic wealth and, as such, was not authorized under any circumstances to redistribute wealth from the industrious to the quarrelsome.

Locke draws his understanding of the function of government from his conception of the state of nature. Although human beings have appetites and aversions that guide their behaviours, they have sufficient reason to live in accordance with evolved principles of morality and conduct in civil society without the need for a government. While Thomas Hobbes derived an obligation to the state from a fear of a state of total war in a world without government, Locke used the state of nature to sketch the natural rights of man (Macpherson 1980). In the state of nature, human beings enjoy the rights to life and liberty as well as the right to pursue their livelihood through the accumulation of property.

Although there will be some transgressors of these principles in the state of nature, they are likely to be in the minority and do not legitimate the need to transfer absolute power to a single authority, as Hobbes suggested (Macpherson 1980). However, the potential of such transgressions means that it is in the rational interest of individuals to leave the state of nature to form civil government, the end of which should be to establish a framework to secure the natural rights of man by enforcing these principles as formal laws.

The authority of the government, however, should be limited and subject to revocation by the community if it violates any of the natural rights that individuals already possess in the state of nature. Accordingly, authority should be vested in a legislative assembly that has the necessary power to make and enforce the laws of nature as well as to secure property by retaining the power to make legitimate use of violence on behalf of these principles.

Although Locke believed that the legislature should be the supreme law-making body within a society, he allowed that its authority should not be sovereign. Since individuals already knew how to live together before government had been established, there was no need for the legislature to make laws beyond the parameters of the laws of nature. Locke believed these laws of nature served "as an eternal rule to all men, legislators as well as others. The rules that they make for other men's actions, must, as well as their own and other men's actions, be conformable to the law of nature" (Locke [1689] 2014, 72).

Any attempts to engage in active legislating beyond these established principles constituted a violation and permitted the public to revoke its authority through the right to revolution. The chief function of Locke's legislature, then, was to formalize these natural laws and to ensure their execution in practice. Locke sought to grant authority to the legislature not to make laws as it desired, but to lay down and protect those natural rights already established before government was formed. In this respect, the legislature served as a sort of trusteeship, one in which a group of individuals was granted the power to make decisions on behalf of others, but only under the conditions that had been previously specified under the agreement (Macpherson 1980).

While liberal theory adapted to the popular struggles of the nineteenth and twentieth centuries, which sought an expansion of the democratic franchise to ever-larger segments of the population, the logical separation between the state's legal and economic roles remained largely unchallenged. In the middle of the twentieth century, Canadian political theorist C.B. Macpherson emerged as one of democracy's most important analysts. He claimed that liberal democracy was grounded in an orthodoxy of "possessive individualism," in which the function of the state was to preserve the rights of individuals to pursue their own ends, as members of both general society and market society.

The job of the liberal state, then, was to uphold market relations through the mediation of trade, the protection of property, and the security of certain individual rights and freedoms. However, these principles were never meant to be applied equally – indeed, from the beginning, only propertied men were given the right to vote. Given that the very logic of liberalism was to legitimize and rationalize the exchange of money as capital, and to protect property from intervention by feudal governments, it required a state form that would not reach so far as to abolish the division of labour, which was necessary for the ascension of this new, liberal class.

The liberal form of democracy, through the responsible party system, was a movement by an emerging bourgeois class to establish a state system that was both logically and substantively consistent with its collective goals (Macpherson 1965). Maintaining a disempowered working class would be crucial to the bourgeoisie attaining its class objectives (ibid.). Representative democracy, then, "came as a late addition to the competitive market society," and, as a "top dressing" to the liberal state, it was admitted only as a means of maintaining the legitimacy of the liberal order as increased demands on the state to extend the franchise became impossible and logically inconsistent to ignore (ibid, 5–9).

Once applied, democracy had to "accommodate itself to the soil that had already been prepared by the operation of the competitive individualist market society and by the operation of the liberal state, which served that through a system of freely competing, though not democratic political parties" (Macpherson 1965, 5). In short, by the time democracy had been universalized, it had to be defanged of its revolutionary and class characteristics, and the liberal state was able to absorb the entire franchise without having to resort to a wholesale change of the liberal system itself.

Jeremy Bentham and "New" Liberalism

It was not until the beginning of the nineteenth century that the liberal tradition began to embrace the concept of universal legal and political rights. English legal and political philosopher Jeremy Bentham argued that the underlying nature of power relations, and the entrenched, comprehensive political systems designed to sustain class power, demanded a radical reconfiguration of constitutionalism.

In his early career, Bentham subscribed to the Enlightenment view that virtue was an inherent human trait that some individuals possessed. Corrupt government could be attributed to the ineffective and unscrupulous nature of public officials rather than being a systemic or structural problem. By the early nineteenth century, however, Bentham had come to recognize that the common law tradition, upon which English political systems were based, was designed to embed and legitimize the authority of a ruling class.

As Don Jackson (1991) has argued, by 1809, Bentham's thought had transformed from a utiltarian theory of virtue to one based upon a phenomenological principle of universal egoism. This shift in Bentham's thinking can be attributed to his development of a single, psychological maxim, which, he argued, could explain all social behaviour: the self-preference principle (SPP). According to the SPP, the impulse for individuals to pursue pleasure and avoid pain guides human action at the expense of the pleasure or suffering of others. The SPP, for Bentham, functioned as an "all-comprehensive" view of human nature, in which "the self-regarding interest is predominant over all other interests put together" (Bentham 1830, 5).

Bentham was able to see political institutions as vestiges of historical power relations, structurally embedding the hegemony of the ruling class by designing systems with laws, systems, and norms that consolidated its authority. The implications of the SPP as a philosophical principle threw off the illusions of the natural law tradition, which had been used to justify the preservation of class privilege. Instead, using the SPP as a foundation, one could study government in the abstract, as a coherent system with predictable outcomes. It followed that those public functionaries who acted without some other incentive to serve as a counterweight to their private interests would inevitably behave with "sinister interest" or intent. Bentham contended that this had been true of the role of government throughout history:

> At all times – on every occasion – in every instance, the end actually pursued by the several sets of rulers, has been the promotion of the particular, and thence sinister interest of these same rulers. Look the world all over, in no one place, at no one time, has any arrangement of government and for its object, any other object than the interest by whom it has been made. (Bentham 1830, 2)

There could be no Great Men or Philosopher Kings, only pleasure-seeking and pain-averting beings, all of whom were subject to the SPP. Notions of "character" and "position-in-life" were the grounds upon which sinister interest had been justified over the centuries and "locked in" by legal structures that had been organized to benefit the ruling few. Having come to understand human behaviour as being conditioned by interest based upon circumstance, Bentham believed that establishing a radical constitutional system was the only way to bring an end to the corrupt, self-interested rule of the aristocratic class.

Bentham devised a complex constitutional structure in which the legislature would be sovereign and elected by way of universal suffrage – extended to all adult citizens, regardless of gender, class, or social status. The legislature would become, in effect, a "public opinion tribunal," which would function like a large jury, while providing a forum to keep rulers "in check and keep its course within the paths indicated by the greatest happiness principle" (Bentham 1830, 41). Those officials who failed to behave in ways consistent with the greatest happiness principle would have their authority counterbalanced or taken away by the public opinion tribunal. The legislature's role was not simply to pass laws but also to serve as a counterforce to the abuse of executive authority. Though the executive would retain the authority for carrying out the law, it would be responsible to the legislature, which would, in turn, be accountable to a universally representative electorate.

Constitutional artifices, established to hold governors to account, were designed to subordinate the ruling class to those over whom they ruled, thereby ensuring that their own egoistic interests would be under the constant scrutiny of the public opinion tribunal. A sovereign parliament was a necessary condition of good government since those officials not subject to accountability mechanisms were certain to pursue their own ends at the expense of the public interest.

Hayek and Constructivist Rationalism

It was precisely at this pivotal point in the early nineteenth century, when the liberal tradition embraced a philosophical radicalism based on the principle of universal egoism, that the neoliberals believed liberalism had become fatally corrupted. Writing more than a century after Bentham, Friedrich Hayek, one of the most important thinkers in the development of the neoliberal school of thought, advocated a reconfiguration of the principles of liberalism as part of an effort to undermine the "constructivist rationalism" upon which modern political institutions had been structured (Hayek 1982, 1:28). He believed that the beginning of the nineteenth century, and the conferral of sovereignty upon parliament, was the moment that liberalism had lost its way.

Hayek claimed that the history of liberalism could be characterized by two forms of rationalism. First, the seventeenth- and eighteenth-century approaches to the character of knowledge viewed reason as a guide for selecting, although not transcending, the laws of nature. Second, a form of rationalism emerged in the nineteenth century, based on a universal maxim that saw human egoism as the foundation of all public institutions (Gamble 2006). It was this second form of post-eighteenth century rationalism, embodied by Bentham and his followers, that Hayek considered the most dangerous. Granting the authority to legislators to design society in accordance with notions of equality or social justice represented encroachments upon the common law, which had emerged over centuries.

Hayek believed that most of history had been guided by a series of practical lessons, traditions, customs, and norms, which had been learned and passed down collectively through the ages and established as general rules upon which political community was structured. The trouble with efforts to structure the law upon the dictates of reason was that it conceived of humans as having "an independently existing mind substance which stands outside the cosmos of nature," thus granting to each person the authority and right to "design the institutions of society and culture among which he lives" (Hayek 1982, 1:17). Indeed, he argued that "the whole history of constitutionalism" had been characterized by "a struggle against the positivist conception of sovereignty and the allied conception of the omnipotent state" (1:6).

Constructivist rationalism, in which political decisions are made by deliberate design, leads to "false conclusions" because it is not possible for any single person, or assembly of people, to understand "circumstances which we are not aware of and which yet determine the pattern of our successful actions" (Hayek 1982, 1:12). Those who subscribe to the rationalist view, Hayek argued, exist under the spell of a "synoptic delusion," in which they believe that "relevant facts are known to some one mind, and that it is possible to construct from this knowledge of the particulars a desirable social order" (1:14).

Hayek contended that, since the development of capitalism, the "Great Society" had been arrived at by the establishment of a market-based order. Since there exists no overarching structure in which the facts are known, or a single mind that can know all, the market offers "a procedure that is on the whole likely to bring about a situation where more of the potentially useful objective facts will be taken into account than would be done in any other procedure which we know" (Hayek 1982, 3:68). Market relations establish "agreement on common ends which in turn are mostly non-economic" and function as a way for societies to adapt to that which is unknowable in a dispersed manner (2:112). He turned to metaphor to explain the importance of competition, suggesting that it was like an "experimentation in science, first and foremost a study in procedure," one in which the outcomes were unpredictable (3:68).

The variables that condition the development of the law "inevitably come in part from outside the law and can be beneficial only if they are based on a true conception about how the activities in a Great Society can be effectively ordered" (Hayek 1982, 3:70). Both the market and traditional values function as ideal guides for social organization because they are the result of abstract processes that generate knowledge, which no individual has consciously planned.

Their outcomes are not planned in any kind of sequential manner, but are the result of individuals pursuing their own rational self-interest in ways that benefit the whole community.

In the market, ideas are reaffirmed by the price mechanism, which confers the wisdom of the many. Similarly, traditional values represent the outcome of a dialectic of trial and error carried out by community members over centuries. This process leads to the emergence of certain spontaneously arrived-at truths, which are dictated by no one, but which convey the essential will of the community.

Hayek believed that preserving these spontaneously evolved principles ought to form the foundation of the law. Following the Lockean tradition, he believed that the legislature should be restricted from actively making the law and should instead focus on laying down and securing the intrinsic principles common to all members of the community. Such laws should be derived from knowledge "of which we are not aware, and which does not appear in our conceptual thought, but which manifests itself in the rules which we obey in our actions" (Hayek 1982, 2:21).

This belief necessarily also meant that Hayek rejected the principle of popular sovereignty upon which the liberal tradition, dating back to Hobbes, had been based. However, while he believed that the idea of popular sovereignty being vested in a leviathan was a misguided, "anthropomorphic" fantasy, he did not reject the idea of popular rule outright (Hayek 1982, 1:10). The "constructivist-positivist superstition" led to the emergence of the perspective that "there must be some single unlimited supreme power from which all other power is derived" (3:129). The conceptual error made by the Western liberal tradition, then, lay "not in the belief that whatever power there is should be in the hands of the people, and that their wishes will have to be expressed by majority decisions, but in the belief that the ultimate source of this power must be unlimited, that is, the idea of sovereignty itself" (3:27).

For Hayek, the problem with the idea of popular sovereignty was that it granted unlimited power to the state, which would inevitably trend towards tyranny. Instead, sovereignty should be located within the community itself, exercised through decentralized power structures in civil society such as the market, thereby preserving against abuses by public officials. This is a critical point because it helps to explain why Hayek and the neoliberals took issue with the turn to philosophical radicalism and parliamentary sovereignty that had occurred at the beginning of the nineteenth century.

The issue, for Hayek, was not that the law should be based on the principle of majority rule, but that the legislature should be granted unlimited power to make laws without being restricted by the common law or these general principles passed down through the ages.

It was for this reason that Hayek believed modern parliament to be the "root of evil," since it grants formal legal and political sovereignty to a collective body to render decisions on behalf of the body politic. The existence of disparate interests in society creates a "constant necessity of satisfying special interests," which ultimately leads to excessive government action over the free will of individuals. Politicians take this action, he argued, "not because the majority is interventionist, but because the ruling party would not retain a majority if it did not buy the support of particular groups by the promise of special advantages" (Hayek 1973, 10). An institutional arrangement in which parliament has ultimate law- and policy-making authority "can only lead to a steady growth of the preponderance of government over law" (Hayek 1982, 3:31).

Granting a legislative assembly unlimited power, Hayek argued, was akin to "leaving the cat in charge of the cream-jug – there soon won't be any, at least no law in the sense in which it limits the discretionary powers of government" (Hayek 1982, 3:31). "Permanent limits" should be placed on the coercive authority of government intervention in the market, which "even the democratically-elected governmental assembly could not overstep" (Hayek 1973,

21). An ideal legislature would be stripped of its supremacy as the ultimate source of authority and required to function within a framework of limited technocratic power.

Hayek suggested his own radical constitutional reforms, in which power would be divided between a Legislative Assembly (upper house), responsible for the mediation and evolution of the rules of just conduct, and a Governmental Assembly (lower house), which would provide for health and safety, while creating the conditions necessary for market relations and looking after the daily operation of government. The upper chamber would be comprised of legislators between the ages of 45 and 60, assigned to 15-year terms, and would function as a common-law judge might, gradually redefining the just rules of conduct in accordance with tradition and custom. Meanwhile, the Governmental Assembly would be responsible for establishing the concrete form of the law, making decisions only within the confines of the rules set out by the legislature.

In *Economic Freedom and Representative Government*, Hayek pointed to Locke's model of limited government within a framework of market relations as a model of how a legislature ought to function.

> John Locke made it very clear that in a free state even the power of the legislative body should be limited in a definite manner, namely to the passing of laws in the specific sense of general rules of just conduct equally applicable to all citizens. That all coercion would be legitimate only if it meant the application of general rules of law in this sense became the basic principle of liberalism. (Hayek 1973, 10)

Under the Hayekian model, parliament's role would be returned to the functions established by John Locke's conception of a supreme, but not sovereign, legislature. The legislature should be "not all comprehensive," but rather "confined to restraining both organized government and private persons and organizations by the enforcement of the general rules of conduct" (Hayek 1982, 3:135). Its authority should be constrained by the establishment of "long run rules which nobody has the power to alter or abrogate in the service of particular ends" (3:129). Parliament's primary function would be comparable to that of the Lockean legislature in that it would both secure and nurture the wisdom inherent in tradition as contemporary jurisprudence, while surrendering its capacity to arbitrarily create the law. Hayek's issue with contemporary liberalism, then, was primarily a political and institutional one. The nature of the sovereign parliament established an institutional imperative for legislators to continually satisfy the needs of those interests upon whom they depended for their support. Legislators were "forced" to make use of their discretionary powers "to favour particular groups on whose swing-vote their powers depend" (3:139).

Regardless of whether the legislators were "angels or profoundly convinced of the supreme value of personal freedom," the incentive structure of parliamentary democracy caused them to assume the view that "they can obtain power to do any good only if they commit themselves to secure special benefits for various groups" (Hayek 1982, 3:135). In this way, a sovereign parliament was "the main cause of a progressive and accelerating increase of the power and the weight of the administrative machine" (3:138).

A sovereign parliament was institutionally predisposed to use its power to expand the welfare state ad infinitum. Accordingly, the idea of a sovereign parliament was "wholly in conflict with the conception of a constitutional limitation of governmental power, and irreconcilable with the ideal of a society of free men" (Hayek 1982, 3:134). So long as parliament was authorized to "use force to effect a redistribution of material benefits," something Hayek referred to as constituting the "heart of socialism," there could be "no curb on the rapacious instincts of all groups who want more for themselves" (3:150).

Constitutional reform that stripped parliament of its sovereignty was among the few solutions that could achieve the "dethronement of politics" from the operation of government. It would reorient political concerns towards more worthwhile endeavours, such as regulating the market and laying down the rules of conduct, while making "all socialist measures for redistribution impossible" (Hayek 1982, 3:149–50). This "depoliticization" of state activities, replacing the virtue of political discourse and consensus-building with the logic of market rationalism, has been a central feature of neoliberal governance, and it is discussed further in the chapters to follow.

Hayek viewed the growth of the welfare state in the decades after the Second World War as a particularly dangerous overreach of deliberate design, contending that "so long as the belief in social justice governs political action, this process must progressively approach nearer and nearer to a totalitarian system" (Hayek 1982, 2:68). Later, he wrote,

> The dispute between the market order and socialism is no less than a matter of survival. To follow socialist morality would destroy much of present humankind and impoverish much of the rest. (Hayek 1988, 7)

It was with this level of urgency that Hayek thought that the radical, rationalist overreach of the twentieth century had to be unwound through constitutional reform. In his proposed constitution, Hayek argued that there were circumstances in which the use of emergency powers, concentrating authority at the centre of the political apparatus, might be justified. He contended that circumstances might arise "when the preservation of the overall order becomes the overruling common purpose." Thus, he argued, there may come a time when "the spontaneous order, on a local or national scale, must for a time be converted into an organization" to consolidate power as a means of preserving the rules of conduct (Hayek 1982, 3:124). He wrote that "like an animal in flight from mortal danger society may in such situations have to suspend temporarily even vital functions on which in the long run its existence depends if it is to escape destruction" (ibid.).

However, Hayek was willing to go even further in his rationalization of the use of emergency law. Though he admitted that there were "major dangers" with dictatorships, he argued that there were circumstances in which they were justified. For example, in an interview with the press while visiting Chile in 1981, he suggested that the institution of an authoritarian regime could be necessary in some cases during a "transitional period" to a liberal-democratic, market-based order.

> Sometimes it is necessary for a country to have, for a time, some form of dictatorial power. As you will understand, it is possible for a dictator to govern in a liberal way. And it is also possible for a democracy to govern with a total lack of liberalism. I personally prefer a liberal dictator to a democratic government lacking liberalism. (Friedrich Hayek, quoted in Caldwell and Montes 2015, 298)

Thus, though dictatorships should not be a long-term solution, they could serve to stabilize regimes while the conditions necessary for market relations were being cultivated. Hayek's chief concern was not securing popular consent, but rather establishing the conditions necessary to allow the fragmented wisdom of individual transactions in the market to serve as the foundation of government. While liberty required "a certain degree of democracy," Hayek viewed it as incompatible with "the existence of a representative legislative assembly with all-embracing powers" (Friedrich Hayek, quoted in Caldwell and Montes 2015, 301).

Conclusion

Although they represented a radical departure from the complexion of modern democratic institutions, Hayek's constitutional reforms were an essential element of his thought. Parliamentary sovereignty was not a mere inconvenience, but the central cause of liberalism's decline because it granted arbitrary authority to the legislature to design the law in accordance with its will. Rent-seeking democracies were limited by their inability to assess the quality of decisions since they, unlike the market, did not contain a mechanism for measuring policy effectiveness, and they were structurally prone to the state expanding by privileging those special interests whose support its members required for political survival.

It was the conferral of sovereignty to parliament that incentivized and facilitated the irreversible trend towards state expansionism. Until constitutional reform could be achieved, society would always be prone to varying degrees of socialism as politicians privileged the interests of the few at the expense of the many. In the spirit of the Lockean tradition, the state's objective was to lay down the general principles as they had been agreed upon by the community; parliament was consigned to a largely administrative role, fine-tuning the application of the general rules, and regulating the market. A sovereign parliament retained the capacity to transcend these general principles on the supposition that it knew best how to govern the lives of others.

The Hayekian perspective contradicted the recognition at the root of the modern liberal-democratic state that human egoism requires the presence of constant scrutiny to counter governmental authority. Bentham's SPP rejected the Hayekian principle that rulers throughout history had acted in the interest of the collective by formalizing into law spontaneous principles that were selected because they were the most useful to the survival of the community. History demonstrated that members of the ruling class had established laws, structures, and ideologies that preserved their own positions of authority and their own interests. Political institutions that were not organized to maintain constant scrutiny of those vested with the power of the state were opposed to the interests of the community.

In the neoliberal era, the idea of responsible government has been flipped on its head, as the executive authority has commonly functioned as a shell for the advancement of a market-based order, protecting controversial decisions from the reach of a sovereign legislature. Using procedural techniques, the executive has increased its influence over parliament, increasingly shielding policy reforms from its purview and rendering decisions without consulting it. This has had the practical effect of limiting the authority of the legislature and enabling contentious neoliberal policies to pass through its chambers with minimal disruption from the opposition. In other words, the concentration of political authority in the executive has served as a way for public officials to evade the sovereignty of the legislature without undertaking the kind of radical constitutional reforms that Hayek suggests are necessary to repair liberalism.

In Ontario, governments have repeatedly invoked the notion of economic and fiscal crises to rationalize placing restrictions on the legislature, or rushing a piece of legislation through the assembly. To leave critical decisions about the economy subject to parliament was to invite stasis and ineffective decision-making. Only the executive, freed from the constraints of legislative process, was sufficiently clear-eyed to make the decisions necessary to promote collective prosperity and establish the conditions for market rule. Chapter 4 discusses the extent to which the concentration of political power at the centre of the political apparatus has been an essential feature of actually existing neoliberalism and demonstrates ways in which evolving attitudes towards the role of legislative procedure in the neoliberal era have contributed to this changing dynamic.

4 Neoliberalism and the Strong State

Introduction

Although neoliberalism is popularly associated with the enhancement of freedom, it emerged from a theoretical tradition that recognized the concentration of political power in the executive as being essential to the cultivation of the preconditions for a market-based order. One of the common themes linking the neoliberal tradition with its intellectual cousin, the German ordoliberal school, is that both viewed modern representative-democratic institutions as practical impediments to implementing their ideas; they saw a strong state as a remedy to this problem. While the neoliberals sought to reduce the role of the state in the economy, except where necessary to create the circumstances necessary for free market exchange, the ordoliberals were more explicitly committed to using state institutions to consolidate and manage a competitive market order. Many of the ideas promoted by the ordoliberal school, even some of the more extreme elements, such as bringing in constitutional reforms to tie the hands of legislators to neoliberal principles, have become increasingly conventional aspects of political discourse today (Biebricher 2019).

The ordoliberals, like their neoliberal counterparts, were concerned with the ways in which rent-seeking, representative democratic systems led to inefficiencies in the market and what they considered to be the ceaseless expansion of the welfare state. They believed that the economy should be guided by a constitutional order that could protect a well-functioning market economy, even as political attitudes and cultures evolved over time (Karsten 1985).

German ordoliberal Walter Eucken noted that institutional reform was necessary because the problem of the perpetually expanding state would "not solve itself simply by letting our economic system grow up spontaneously." Eucken insisted that the state required "an economic constitution" to protect the price mechanism from rent-seeking interest groups. The "economic system had to be consciously shaped" and reformed to ensure its proper functioning and to adjust to changing social, political, and cultural conditions over time (Eucken 2012, 314).

Fellow ordoliberal Wilhelm Röpke also insisted on the need for a strong state to shape economic relations. He claimed that economic policy should be based upon "definite rules and fixed principles to restrict the sphere of arbitrary action as much as possible." The economy ought to be protected from the excessive reach of the state and treated as though it were "an unbreakable toy." To avoid what he called the "ruthless exploitation of the state by the mob of vested interests," it was necessary to have "a really strong state, a government with the courage to govern" (Röpke 1950, 192).

The idea of establishing a constitutional order to bind the legislature to market principles was also consistent with several variants of neoliberal thought. As discussed in chapter 3, Hayek believed that the legislature should be deprived of its sovereignty and reduced to performing technocratic functions within the confines of an economic constitution. American neoliberal thinker James Buchanan argued in favour of a "contractarian" approach to economic relations, which held that political systems should be evaluated in terms of "the comparative ease or facility with which voluntary exchanges, contracts, or trades may be arranged between and among members of the community" (Buchanan 1988, 135).

Buchanan believed that the legislature should be restricted to essential functions such as taxing and spending, within strict constitutional limits that demanded conformity to market logic. He recommended that governments pass constitutional amendments requiring balanced budgets to restrict democratically elected legislatures from excessive spending. These constitutional limits should be absolute and enforceable by the judiciary if a legislature attempted to violate them (Buchanan 1988).

The solution for neoliberal and ordoliberal thinkers to the problem of democracy was to place limitations on legislative institutions to protect the market from the overreach of parliament. Given its need to actualize programs that were opposed by considerable segments of the population, actually existing neoliberalism required a strong, centralized state that could secure the rule of the market and implement its policies through its legislative and administrative branches. This chapter offers an assessment of the ways in which neoliberalism has used the strong state as a political shell to transfer class power, while maintaining social order.

Poulantzas and the Relative Autonomy of the State

Given that neoliberalism's central impact has been to privilege the interests of owners of private capital, it has required a political form that could insulate it from a shift in the balance of class forces. Marxist theorist Nicos Poulantzas's thought offers insight into the development of this phenomenon. He claimed that forces comprising the state are born from historically determined social relations between competing classes. For Poulantzas, the state's chief responsibility is to maintain a "unity of formation" in society by privileging the dominant class over others and embedding its hegemony in the state's institutions (Poulantzas 1978, 49). The state does not protect the interests of the dominant class because it is an instrument of their rule, but rather because it has "the particular function of constituting the levels of cohesion between the levels of a social formation" (44).

The fact that the state gives preference to one class at the expense of another does not infer that it owes its legitimacy to the dominant class; rather, it is the dominant class that owes its existence and legitimacy to the sovereign power of the state, which retains a "structural selectivity" to choose a dominant group according to the material relations of that particular society (Jessop 1990, 146).

The Poulantzian view understands the state as a mediator among various interests, which have a "relative autonomy" from the influence of the dominant class (Poulantzas 1978, 301). However, this relative autonomy is always conditioned by the state's obligation to act in accordance with its central function to maintain cohesion in society. The state retains the right to determine which of the various classes will form the dominant class as well as the form of government under which their influence will be enforced.

As the balance among social forces changes, so too does the extent to which the state must support the dominant class to maintain a unity of formation. To fulfil its responsibility to keep society from breaking apart, the state requires the capacity to rearrange power relations in society in response to the constantly evolving dialectic of the class struggle. When the subordinate classes provide a significant counterforce to the power of the dominant group, the state may have to make certain concessions to the working class that are contrary to the short-term economic interest of the dominant class, but that secure their long-term interests by maintaining their legitimacy (Poulantzas 1978).

The state's power, then, is relative in the sense that its function to preserve social order requires it to have autonomy from any external influences. However, this power also implies that the state can operate only within the limited space provided to it by the social and economic context over which it governs. Thus, the state is neither a thing, nor is it a subject. By understanding it as an expression of power relationships within the social formation, it is possible to see the state as a distinct entity with the capacity to establish and consolidate political direction. Such political outcomes are "inscribed in the very structure of the state" and, thus, serve as a "material condensation of a relation of forces between classes and fractions of class" (Poulantzas 2008, 308).

Since the dialectic of class conflict is in constant motion, the state must adapt its policies to best achieve the objective of preserving social order. The power struggle between the executive and the legislative branches comes to reflect the struggle of the social formation, as Poulantzas understood it more broadly, metabolized through formal institutions. The legislature functions as an institutionalized counterforce through which the subordinate classes may locate and dislocate those functionaries who will exercise state power. While it provides formal channels for the subordinate classes to challenge the dominant class, political representation is nonetheless predominantly organized around the consolidation of the hegemony of the dominant group.

The relevance of Poulantzas's thought today is that it provides a framework by which to view the transfer of class power that has occurred over the last several decades under neoliberalism, as the state has gradually shifted its prioritization from ensuring its legitimacy within a militant working-class movement to nurturing the optimal conditions for the accumulation of capital among the dominant class in society (O'Connor 2003). As the state has sought to reconfigure power relations, it has altered the character of political institutions to secure the implementation of contentious legislation that is contrary to the interests of significant segments of society, chiefly the subordinate classes. As an embodiment of the broader class struggle, an analysis of the shifting power dynamics between the executive and the legislative branches within parliament offers the opportunity to examine a concrete representation of the reconstitution of power relations among social forces in recent decades.

The Strong State and the Decontestation of Politics in the Age of Neoliberal Hegemony

Leftist critiques have long observed that neoliberalism is inherently authoritarian. Andrew Gamble argued that neoliberals hold a paradoxical view of the world, which combines "a traditional liberal defence of the economy with a traditional conservative defence of state authority." The result is that contemporary neoliberal policy has witnessed a situation in which the state is "simultaneously rolled back and rolled forward. Non-interventionist and decentralized in some areas, the state is to be highly interventionist and centralized in others" (Gamble 1988, 28). Thus, while neoliberalism presents itself in the political cloak of enhancing freedom by reducing the role of government in social and economic life through the scaling back of welfarist policies, it is at the same time increasing the repressive function, seeking to fill the social vacuum that is created by the erosion of social programs through a more militarized state apparatus.

The competitive pressures placed on the state by globalization have given rise to what Phillip G. Cerny has called the "competition state." In its efforts to adapt to the changes brought about by the freeing of capital from national boundaries, "both the state and market actors are attempting to reinvent the state as a 'quasi-enterprise' association" on the basis of competitive market principles (Cerny 1997, 251). For Cerny, then, the competition state implies not a withdrawal of the state from intervention in the market, but rather a reorientation of its energies from a Keynesian, demand-oriented approach to an accumulation-oriented, neoliberal strategy. While neoliberal philosophy advocates a reduction in the activities of the state, Cerny (1997) argues that this is an illusion. Instead, in the age of the competition state, the interventionist role of government is expanded, with the government assuming responsibility for creating a policy climate most conducive to attracting foreign investment. He contends that the "crosscutting and overlapping government structures and processes" of the competition state take on "increasingly oligarchic forms where hegemonic neoliberal norms of economic freedom and personal autonomy are delegitimizing both democratic governance in general and the credibility of those who try to make democracy work" (Cerny 1999, 2).

Stephen Gill's notion of "new constitutionalism" (Gill 1995, 1) marks an important contribution to the question of the state's capacity to uphold the central pillars of representative democracy in the age of neoliberal globalization. He argues that governments have entrenched neoliberal policies in international trade treaties as a means of locking in such reforms by insulating them from democratic or parliamentary control and assuring that such policies "become the only method for future development" (Gill 2008, 139). These provisions "imply or mandate the insulation of key aspects of the economy or citizens by imposing, internally or externally, binding constraints on the conduct of fiscal, monetary and trade and investment policies" (138).

In addition to the centralizing tendencies that have characterized neoliberalism over the last several decades, and as parties throughout the West have adopted similar platforms and approaches structured around its general principles, neoliberalism has led to a flattening of ideological divisions within political institutions. This transition has been symbolized most clearly by the rise of what Anthony Giddens (2013) called the "Third Way" among social democratic parties, leading to the left's ideological embrace of the essential principles of neoliberal economic policy. The result has been to achieve the "dethronement of politics" from the process of governance, as an ideological consensus has emerged around certain principles of economic rationalism (Hayek 1982, 3:128).

The rise of the Third Way in the 1990s and 2000s arguably marked the moment at which neoliberalism attained complete hegemony. This approach to social democratic politics led to the "demise of socialism as a theory of economic management" and the rise of competitive market rationalism as the hegemonic paradigm (Giddens 2013, 29). Although this new brand of politics acknowledged the potential consequences of globalization, it also recognized that "protectionism is neither sensible nor desirable" and that the state must adjust to the realities brought about by an age of international economic competition (37). In short, it claims that there are no longer any realistic alternatives to neoliberal capitalism, reducing political discourse to conversations about "how far, and in what ways, capitalism should be governed and regulated" (29). It closes off all alternatives to the status quo, leaving an embrace of the market as the only plausible path for governments of all political affiliations. In Ontario, the politics of the Third Way were represented most clearly by the Rae government in the 1990s and the McGuinty/Wynne governments in the 2000s and 2010s. In each case, these governments embraced the essential economic logic of neoliberalism, while attempting to offset some of its more exploitative elements through modest efforts at redistribution and the embrace of socially progressive politics.

Social and cultural theorist Slavoj Žižek (2000) maintains that we have entered an age of post-politics, in which there are no real antagonisms left within the liberal-democratic frame. To illustrate this point, he claims that Fukuyama's infamous 1989 proclamation that humanity had reached "the end of history" in the form of liberal democracy has proved to be true thus far (Francis Fukuyama, quoted in Žižek 2008, 101). Today, he argues, meaningful disputes about the nature of our political systems are not taken seriously, even by the left. The real, substantive ideological debates about political, social, and economic systems have been deprived of their standing as legitimate alternatives to the existing neoliberal order.

What are left in their place are disputes about cultural accommodation and human rights, but they have been stripped of their counter-hegemonic ideals. The erosion of ideological contestation about the legitimacy of capitalism and liberalism, Žižek contends, poses a significant threat to democracy since democratic societies must present legitimate alternatives to the status quo to mount a meaningful challenge to the ruling class. The left's failure to challenge the foundational principles of neoliberalism, he argues, is symptomatic of the undemocratic nature of post-political society. A society in which alternatives to the existing system of order are not considered part of the political dialogue is unable to oppose elite rule.

Colin Crouch contended that politics has become so deprived of its essential content that we have entered an age of post-democracy, in which democratic institutions have been purged of their content by an elite class that has seized control of the state apparatus. While concrete democratic institutions remain throughout the Western nations, "politics and government are increasingly stepping back into the control of privileged elites in the manner characteristic of pre-democratic times" (Crouch 2004, 6). Public policy today is determined "in private interaction between private government and elites that overwhelmingly represent business interests" (4). This process, he argues, occurs on both the political and economic terrains. For Crouch, one of the central outcomes of the scaling back of the state has been that business interests have been empowered to control it by transferring as many of its social functions as possible to private ownership. Thus, while formal democratic institutions may remain in place, their potency to represent the public interest has been undermined by powerful, private influence on government representatives (Crouch 2004).

Chantal Mouffe has advanced the view that the decline of politics in the neoliberal era is the result of the emergence of what she called a "post-political consensus" (Mouffe 2005, 51). Neoliberalism, she argues, has led to the removal of "most crucial decisions concerning social and economic relations" from the realm of politics (53). As a consequence, modern political parties "have become unable to face societal problems in a political way," leading to an increased role for the "juridical sphere as the realm where social relations can find a form of expression" (53). This has created conditions that "are ripe for talented demagogues to articulate popular frustration" (55). It is, therefore, the "lack of an effective democratic debate about possible alternatives that has led in many countries to the success of political parties claiming to be the 'voice of the people'" (51).

In the political realm, Peter Mair has argued that the decline of parliament has been partially attributable to the "transformation of political parties" (Mair 2006, 25). Political parties are the lifeblood of parliamentary politics, providing forums for the organization of ideological divisions, connecting the legislature to the citizenry through party membership, and serving as the primary vehicle through which electoral politics are contested. Within Parliament, parties also play a critical role, aligning policy deliberation, votes, and communication of policy ideas with the public.

Mair claimed that the contemporary age has been characterized by a "depoliticizing" of political parties. Parties, on this view, proceed from the perspective that modern society is "self-organizing," no longer requiring sharp, ideological divisions that contest popular ideas of what constitutes the good life (Mair 2006, 26). Accordingly, the "government no longer seeks to wield power or even exercise authority," but rather plays a technocratic role, supervising the market and the social realm, while attempting to shore up political support by providing policy initiatives targeted only at those demographics likely to improve its electoral prospects (Mair 2013, 26).

The result has been a de-emphasis of popular sovereignty, replacing popular democracy with a more limited definition based upon the demands of the economy. Neoliberal hegemony has incentivized parties to focus primarily on minor differences between themselves and their political opposition. As a result, parties "can no longer adequately serve as a base for the activities and status of its own leaders, who direct their ambitions towards, and draw their resources from, external public institutions." Parties, Mair contended,

> are failing as a result of a mutual withdrawal, whereby citizens retreat into private life or more specialized and often ad hoc forms of representation, while party

> leaderships retreat into institutions, drawing their terms of reference ever more readily from their roles as governors or public-office holders. (Mair 2006, 33)

The same period has also witnessed the "steady erosion of the parties' political identities, and the blurring of inter-party boundaries," as they adopt similar stances on issues with appeals to leaders' personal attributes as a means of distinguishing among their options (Mair 2006, 45). Parties have become at once less responsive to the needs of those they purport to represent, while at the same time more closely aligned with those whose ideas they are meant to compete with (45). Most opposition comes from "outside conventional party politics" in the form of social movements and popular protest, while parties remain preoccupied with "governing or waiting to govern" (47). With weakened political parties, Mair contended, "we are left with a stripped-down version of constitutional democracy, or with some system of modern governance that seeks to combine 'stakeholder participation' with 'problem-solving efficiency'" (32).

This idea, which is expanded upon in the section to follow, can be explained in part by the view, advocated by Michel Foucault, that neoliberalism functions as a governmentality that swallows society and reshapes it in accordance with a market-based interpretation of the world. Though the de-contestation of politics in the neoliberal era may seem at odds with the notion that this period has been characterized by increased political conflict, the evidence in the Ontario case demonstrates that while the NDP and the Liberals have governed and campaigned in accordance with neoliberal principles, they have been willing to confront neoliberal policy – often forcefully – while in opposition. This was evidenced during the Davis, Harris, and Ford efforts at austerity, all fiercely opposed by both parties. During the period of Liberal rule from 2003 to 2018, the NDP, though through much of this period reduced to a rump in the legislature, functioned as a counterforce to Liberal austerity measures. The Liberals performed a similar role during the NDP's mandate and the Rae government's efforts to implement its restraint agenda.

Foucault and Neoliberal Political Rationality

One of the most relevant explanations for the decontestation of politics can be found in Foucault's lectures on biopolitics from the late 1970s. Foucault contended that neoliberalism was characterized by a political rationality that viewed competition as the primary end of state activity. He argued that the transition in logic from liberalism to neoliberalism involved a shift in the governing rationality of society – and thereby of the "raison d'état" – from one based on exchange to one structured around the notion of competition

(Foucault 2008, 4). Non-economic issues took secondary priority to the prudent management of the economy.

This process of self-governance in accordance with the rationality of the hegemonic system of the age is what Foucault referred to as "governmentality" (Foucault 2008, 192). Neoliberal governmentality has involved governments and individuals alike imposing restraints on their behaviours; rational thinking becomes associated with those things that are conducive to market logic. Whatever might enrich society in other ways, but is unprofitable, is mocked as being irrational or idealistic. Government is something that can be managed only by rational individuals or those with such "expert" knowledge that they are deemed to be sufficiently responsible to govern. In a society where competition guides action, there is little room for signs of dependency.

Foucault describes "*homo economicus*," a metaphor for the individual in neoliberal society, as "someone who accepts reality" (Foucault 2008, 269). *Homo economicus* accepts the logic of competition and transforms their behaviours in accordance with it. In this respect, they are a rational entrepreneur, living for their own interest and for their own satisfaction (226). The language of collectivism and solidarity is gradually replaced by that of individualism and competitiveness. The introduction of *homo economicus* as the model of rationality in contemporary society entails a "complete reorganization of government reason," with the notion of market pre-eminence appearing as an absolute truth.

Wendy Brown (2006, 695) has argued that neoliberal political rationality results in the "saturation of the state, political culture, and the social with market rationality," undermining the importance of the political and social spheres by reorienting the primary logic of all governance to focus on market competition. One of the most salient features of this shift in reason has been its capacity to undermine both the idea of politics *itself* and the pursuit of equality as legitimate activities of the state. As neoliberal political rationality reframes phenomena such as poverty as issues of private concern, it "depoliticizes capitalism" and all elements of political and social life, eclipsing them as legitimate domains of action for the state (Brown 2006, 704). The "relentless diminution of non-monetized existence" reconceptualizes the ways in which political actors understand the nature of the legislative institutions they are charged with steering (Brown 2019, 6). The idea of politics – that is, debate, negotiation, deliberation, and compromise – is viewed distrustfully, as part of an effort to stand in the way of the progress of economic reason.

This devaluing of the democratic has been aided by undermining the idea of promoting equality and social justice as a legitimate activity of the state. Political authority detached from the social, Brown argued, "becomes not just unlimited, but legitimately exercised without concern for social context or consequences, without restraint, civility, or care for society as a whole, or individuals within it" (Brown 2019, 42). The attack on the state's social functions "vanquishes a democratic understanding of society tended by a diverse people equally entitled to share in self-rule" (29). Instead, neoliberalism undermines the idea that the public is entitled to self-rule. The realm of politics becomes a host for "extreme and uncompromised positioning, and liberty becomes a right of appropriation, disruption, and even destruction of the society – its named enemy" (29).

However, while the early neoliberal canon seeks to place "radical limits on the political" by restricting the authority of legislatures, Brown laments the notion that early neoliberal thinkers "would be horrified by the contemporary phenomenon of leaders at once authoritarian and reckless, riding to power on this tide." The result is that the rise of right-wing populism is not "neoliberalism's intended spawn," but rather its "Frankenstein creation" (Brown 2019, 10).

Conclusion

Given that the kinds of radical constitutional reforms that the neoliberal and ordoliberal schools envisioned were practically unfeasible in most Western democratic societies, undertaking a shift in the balance of class forces away from centralized state planning and towards an accumulation-centric public policy required developing alternative approaches to institutional governance. Neoliberals such as Buchanan were keenly aware of this practical problem, which is why they recommended establishing constitutional artifices, which would be guaranteed to enact neoliberal reforms, and placing them in the executive, beyond the jurisdiction of legislative assemblies.

In Ontario, the case that political power needed to be centralized in the executive to ensure that the legislature did not have the capacity to overstep its boundaries was made explicitly by the Mike Harris and Doug Ford Progressive Conservative governments, but also more subtly by other governments, which commonly invoked the spectre of economic or fiscal crises as a rationale for the need to place limitations on legislative power. The consequence of a prevailing logic of economic rationalism towards political institutions over a period of decades was to gradually but consistently deprive the legislature of its authority to serve as a counterforce to the executive, resulting in an increasingly pro forma institution that had lost its capacity to meaningfully hold government to account.

The concentration of power in the executive has occurred in lockstep with the rise of anti-politics under neoliberalism. Contemporary, right-wing populism has capitalized on the anti-parliamentarism at the root of neoliberal thought, conflating the supposed cultural elitism of the leftist parties with legislative processes themselves. As the chapters to follow show, legislative debates are increasingly understood, particularly among those on the right, to be wasteful exercises of politics that are opposed to the actual public interest.

Using the logic that parliamentary debate is an inefficient and necessarily political exercise, politicians can frame the concentration of power in the executive as an act of resistance against the myth of a cultural elite that exercises substantial power over the legislature. Efforts to hold the executive to account between elections are viewed as needless interventions of "politics" in otherwise rational policy-making processes.

Although early neoliberal thinkers might have been dismayed at the perverse form that modern, right-wing populism had taken, they likely would have supported many of its essential features, including its anti-parliamentarism. Concentrating power in the executive within a system of parliamentary sovereignty came well short of the ambitious reforms that Hayek thought necessary to repair the liberal tradition, but it nevertheless offered the most functional way to implement the essential ideas of neoliberalism in the context of already existing political institutions. It also allowed the executive to function as a "check" on the sovereign legislature by ensuring that parliament did not use its authority to impose socialism. In other words, this process I have referred to as neoliberal parliamentarism, or the systematic concentration of power in the executive, served the purpose of restricting a sovereign legislature from behaving in ways that contradicted the principles of economic rationalism and undermined the effective functioning of the market. The chapters to follow provide an overview of the ways in which this process occurred at the Ontario Legislature from 1981 to 2021.

5 The Origins of Neoliberal Parliamentarism: The Davis Years, 1981–1984

Introduction

When Bill Davis was elected as the leader of the Progressive Conservative Party of Ontario in February 1971, he inherited a political machine that had governed the province since 1943. During the previous twenty-eight years, the Tories had overseen the tremendous prosperity that had accompanied the post-war upswing in the capitalist economy and the subsequent expansion of the welfare state. By the middle of the 1970s, however, rising inflation rates were beginning to act as a brake on economic growth, and the situation was depriving the provincial Treasury of the revenue that had financed the growth of the welfare state during the governments of Leslie Frost and John Robarts.

The story of the Bill Davis era is that of a government coming to terms with the challenge of governing through a period of economic upheaval that threatened to undermine the truce between business and labour that the Progressive Conservative dynasty had nurtured throughout the 1960s and 1970s. As the political winds began to shift towards an embrace of neoliberalism throughout the West, the Progressive Conservatives came under increased pressure from the financial sector to bring its deficits under control so that the province could maintain a favourable credit rating.

By the early 1980s, inflationary pressures throughout the West were prompting the government to take more severe measures to curtail government spending growth. After winning a majority government in the 1981 general election, the Progressive Conservatives adopted a more aggressive strategy of public-sector retrenchment. While the Davis government's approach to the economic downturn did not result in a complete abandonment of Keynesian policies, this period would mark the first significant undertaking in the province's transition to a policy of retrenchment.

The government confronted two obstacles in its efforts to impose a regime of austerity on the province's public-sector institutions. First, the opposition

NDP, whose political base relied upon the support of the public-sector unions, clearly indicated that it intended to do everything possible to stop the government from enacting its signature inflation-restraint measures, even if this meant jamming the parliamentary process through the use of delay tactics. Second, in order to overcome path resistance internal to the public administration, as well as local boards and councils, the government increasingly centralized authority in the executive as a means of imposing austerity.

Given the acute nature of the inflation crisis, the Davis government sought to pass its policies in relatively short order. This placed it in conflict with the opposition NDP in the legislature and required it to overcome the problem that retrenchment efforts are often met with: political resistance (Pierson 1994). The government required a parliamentary apparatus that could facilitate the implementation of its highly controversial retrenchment agenda – not simply one bill, but multiple legislative initiatives – and move it through the legislature. When the NDP refused to compromise and stand down from its efforts to obstruct legislative proceedings, the Davis government intervened, using time allocation for the first time in the province's modern history to break the parliamentary deadlock and ensure that its legislation received royal assent.

The political contradictions of retrenchment policy were played out on the floor of the legislature during these early efforts at restraint in Ontario. By resorting to such heavy-handed tactics to implement its agenda, the Davis government laid the building blocks for an approach to parliamentary governance that has culminated in what I have called neoliberal parliamentarism. Although the measures the government put in place were temporary fixes, designed to address a severe recession, the precedents it established left a permanent mark on the Ontario Legislature, functioning as a blueprint for how to overcome the political tensions of the neoliberal era without having to significantly compromise its broader agenda. Future governments, even during times of relative prosperity, built upon the approaches and strategies set out by the Davis government during this period.

Reforming the Public Sector

One of the most common ways in which neoliberalism has been implemented in Ontario has been to use delegated legislation to insulate certain decision-making processes from the reach of democratic or moderating impulses. The Davis government used this approach to establish centralized control over the finances of public-sector institutions, imposing on them a regime of strict fiscal discipline.

Arguably the most controversial and sweeping example of the government's use of this approach was the Inflation Restraint Act, brought forward in the fall of 1982. Its intent was to grapple with the economic downturn of the early 1980s by freezing increases in public-sector wages to a maximum of 5 per cent for the ensuing year and setting fixed prices for goods and services provided by the government.

Under section 29 of the bill, a Cabinet-appointed Inflation Restraint Board was empowered to make recommendations to arbitrarily roll back or disallow price increases and to set public-sector salaries for the upcoming year (Bill 179, 1982). In addition to its responsibility to control prices, the board was given the authority to determine wage increases so long as they did not exceed the mandated 5 per cent ceiling. The Act also restricted scheduled merit increases in existing contracts for employees earning more than $35,000.

The government contended that such measures were necessary to bring public spending practices in line with the private sector in Ontario. As Treasurer Frank Miller put it, "We cannot permit unconstrained growth in the public sector when the private sector is undergoing its most serious crisis since the end of the Second World War" (Miller 1982). Attempting to justify the decision, Minister of Finance Bette Stephenson suggested that the bill would provide "a time for us to catch our breath, to reflect upon the future as well as on the past and the present and to move towards combating inflation, which has been a virulent attack on our spiritual and physical wellbeing over the past decade." She continued her defence by lamenting, "There is no doubt at all that there are those in our society who will continue to disagree with the program; they will still want to take out more than they are willing to contribute" (Stephenson 1982). However, as NDP MPP Odoardo Di Santo pointed out, the government would save only an estimated $420 million, which constituted "a minimal percentage of the provincial budget and an even lower percentage of the gross provincial product" (Di Santo 1982).

Predictably, the opposition parties in the legislature took considerable issue with the authority granted to an unelected, unaccountable board to make arbitrary decisions about public-sector wages for the tenure of the bill. NDP leader Bob Rae (1982b) argued that the name of the board ought to be changed to the "wages expropriation board" since it "has everything to do with expropriation of wages in the public sector" (Rae 1982a). He maintained that the bill gave the board "extraordinary, unusual, emergency, peremptory and dictatorial powers" (ibid.). In a speech to the Legislative Assembly on 30 November 1982, Rae laid out his stance on the Inflation Restraint Act in the clearest possible terms:

> Basic rights and assumptions of due process, rights to a hearing, rights to a rational and arbitrated decision, all of which have become an essential part of the fabric of public law in Ontario, have all been wiped out [with] a single stroke of the pen.
>
> Those rights have been replaced by a regime of unilateral power, enforced wages and working conditions, and one-man rule. There is no other way to describe it. (Rae 1982a)

NDP MPP Jim Foulds argued that although the bill contained "draconian, arbitrary measures" for the wages sector, the same could not be said of government fees and charges, which were subject to maximum increases of 5 per cent, but were ultimately left to the discretion of Cabinet (Foulds 1982). The contradiction inherent in this provision, as Foulds recognized, was that while the government imposed mandatory restrictions on wage expenses, it did not impose the same restrictions on its own behaviour. This, he argued, revealed that the true intent of the bill was to undermine the efforts of labour by imposing restrictions on wage increases and the right to strike. Bill 179 was "a piece of class legislation that makes ordinary people suffer under oppressive laws but lets the privileged, well-to-do corporations accumulate wealth almost at will" (ibid.). Foulds called the bill an attack "on democracy itself," which "established a czar with rights and privileges that Louis XVI would have envied" (ibid.).

Finance Minister Frank Miller encapsulated the government's position, citing a quote from economist Alfred Kahn:

> The problem in our economy is that we have these persistent, well-organized pressures by each individual and group to preserve his or her absolute position regardless of what happens to the country as a whole. What this does is create, on the part of everyone in society, the expectation that no matter what happens to the aggregate, each of us is individually entitled to CPI plus three per cent. What we have got is those constant forces to increase expenditures, to increase nominal incomes and to expand government programs. It is clearly something that has to do with a lack of social discipline. (Miller 1982)

The problem for Miller was that competing social interests in society tended to interfere with taking the steps necessary to curb inflation. This lack of social discipline could be achieved only by vesting those individuals who had an appropriate understanding of how to fix the problem with the authority to make decisions, free from external constraints. Miller claimed that he believed "a democracy can discipline itself," but that he would first require that the opposition support his government's legislation to undermine the bargaining rights of labour and to centralize authority over the governance of the economy in the hands of Cabinet (Miller 1982). While the Davis government was willing to work with union leaders, opposition members, and social activists to achieve certain goals, broader issues of economic governance were to be sheltered from the public forum to give the government a free hand to establish fiscal stability.

Centralizing Local Politics at Queen's Park

One of the most important ways in which the Davis government imposed its restraint agenda was to use its constitutional authority to enforce restraint upon local governments and institutions. From the early 1980s onwards, the government began to design policies to discipline wayward locally administered and managed institutions, such as city councils and school boards, that had strayed from the objective of cutting costs and reducing inefficiencies. Arguably the most extensive of these policies was the Municipality of Metropolitan Toronto Amendment Act. It allowed the government to reorganize the financing and negotiating schemes of the Toronto school board system at the expense of local autonomy. It also mandated compulsory joint bargaining between teachers and the city's six district school boards under the umbrella of a single, region-wide negotiating unit.

The purpose of this new directive was, as MPP Jim Bradley put it, "an attempt to centralize control of education" in the province. He continued that his party's "vehement opposition" to the bill stemmed from "our view that this bill represents an assault on local autonomy in teacher-board negotiations in Ontario and in certain aspects of the financing of education at the local level in Metropolitan Toronto" (Bradley 1983). The benefit of requiring compulsory joint, regional bargaining, from the province's perspective, was to centralize negotiations so as to exert more influence over the terms and conditions of collective agreements. A further inclusion in the bill required that teachers and the new regional bargaining unit negotiate a fixed cap on the number of teachers who could belong to a board at any given time and agree that no board exceed this number (Bill 127, 1982).

In short, through what NDP leader Bob Rae called its "two-tiered monstrosity," the province was able to wrest control over the financial operations of Toronto's school boards by centralizing power in a provincially controlled, regional body, while allowing the local boards to retain authority over day-to-day operations. The clear intent of this legislation was to harness costs by placing the collective bargaining process in the hands of a board accountable to Queen's Park, designating caps on the hiring of new teachers, and establishing more budgetary accountability for school boards.

The Davis government adopted a similar approach in its relations with Ontario's self-governing post-secondary institutions. An advisory report from the Ontario Council on University Affairs, provided in the government's background documentation on a bill it was drafting, lamented the problem of growing deficits at Ontario's universities. It claimed that some institutions were at risk of financial insolvency if the government did not intervene to force Ontario's higher education institutions to become accountable to the Ministry of Training, Colleges and Universities' deficit targets (Ontario. Council on University Affairs 1982). While the tradition of self-governance should be respected, the report maintained, "It cannot be successfully argued that institutional autonomy must be absolute, particularly when the major portion of the operating cost comes from the public purse" (ibid., 2).

In response to the report, in the fall of 1982 the government introduced Bill 213, An Act to Amend the Ministry of Training, Colleges and Universities Act, which sought to use its control over the state administrative apparatus to dispense severe disciplinary measures to post-secondary institutions that ran deficits. The bill stipulated that "no university incur a deficit in its operating fund in excess of two per cent of its revenue for the year." For universities that failed to meet this standard, the bill provided for the appointment of an arbitrator to "investigate and report upon the financial situation of the universities." Cabinet was also authorized to appoint a university supervisor, accountable to the minister, who had the power to control the finances of the university and to make the changes necessary to restore it to surplus conditions (Bill 213, 1982).

During the period in which the supervisor served at the minister's request, "no act of the governing body is valid unless approved by the university supervisor" (Bill 213, 1982). This provision marked an important step for the Davis government in that it undermined the tradition of an autonomous academic institution by threatening the complete transfer of its sovereignty to a financial czar, who was authorized to force a policy of austerity upon it. It is important to note that although Bill 213 was reintroduced in the third session, and once again in the fourth, both times under the name Bill 42, at no time did it ever proceed beyond second reading in the legislature. It was intended mostly as a mechanism to indirectly incentivize universities to adopt the government's policy of fiscal restraint, and, in this respect, it had its intended effect, coercing universities into adopting their own restraint policies.

Bringing Down the Hammer of Closure: The Realities of 19 March

Despite the relative harmony that characterized the two minority Parliaments at the end of the 1970s, the tenor of the debate shifted markedly after the Progressive Conservatives won their long-sought majority in the general election of 1981. When the dust settled on the evening of 19 March 1981, the party had gained twelve seats, for a total of seventy in the 125-seat legislature. Two factors, I argue, resulted in a general erosion of decorum in the legislature and the government's eventual turn towards the most consistent and severe restrictions on debate in the Assembly's history.

First, after the government had won its majority, a degree of hubris appeared to set in. It took less care to consult the opposition before introducing legislation, and, as a consequence, efforts at collegiality with the opposition parties slowed considerably. This was perhaps best illustrated by Bill Davis's answer to a question from the NDP by making reference to the realities of 19 March, reminding the opposition that as a consequence of his party winning a majority of seats, "The reality is that things have changed." The premier continued:

> I am not going to give an undertaking to the leader of the New Democratic Party on the contents of proposed legislation. Traditionally they are made apparent when legislation is introduced, and that is when members will find out what is in it. (Davis 1981)

Years later, Liberal MPP Jim Bradley would recount the impact of Davis's dismissal of the NDP question.

> The government came back in here, having been a fairly conciliatory government from 1975 to 1981, and the Premier of the day referred to "the realities of March 19," and you could see it start to deteriorate from there, because they were back in the driver's seat, not having to be accountable. (Bradley 1993)

The second factor was that the inflationary crisis of the early 1980s impelled the government to escalate its restraint and inflation-control agenda by targeting public-sector salaries. The aggressive approach it took, and the ensuing reaction from the opposition to obstruct such efforts, meant that the government would have to either deal with an obstructionist opposition, which would delay the implementation of its key anti-inflation legislation, or act pre-emptively, applying the rarely used parliamentary mechanisms available to it to end debate and usher its crisis management agenda through the legislature. In choosing the latter course, the government permanently altered the complexion of parliamentary procedure at Queen's Park.

One early example of this transition in legislative governance involved the use of closure. The issue in question was the government's acquisition of a 25 per cent stake in Suncor Incorporated and the government's subsequent refusal to produce documents in the Assembly related to the purchase. The opposition, which had been calling for the release of the compendium detailing the purchase of the Suncor shares since shortly after Davis had announced it in the legislature, used a routine motion for interim supply to filibuster in protest. It stalled the proceedings of the legislature by speaking against the motion, running the clock through to the evening adjournment. Under the existing Standing Orders, the debate on the matter would have to resume the following evening, when the Orders of the Day were called. Theoretically, the opposition could continue to filibuster until it could reach an agreement with the government.

Given the opposition's steadfast refusal to end its filibuster until the government released the compendium, Davis decided to invoke closure in the legislature to put an end to the stalemate on the grounds that the deadline for the government to write cheques had passed and it needed the approval of the legislature to pay wages and attend to other financial obligations.

During the night session of 3 November 1981, Bob Welch invoked Standing Order 36 without notice and closed debate when he motioned that "this question be now put." He argued that where the compendium was concerned, "It is clear from the record that the House has considerable information at its disposal on this transaction. Moreover, it is clear there are legitimate reasons why it is not appropriate to provide the kind of information being sought." Furthermore, he explained, "The business of government must proceed in an orderly manner. While dissent is the spice of democracy, decisions have to be taken at some time" (Welch 1981). The opposition derided the decision as "a black day for this legislature," contending that using such a severe parliamentary procedure to conceal documents from the legislature exemplified "the high-handed arrogance, the contempt for the people and for democracy" that had come to characterize the Davis Tories (S. Smith 1981a).

The events of 1981 were a prelude to the shift to neoliberal parliamentarism in Ontario. The Davis government's approach to the legislature foreshadowed some of the political tensions that rose to the surface during the following year, when the government attempted the most serious effort at public-sector retrenchment up to that point in the province's history. The political conflict that manifested itself on the floor of the legislature during this period, and, more importantly, the tools that were used to resolve it, left a permanent mark on the practice of parliamentary governance in Ontario.

The Emergence of Time Allocation as a Procedural Norm

While the use of closure on the interim supply motion in 1981 was the first time in decades that a government had resorted to such an extreme measure to pass its agenda through the legislature, it would not be the last. The next time the Davis Tories attempted to restrict debate, they resorted to the use of time allocation. Time allocation was not formally provided for in the Ontario Standing Orders, but there was a precedent for it in the British parliamentary tradition dating back to the late nineteenth century.

It was significant that the Progressive Conservatives chose to use time allocation for the first time in the province's modern history on its most controversial bill, the Inflation Restraint Act (Bill 179, 1982). The Davis government appeared to realize, after its experience the previous year on the interim supply motion, that the passage of such highly controversial legislation would be no fait accompli unless measures were taken from the outset to restrict debate. When the third-party New Democrats began to obstruct the passage of Bill 179 in the legislature – its leader, Bob Rae, declared that he would accept nothing short of a full withdrawal of the legislation as a compromise – the Davis Tories took pre-emptive action by introducing the guillotine motion (Duffy 1983). Its purpose was to ensure that debate was brought to a timely conclusion at all stages of the legislative process. It read as follows:

> Notwithstanding any order of the House, the consideration of Bill 179, the Inflation Restraint Act, 1982, by the committee of the whole House, be concluded not later than 10:15 p.m. on the first sessional day following the passage of this motion unless such a date be a Friday, in which case the conclusion of the consideration will be not later than 10:15 p.m. on the following Monday, at which time the Chairman will put all questions necessary to dispose of every section of the bill not yet passed, and the schedule, and to report the bill, such questions to [be] decided without amendment or debate; should a division be called for, the bell to be limited to 10 minutes;
>
> And, that, any debate on the question for the adoption of the report be held on the next sessional day and be concluded not later than 10:15 p.m. on that day, unless it be a Friday when again it will be on the following Monday, at which time Mr. Speaker will interrupt the proceedings and put the question for the adoption of the report without amendment or further debate and if a division is called for, the bell to be limited to 10 minutes;
>
> And, further, that, the bill be called for third reading debate on the third sessional day following the passage of this motion and be completed not later than 10:15 p.m. on that day unless it be a Friday, when again it will be called on the following Monday, at which time Mr. Speaker will interrupt the proceedings and put the question without further debate and if a division is called for, the bell to be limited to 10 minutes;
>
> And, finally, that, in the case of any division in any way relating to any proceeding on this bill prior to the bill being read the third time, the bell be limited to 10 minutes. (Wells 1982)

Rae raised a point of order: the time allocation was out of order because provisions for its use were not explicitly included in the Standing Orders. "There is no right on the part of the majority to bring in a motion for time allocation that falls outside the standing orders of this Assembly" (Rae 1982b). MPP Tom Wells, however, countered that while there was no formal provision in the Standing Orders for time allocation, there was ample precedent in the British parliamentary tradition. To this end, he claimed that the use of the guillotine motion under the existing circumstances "sets out a democratic way to lay out procedures for the passage of this bill. It does not attempt to change the orders" (Wells 1982). The Speaker ultimately ruled that the motion was in order on the basis that it did not need to be included in the Standing Orders to be consistent with proper procedure:

> I submit to the members that, to deal with the argument put forward by the member for York South [Rae] that this is not closure and that there is provision for closure as such, I do not know why the government has not chosen to go that route, but it has chosen this route.
>
> All I can say is that the motion has been made properly. There has been proper notice. It has been printed. It was properly moved and put before this House. I find, therefore, that there is nothing out of order and that the motion, which is a regular substantive motion, is in order. (Turner 1982)

Despite losing on his point of order, Rae continued to make the case that the procedure violated the spirit of democracy. He argued that the government's use of time allocation, "for reasons of sheer administrative convenience ..., eliminates the ability of the opposition to do its job." He continued, contending that the time allocation motion under such circumstances was, in fact, more undemocratic than the use of closure:

> This is a government which introduces a motion that has absolutely no precedent in this Legislature; it cuts off committee of the whole discussion, it cuts off report-stage discussion and it cuts [off] third reading discussion. This is a government which says it is not introducing closure. It is correct; it is introducing closure not just once but three times. So it is not a closure motion; it is a triple closure motion, that is what it is. (Rae 1982b)

For its part, the government contended that it was important to get the bill passed and move on with other business. Wells pointed out that Bill 179 had already received 138 hours of consideration after accounting for debate both in the legislature and in committee. He claimed that this was more than enough time to debate legislation and said, "We acknowledge that there is a political impasse here." But, "At some time the House must come to some means of deciding how this can be brought to a conclusion." Furthermore, the motion represented "a sensible way of allocating time when it becomes obvious that a political impasse has been reached" (Wells 1982). The time allocation motion ultimately passed, and the Inflation Restraint Act received royal assent without amendment shortly before the legislature adjourned for winter recess.

The government attempted to use time allocation again just a few months later, on another controversial piece of fiscal-restraint legislation, Bill 127, the Municipality of Metropolitan Toronto Amendment Act. The New Democrats, who were fiercely opposed to the bill since it undermined the collective bargaining rights of Toronto teachers, vowed to block its passage. In response, on 16 February 1983, the government brought forward a time allocation motion to bring the debate to a resolution so that it could proceed with its plan to prorogue the legislature shortly thereafter. Premier Davis defended the decision on the grounds that the government had already debated the issue for ninety-six hours and saw little chance at a resolution, given the NDP's opposition to the bill:

> We are not expecting the leader of the third party to change his mind. If he reads Hansard, if he reads the transcript of the committee hearings, he will not find any new arguments being presented. No new facts have come to light that we are not all aware of. We have agreed to disagree on this legislation. We think it is important in terms of our responsibilities as a government to see this brought to a conclusion. (Davis 1983)

In contrast, NDP MPP Eli Martel argued that the government was "playing around" by maintaining that adequate debate had been held. He reminded members that while considerable time had been spent on the bill in committee, it had been subject to only ten hours of clause-by-clause consideration in the legislature, which was "certainly not a lengthy time in which to pass legislation which the premier should be worried about because there is so much controversy around it" (E. Martel 1983).

The day after the time allocation motion had been introduced, however, Sean Conway noted that the way it was worded left room for the opposition to continue with its obstruction of the bill's passage. The first paragraph of Bette Stephenson's motion had read as follows:

> That, notwithstanding any order of the House, the consideration of Bill 127, An Act to amend the Municipality of Metropolitan Toronto Act, by the committee of the whole House, be concluded at 5:45 p.m. on Thursday, February 17, at which time the Chairman will put all questions necessary to dispose of every section of the bill not yet passed, and to report the bill, such questions to be decided without amendment or debate; should a division be called for, the bell to be limited to 10 minutes. (Stephenson 1983)

While the motion stipulated that the vote "be concluded at 5:45 p.m." on 17 February, it did not include a provision instructing the Speaker to end the debate and begin the Committee of the Whole, as the motion set out. As a consequence, the opposition determined that so long as it managed to keep debate on the motion going through to the end of the sessional day on 16 February, the Speaker would have no choice but to begin the Orders of the Day on 17 February with a resumption of the debate on time allocation, thus making it impossible to begin the Committee of the Whole House.

According to procedure, if a government is unable to maintain the timeline set out for it in its time allocation motion, the entire resolution before the legislature is considered to be void. Having recognized this crucial mistake on the part of the government, the opposition proceeded to hold debate throughout the afternoon of 16 February in order to delay the vote on the time allocation motion to the following day. Sean Conway rose in the legislature to speak for nearly two hours to run out the clock on the debate. Unable to extend the session further into night sitting without the unanimous consent of the legislature, and since such notice had not been provided, Wells was forced to "reluctantly move the adjournment of the House" (Wells 1983).

The following day, the government conceded defeat to the opposition, calling the Committee of the Whole on the promise that it would not invoke closure at 5:45 p.m., as the original time allocation motion had called for. Liberal MPP Bob Nixon said, "Actually, I am delighted that the government House leader is calling the second order, because we can now proceed with the discussion of the bill in committee stage without the restriction that the government had tried to apply to it." He continued, referring to the government's promise to allow a full debate in the Committee of the Whole House, "There is some indication that maybe the government House leader, being kind of a slippery and fast operator, is going to do a double-shuffle at 5:45. I do not believe for a moment that he will do that to restrict the debate on the government" (Nixon 1983). Fellow Liberal Jim Bradley called the defeat on the motion "a major victory," in which the government "was out-foxed by the opposition" in its attempt to "bulldoze through the House its legislation through a time allocation motion" (Bradley 1983). As a result of the opposition's obstructionist tactics, Bill 127 made its way through the legislature using the normal procedures. However, on 23 February, the government invoked Standing Order 36 to enact closure on the debate and bring about a vote on third reading.

The government used time allocation one final time before Davis left office at the end of 1984. Bill 142, the Barrie-Vespra Annexation Act, was a controversial bill in the Simcoe Region of Ontario because it involved the province using its constitutional authority to annex the small farming township of Vespra to the City of Barrie (Bill 142, 1984). The government established 1 July 1984 as the operative date for the bill, but when the opposition made it clear that it would delay proceedings unless the government held further public consultations, Davis made the decision to time-allocate the bill rather than delay the start of summer recess indefinitely. New Democrat MPP Michael Breaugh called the decision "one of the greatest disservices to parliamentary democracy that I have ever seen" (Breaugh 1984). Bob Nixon argued that such a decision "to allocate time for the completion of the Barrie-Vespra bill was unnecessary since we are not labouring under any time pressure." He explained that

> we all know if it were to carry even after July 1, which is still some days in the future, the retroactive aspect would apply. We hope the bill will not carry, but even if the government, with its overwhelming majority, eventually had its way, there

> would still not be any significant inconvenience in the application of the measures in the bill. (Nixon 1984)

Tom Wells reminded the opposition that the bill had first been brought forward in December 1983 and was sent for thirty-eight and a half hours of committee hearings, "during which time changes were made, and all those communities and people affected were given the opportunity to come in and meet with a committee of this legislature." He maintained that the government would be willing to operate according to normal House procedure if the opposition were to end its obstruction of proceedings, "but they will not do that." Consequently, he told the legislature, "We have reached the time when, after full and frank debate, we can move ahead" (Wells 1984). The time allocation motion eventually passed, with support from the Tory majority, and received royal assent before the Assembly adjourned for the summer.

Liberal Sean Conway proved to be most prescient on the day after the government's introduction of the time allocation motion for the Inflation Restraint Act: "I am deeply concerned that in the course of this difficult passage we are going to write very bad new rules into our practice here in this Assembly" (Conway, quoted in *Globe and Mail* 1982). The government's use of the guillotine as a means of passing Bill 179 was a precedent-setting development for the Ontario Legislature. From this moment forward, governments belonging to all three parties became gradually, but ever increasingly, more aggressive in their use of this procedural tactic to usher legislation through the Assembly. Indeed, by the 1990s, the use of time allocation had become commonplace; motions were often introduced at the same time as legislation, in anticipation of obstruction from the opposition and formal recognition in the Standing Orders.

Conclusion

Ultimately, the Davis era's sustained impact on legislative governance in the province of Ontario was felt most profoundly through the parliamentary precedents it set as it attempted to bring inflation under control. Not only did the Davis government take the first important steps to abandon Keynesianism, but also, in its efforts to overcome political resistance in the legislature, it established new, customary practices in the parliamentary tradition that contributed to an increasingly impoverished role for the legislature. The struggle with the New Democrats over the Inflation Restraint Act reflected the challenges associated with balancing the opposition's right to delay the proceedings of the House with allowing the government to continue with their agenda. After hours of debate, the government elected to set a new legislative precedent rather than compromise on its restraint agenda. The inflation crisis made it urgent for the government to intervene with policy solutions to address the crisis, but it also gave it a justification for rolling out restraint policies whose virtues it had long rhetorically extolled.

The trend that emerges is that the government resorted to these mechanisms when confronted with acute political opposition in the legislature. The most path-breaking and common examples of the Davis government's misuse of the legislative process related to its attempts to deal with the problem of inflation. It is during this period that we see the foundation for a new approach to parliamentary governance in Ontario most clearly and coherently laid out.

To break parliamentary deadlock, the government set the precedent that time allocation could be used to end debate on bills that it sought to move through the legislature quickly. In so doing, the Davis Tories drew up a blueprint for an approach to parliamentary governance that could overcome contradictions both outside and within institutional processes and ensure that they could actualize their retrenchment agenda in the face of widespread opposition.

In the following decades, time allocation and closure became the conventional means through which governments advanced their agendas through the Assembly. Furthermore, when the next economic crisis confronted the province less than a decade after Davis had left office, governments became increasingly emboldened in their use of these tactics to implement extreme measures to deal with it. The patterns laid down during this early period are ones that would be returned to repeatedly when future governments were confronted with similar dilemmas, and they are a critical part of the story of the implementation and entrenchment of neoliberalism in Ontario.

6 Ontario in Transition: The Peterson Era, 1985–1990

Introduction

With the benefit of hindsight, it is possible to argue that the dramatic turn of events in Ontario over the period from 1985 to 1995 was intrinsically connected to the reorganization of economic and social capital that was already well underway in the Western world. While the stench of decline had been lingering since the late 1960s, when a crisis of overproduction had begun to act as a drag on the average rate of profit in the West, it was only when inflation rates soared to unprecedented levels in the early 1980s that the province began to take meaningful action to restrain public spending. Ontario's fading exceptionalism articulated itself through a profound shift in political loyalties that shattered the stable, one-party rule that had characterized its post-war political complexion (Courchene and Tellmer 1998).

In 1985, Ontarians rejected the Frank Miller–led Tories' retrenchment-based approach to policy, opting instead to transfer power to parties that promised to maintain and revive the province's Keynesian architecture. The 1985 Liberal-NDP Accord, discussed below, was a watershed moment for the province of Ontario in more ways than one: not only did it mark the end of the Progressive Conservatives' four-decade reign, but it also, in many ways, signified the end of the old Ontario. The political turmoil that was to follow was rooted in the reality that the province's long tenure as Canada's economic heartland had come to its end, to be replaced by a period of uncertainty and transition.

Thomas Courchene and Colin Tellmer (1998, 70) have referred to the period following the end of the Tory dynasty as Ontario's "Quiet Revolution" due to the interventionist strategies pursued by the Peterson government during its five years in power. The Liberals had the good fortune of governing in a political climate that was ideally suited to both its agenda and the youthful, progressive image of its leader, David Peterson. They could take full credit for social reforms by following a generally popular, expansionist agenda since they controlled the keys to the provincial Treasury and were responsible for directing the government. This was evidenced by the substantial majority government that they won in 1987, while running on a blueprint that had been drawn up by the New Democrats.

In contrast to the final years of the Davis government, the Peterson government also benefited from improving economic conditions. Rather than proceed with caution, as Ontario governments had traditionally done, the Liberals, temporarily freed from the constraints of declining government revenues, were able to expand the welfare state and invest in social initiatives that had been neglected by the Tories. Taxes from non-corporate and business sources more than doubled in just five years, between 1985 and 1990, despite a population increase of only 10.77 per cent, and the Liberals used them to make significant investments in education, health care, energy, and the cultivation of a knowledge-based economy, among other initiatives (Statistics Canada 2011, 2015a).

Because the Liberals did not serve their full-majority mandate before losing the 1990 election, their response to the recessionary economics that set in shortly thereafter must remain a matter of speculation. Ultimately, their legacy is that of pragmatic leadership under favourable economic circumstances. The economic buoyancy of the late 1980s put them in the luxurious position of allowing political expediency to trump ideology. In doing so, they pursued a political implementation strategy that complemented the general public's acceptance of its expansionary policy agenda. The popularity of the government's interventionist agenda meant that it had less incentive to resort to the undemocratic procedural mechanisms used by the Davis Tories.

In the broader trajectory of Ontario's history, the Peterson era can be best described as what Gramsci (1971) called an "interregnum period" in the marginalization of the legislature. With a few notable exceptions, Peterson's tenure in office witnessed a reduction in governance through delegated legislation, which had become a crucial part of the Tories' fiscal-restraint strategy. These years were a high-water mark, rivalled only by the minority Parliaments from 1975 to1981, for the influence of the opposition at Queen's Park. Beginning in 1985 with the Liberal/NDP Accord, and ending with a series of obstructionist tactics that resulted in a number of significant victories for the official opposition New Democrats, the Peterson era saw an unprecedented expression of assertiveness from the opposition.

While the government continued the trend of bringing forward time allocation motions, and implemented more restrictive Standing Orders governing parliamentary debate, it did so, in large part, to break the deadlock brought about by the uncooperative behaviour of the New Democrats. Some of this may have had to do with the introduction of a new, competitive dynamic at Queen's Park after the end of the Progressive Conservatives' forty-three-year reign over the province.

Although the Peterson years were ultimately defined by the establishment of more restrictive Standing Orders, a more fractured and partisan legislature, and the continuation of a number of procedural trends passed down by the Tories to curtail parliamentary debate, it was also a period of momentous change in Ontario. After more than four decades in office, the Tory dynasty had reached its end, but gone with it was the stability and predictability that had characterized post-war Ontario. The Peterson era marked an interregnum in the implementation of both neoliberalism and the use of proactive efforts by the government to insulate key elements of its agenda from parliamentary control. The period's true legacy, however, may be the emergence of a new, hyper-partisan political environment, which poisoned the atmosphere at Queen's Park and, shortly after the Liberals went down to defeat in 1990, set in motion a further tightening of parliamentary procedure.

The achievements made by the opposition during the Peterson years sowed the seeds for the divisiveness and rancour that characterized the politics of the 1990s in Ontario. Although the Peterson government did not contribute to the emergence of neoliberal parliamentarism to the extent that other governments before and after it did, the political contradictions that gave rise to these developments became calcified during this period, as parliamentary deadlock became an increasingly common occurrence.

The Liberal-NDP Accord: The End of the Tory Dynasty

Although the emergence of a more assertive opposition at Queen's Park were rooted in the heavy-handed tactics employed by the Davis government during its final years in office, it was not until the spring of 1985 that the opposition was granted an opportunity to exert meaningful political influence by expressing non-confidence in the government. The series of events that unfolded was not only the most significant expression of power by an opposition in the legislature's history but also a watershed moment in Ontario's political trajectory. In April of that year, just a few short months after winning the Progressive Conservative leadership, and without having ever served a day as premier in the legislature, Frank Miller called an election in the hope of winning his own majority mandate to govern the province. When the returns were tallied on 2 May, the Progressive Conservatives clung to power with a slim minority government in which they held 52 seats, the Liberals 48, and the NDP 25.

The province had recent experience with minority Parliaments – many of the returning members had served in the Davis minorities of 1975–81; however, the cloud of rancour that had hung over the legislature during Davis's final majority mandate emboldened the third-party NDP to seek to use the balance of power it now held in the legislature. Rather than accept the reality of another Tory government, as it had done in 1975 and 1977, the NDP under leader

Bob Rae began discussions with both the Progressive Conservatives and the Liberals to negotiate a pact, whereby the new government would promise to implement several of the NDP's most important policy initiatives in exchange for its support.

The NDP engaged in several weeks of intense bargaining with both parties, seeking a working arrangement on the terms it had set during caucus deliberations. After meetings with the Tories broke down, the NDP set its sights firmly on a deal with the Liberals to topple the Miller government. The resulting agreement set a timetable for the Liberals to push the government to enact laws implementing full funding for separate schools, extending rent protections, implementing employment equity legislation, and ending extra billing by doctors (Cruickshank 1985). In exchange, the NDP agreed not to move or vote for a non-confidence motion for two years.

Shortly after the Accord was announced, Frank Miller reached out to the NDP in the faint hope of reaching a deal to stop it. Miller, a long-time Cabinet minister under Davis, expressed a contemptuous attitude towards the New Democrats, refusing to commit to holding another election for a substantial period or to agree to a timetable for implementing their policy proposals. He contended that giving the opposition such significant power would be the "death knell" for the practice of parliamentary democracy in the province. He asked, rhetorically, "Can you have peace at any price? Or do you have to recognize that the system is more important?" (Frank Miller, quoted in Speirs 1985).

Miller's initial response to news of the accord was to publicly contemplate asking Lieutenant Governor John Black Aird to dissolve Parliament and call another election (Christie 1985). But there were two problems with this course of action. First, according to parliamentary custom, it is the Crown's responsibility to first seek a working alliance with the opposition parties. Given that an election had just been held and that there was a clear, governing alternative constituting a majority of seats in the legislature, it is unlikely that the lieutenant governor would have granted the premier his request. Second, significant segments of the Tory caucus were calling for Miller to simply accept defeat and resign after the Speech from the Throne had been given; this would allow the party to serve its penance before challenging the fragile alliance in two years' time.

The final days in the life of the Tory dynasty were characterized by a marked shift to the left as Frank Miller was admittedly "clinging to hope" that his party could remain in power (Miller, quoted in Harrington and Walker 1985). In its Speech from the Throne, the Miller Tories promised to implement the NDP's long-sought policy demands. They committed to

> eliminate barriers and assist all individuals, particularly women, young people, visible minorities, native people and the disabled, who seek employment and who pursue excellence; to protect our environment and enhance our diverse regional

> economies; to maintain and expand our investment in essential social services; to introduce and amend laws which serve our community values; and to encourage co-operation and trust by improving the openness and accountability of all our public institutions. (Aird 1985)

Premier-in-waiting David Peterson called the decision "deathbed repentance" from a government that had indicated during the election that it would take a hard shift to the right (Peterson, quoted in Harrington and Walker 1985). Meanwhile, Bob Rae quipped, "It almost makes you wish you could defeat governments all the time if this is what kind of legislation it produces" (Rae, quoted in B. Walker 1985a).

Despite Miller's efforts to reach out, the NDP kept its pact with the Liberals. On the day of the confidence motion, Miller gave an acerbic final speech as premier that reinforced his view of executive entitlement. He argued that the accord was an affront to democracy and accused David Peterson and Bob Rae of "prostituting themselves for power" (Miller 1985) in an effort to "highjack the parliamentary process" (Frank Miller, quoted in Cruickshank 1985). He continued, suggesting that the NDP was "throwing out 700 years of parliamentary tradition without consulting the legislature for two reasons: One man (Peterson) who wants to be premier so badly he'll give in; and another (Rae) so afraid of an election he'll make compromises" (Frank Miller, quoted in B. Walker 1985b). Miller added that the confidence motion amounted to a coup d'état:

> I would like the Bobbsey Twins in Queen's Park to come clean. If they are determined to govern as a coalition, which does have lots of historic precedent, they should have the intestinal fortitude and fess up. If they are really as united as they pretend to be, they should legitimize their relationship and face us in the legislatures [as] the coalition party they really are. This province and its people deserve better than a puppet Liberal Premier with the NDP pulling the strings. (Miller 1985)

He concluded with a warning to the NDP that the "opportunistic" Liberals would seek to call an election to take the "socialist monkey off their back" (Miller 1985).

For their part, the opposition parties reminded the premier of the "realities of May 2nd," which was a play on former premier Bill Davis's comment in the legislature of the "realities of March 19th" (Nixon 1985). The new reality, they claimed, was that, in a minority Parliament, the opposition controlled the majority of the seats and was well within its rights to defeat the existing government and replace it with the majority will of the Assembly (ibid.). Liberal MPP Bob Nixon chastised the premier for failing to understand the parliamentary process; he claimed that his government had engaged in "an embarrassing series of changing positions, attempting day by day to find a formula to remove the risk of the final defeat of conservatism in this House after 42 years." He continued, implicating the entire Tory Cabinet of complicity in the act of denial; Conservative ministers, he said, "rose in their places day by day as the Tory political corpse twisted in the wind, there was something unnatural, something shocking. It was like looking at a corpse that winks" (ibid.).

The historic Liberal-NDP Accord had shaken the foundations of politics in Ontario by using the principle of majority rule to replace a government that had, during its last mandate, demonstrated a propensity to centralize authority in the executive branch with increased fervour. The new Liberal regime promised to govern according to the principle of collaboration between the executive and legislative branches of government. The use of the opposition's majority in the House to leverage a change in government was structured upon what Peterson called "a high level of trust" between the Liberals and the NDP; it held the promise of a more decentralized and collegial atmosphere in the legislature, along with a productive role in policymaking for the opposition parties (Christie 1985).

No one at the time could estimate the shock to the central nervous system of Ontario's political culture that dislodging the Tory dynasty, after four decades, would have on political dynamics. Despite an uneventful first term, aided in large part by the accord, in Peterson's second term Parliament was beset by an adversarial and partisan tone. The marriage between the NDP and the Liberals, it turned out, was less an expression of a renewed attitude of collegiality than a union of convenience to rid the province of forty-three years of Tory rule and have a hand in power themselves. The end of the Progressive Conservative dynasty, then, represented more than the replacement of one party in power with another; it symbolized the end of the stability of the old Ontario and ushered in an uncertain and competitive dynamic that would permanently reshape politics at Queen's Park.

Accountability Renewed: The Liberal Promise of a More Transparent Government

David Peterson laid out his legislative platform on 2 July 1985, in his first speech as premier, amid a flurry of optimism that the new government, having experienced the alienation of serving in opposition for more than four decades, was serious about taking steps to democratize the legislative process. He promised to make reforms that would see the government be more "open, compassionate and competent" than it had been under the Tories. The public, he contended, "can only achieve the changes they want and need if they are allowed to put their hands on the levers of power and shift gears when necessary." Accordingly, the new government pledged to put out "a welcome mat at the front doors" of the legislature and undertake significant reforms to open up the decision-making process to the public – among other things, to televise legislative proceedings, to pass freedom-to-information legislation, and to strengthen the role of backbench members and committees by establishing a committee to review parliamentary procedures and appointments (Peterson 1985).

The Peterson government's efforts to increase transparency led to the establishment of an integrity commissioner, an independent officer of the legislature with the mandate to oversee the maintenance of ethical standards in government. This new parliamentary watchdog was an important development in government transparency in the province and the first of its kind in Canada. One of David Peterson's legacies will undoubtedly be the political courage he demonstrated to democratize the legislative process by implementing various reforms that have since become an important part of the day-to-day operations of Queen's Park. Installing television cameras and enacting freedom-to-information legislation, for example, did much to improve the public's access to parts of the political process that had been previously inaccessible to most Ontario citizens. However, he will also be remembered as a premier whose final years were plagued by scandal, brought about to some degree by his willingness to run a decentralized government. Having learned from Peterson's stunning 1990 electoral defeat, future premiers would be hesitant to follow his example of transparency and inclusivity.

Parliamentary Procedure under Peterson

The Peterson government opened its second session in office with an attempt to facilitate a more conciliatory approach to daily proceedings in the legislature. On 28 April 1986, Government House Leader Sean Conway announced a series of reforms to the Standing Orders. While most of the reforms were minor, they made important changes to the organization of the sessional day in the House. Among other changes, evening sittings were done away with in favour of a more consistent daily schedule, and Friday sittings were abolished. These reforms were designed to give members of all three parties the opportunity to spend more time in their constituencies. Another change devoted ten minutes to Members' Statements per day. This gave backbench members, who were to be recognized by the Speaker on a rotating basis, a daily opportunity to make statements in the House on issues of importance to them (Conway 1986).

These revisions were significant not only because they made important changes to the conduct of affairs at Queen's Park but also because they were an example of increasingly rare, all-party collaboration towards a common end. The new Standing Orders were the result of deliberations among the three

House Leaders and were approved with unanimous support in the Assembly. They also fulfilled a promise that the Liberals had made upon taking office in 1985 to increase the role of the backbencher in the House.

This spirit of collegiality was short-lived, however. In June 1986, the Progressive Conservatives attempted to obstruct Bill 94, the Health Care Accessibility Act, legislation to ban doctors from the practice of extra-billing, by refusing to stand down from debate on the issue during the Orders of the Day. The legislation was particularly controversial within the medical community because doctors argued that requiring them to cease the practice of extra-billing would result in longer wait times and poorer standards of care.

The Tories, who championed the view of the Ontario Medical Association, were particularly dismayed that the government had introduced the bill under the shadow of Christmas on 19 December, when no work at the legislature would occur and the story would receive only a day or two of coverage in the press before the holiday (Grossman 1986). Once the bill reached committee, they argued that it required clause-by-clause consideration and several months of consultations with concerned members of the community. Becoming impatient with the stall tactics of the official opposition and sensitive to the political damage this issue could cause their party, the Liberals made the decision to invoke closure in committee, bringing the bill back to the House for further debate. Progressive Conservative leader Larry Grossman criticized them for their "impatience" with the clause-by-clause review and argued that when the political heat was turned up, they simply "jumped it back into the House" (ibid.).

When the Tories refused to allow the bill to pass to third reading without further public consultation, the government resorted to time allocation to expedite its passage. Grossman argued that the government "was fed up with the heat it was taking out there, which was a lot worse than he thought," and decided to use "closure" to bring the debate to an end. "Crisis, insults and closure; that is the main theme of this government," he said, claiming that the premier was providing a clear example of the difference "between real leadership and real dictatorship" (Grossman 1986). To this end, Conservative MPP Phil Gillies derided the premier for his "pigheaded attitude" and his refusal to "consider the very constructive options put forward by the leader of my party that could have averted the necessity for this motion" (Gillies 1986).

Perhaps the most surprising response was that of the leader of the NDP, Bob Rae, who had long been critical of time allocation. In 1982, Rae made a statement in reference to the Davis government's use of time allocation on the Inflation Restraint Act:

> Once we enter into the world of time allocation, we are giving an extraordinary degree of power to the executive … A gun is being put to our heads by the

> government and we have absolutely no intention of putting up with that kind of pressure or knuckling under simply because there is that kind of pressure coming from the government. (Rae 1982c)

Given that the Liberals had only a minority of votes in the legislature, Rae was put in the difficult position of having to either support the time allocation motion or refuse to do so and take the risk that the political pressure would become too extreme and the Liberals would lose their resolve about the extra-billing legislation. Ultimately, in a decision that foreshadowed his tenure as premier, Rae chose pragmatism over principle, deciding to support the Liberal motion. He laid out his party's position in very clear terms:

> If this is what it takes to get the bill through, then we are prepared to see that gets done. If at the end of the debate tomorrow we have the completion of third reading and if at the end of third reading we have proclamation, which I am also assuming is going to take place, it will be a historic day in the life of this province. (Rae 1986)

Rae's support of the Liberals marked a significant moment in the evolution of time allocation in the legislature. By this point, all three parties had played at least some role in supporting it. It is not an overstatement, then, to suggest that the use of time allocation on Bill 94 was a monumental step in the evolution of House procedure: it signified the dawn of the use of time allocation as a common mechanism used by all three parties to stifle debate.

Petitioning the Government: The Filibuster of 1988

In the spring of 1988, the opposition parties collaborated to organize one of the most extreme uses of obstructionist tactics in the legislature's history in protest of Bill 113, the Retail Business Holidays Amendment Act, which permitted Sunday shopping in Ontario. The decision to allow merchants to remain open on Sundays had significant support throughout the province, but it was also subject to fierce criticism, particularly within religious communities on the right and labour unions on the left. It had the effect of dividing the majority legislature even further along partisan lines because both the NDP and the Tories had considerable factions within their political bases that were vehement in their opposition to the bill. At stake was the right of employees to have at least one scheduled day off per week. For Bob Rae, the issue was no less fundamental than a question about religious values and "a basic question of how we organize our time together as families and how we organize our time together in the workplace" (Rae 1989a).

The New Democrats and Progressive Conservatives were aware that since there were no restrictions in the Standing Orders on the time set aside for the presentation of petitions, a debate of indefinite length to block the introduction of the Sunday shopping legislation was a distinct possibility. If opposition members were to stand in the House and read petitions on to the record, the Speaker would have little choice but to recognize them for as long as they continued to do so. It was here that the contradiction between the emerging, hyperpartisan culture of Queen's Park and the old, stable system of cooperation was revealed. So long as the opposition was willing to exploit Standing Orders that were sufficiently flexible to allow the House schedule to be set by the House Leaders, and if it wanted to avoid parliamentary deadlock, the government had to close these loopholes.

On 14 April 1988, the NDP and the Progressive Conservatives spent the majority of the sessional day presenting petitions, blocking the House from proceeding to the Introduction of Bills or the Orders of the Day. As a result, the Liberals were unable to introduce Bill 113 for first reading in the House, as they had planned. The government argued that the Speaker was within his rights to rule the endless reading of petitions out of order since he had discretion to rule on any contingencies not provided for in the Standing Orders and since the presentation of petitions, "on a continuous basis," constituted a "clear abuse of the process of this House" (Faubert 1988). Speaker Hugh Edighoffer, however, ruled that the presentation of petitions did not violate the provisions set out in the Standing Orders. In response to the government's arguments, he ruled that the members themselves had "agreed and formed the standing orders that are here before you" and that the Speaker's role was merely to "maintain those orders and to make certain that all members have the right to speak and to be heard" (Edighoffer 1988).

The filibuster continued through the week of 18 April: each sessional day began with Member's Statements, Statements by the Ministry, and Question Period, as planned, before the NDP brought the remainder of legislative business to a halt by reading petitions for the balance of the day. Earlier in the month, the government had informed the House that Finance Minister Bob Nixon would introduce his budget on Wednesday, 20 April. However, as the three House Leaders had yet to come to an agreement to end the filibuster, the NDP refused to cease reading petitions. Unable to proceed to the Orders of the Day, Nixon stood on a point of order to ask for the unanimous consent required under the Standing Orders to bring an end to the reading of petitions. Unanimous consent, however, was denied, and, as a result, for the first time in the legislature's history, the government was unable to introduce its budget motion in the House or to give its budget speech. Nixon was left with little choice but to simply deposit the government's budget with the Clerk, while the New Democrats continued the practice of reading petitions through to the end of the sessional day.

After the NDP had obstructed proceedings for more than a week, its House Leader finally came to an arrangement with the Liberals to end the delay and resume normal proceedings. At 5:10 p.m. on Thursday, 21 April, the NDP filibuster came to an end, and the Speaker called for the Introduction of Bills, allowing the government to, at long last, introduce Bill 113. When Solicitor General Joan Smith introduced Bill 113 for first reading, the NDP did not show up to vote; its absence left the division bells to ring until the following day at 4:00 p.m., when the Speaker announced that a deal had been made among the three parties to delay the vote until the following Monday morning (Mellor 1988). As a part of the deal, the government had agreed to allow the bill to be subject to the scrutiny of a lengthy menu of public consultations and committee hearings throughout the summer months before proceeding to third reading. This being the case, the Speaker was left with little choice but to deem the bells to continue ringing through the weekend until a vote could be taken on Monday.

At just after 1:00 p.m. on 25 April 1988, a week and a half after the delay had begun, the vote on first reading of Bill 113 was recorded, bringing an end to the nearly one-hundred-hour-long sessional day, the longest in the legislature's history at the time (Mellor 1988). The opposition parties' ability to delay House proceedings exemplified the leverage that they could wield to receive additional time for debate and consultation, even in a majority government.

A New Precedent: The Use of a Single Time Allocation Motion for Two Bills

After the government had recalled the legislature in early January 1989, one of its first acts was to bring forward a motion to adopt the reports of the Standing Committee on the Administration of Justice on Bills 113 and 114. Bill 114, the Employment Standards Amendment Act, was a partner legislation to Bill 113, enabling retail businesses to open on Sundays. Having learned from its experiences on the first reading of Bill 113, and facing continued resistance to the legislation from both opposition parties, the government brought forward a motion of time allocation on both Sunday shopping bills. Introduced on 19 January, it was designed to apply to Bill 113 and to bring about both the Committee of the Whole House and third reading in a timely fashion, without obstruction from the opposition. In a speech to justify introducing the motion, Government House Leader Sean Conway argued that the bills had been subject to a weeks-long public consultation process in various locations around the province as well as lengthy committee hearings, and it had received over sixty hours of debate in the legislature. He claimed that the motion did not constitute closure since it permitted debate over the bills to continue within the timelines set out by the government. The time had come to "now move these two bills on to the next stage of debate so that we can continue a good dialogue and bring all of this to an orderly conclusion," he argued (Conway 1989a).

The opposition, however, maintained that the use of a time allocation motion to usher two bills through the House was a violation of procedure and the Speaker should rule it out of order. It claimed that time allocation was not provided for in the Standing Orders, nor was there sufficient precedent for the government to use the guillotine to pass more than one bill. Establishing such a precedent could lead to further abuses in the future if a government chose to use this procedural tactic to expedite the passage of multiple pieces of legislation at once.

Speaker Edighoffer (1989a), however, ruled that there was, in fact, a precedent in the British parliamentary tradition and cited an example from Westminster from 1988, during which the Thatcher Conservative government had used a single time allocation to pass two unrelated bills dealing with school boards in Scotland and firearms. Furthermore, during the previous Parliament, the three parties at Queen's Park had agreed by unanimous consent to allow a package of three bills to be moved and debated together. Nevertheless, that occasion "still represents the will of the House and this does not take anything away from the absolute right of the House to determine its own procedure." Given that, in accordance with Standing Order 1(b), by which the Speaker was required to "base his decision on the usages and precedents of the legislature and parliamentary tradition," Edighoffer was left with little choice but to rule that the time allocation motion was in accordance with the procedures and practices of the House and should be allowed to stand (Edighoffer 1989a).

Predictably, the opposition was upset by the decision, arguing that the use of time allocation motions was becoming normalized at the expense of the democratic process. Bob Rae argued that the Speaker had set a "very dangerous precedent," which implied that "the majority can in effect, without so much as a by-your-leave, amend the standing orders and simply force through legislation as it wishes." The minority parties "need more protection," he argued, but instead, "we are now living with rules and with precedents in this House which will not stand democracy well at the end of the day" (Rae 1989b).

Progressive Conservative House Leader Mike Harris argued that while his party had used time allocation in the past, it had done so out of necessity, as a means of addressing the economic crisis of the early 1980s. To use time allocation for legislation as "insignificant" as Bills 113 and 114, he argued, was to set a dangerous precedent. He claimed that he felt "particularly betrayed" since, as House Leader, he had been promised that if he agreed to limit debate on second reading, another opportunity would present itself. That opportunity, he insisted, had been taken away in an underhanded and unfair fashion and had caused him to feel as though he had "let my members down by trusting in the good faith, by trusting in the sense of fairness, of the government that the opportunity would be provided" (Harris 1989).

Despite the protests of opposition members, on 30 January the government used its majority to pass the time allocation motion. Its use in this instance must be viewed from a different perspective than on previous occasions. While it was undoubtedly a pre-emptive attempt to ensure that the Sunday shopping bills passed in a timely fashion, opposition obstruction efforts had reached new heights: the NDP's tactics of April 1988 had prevented the Progressive Conservative government from introducing its budget in the House. In light of the recent willingness of the opposition to resort to its own extreme methods to hinder the government from implementing its agenda, time allocation could be viewed as an unavoidable method of confronting the more adversarial nature of House governance. Whether or not this was the case, the motion was an expression of the continued decline of decorum and collaboration between the government and the opposition at Queen's Park.

The government prorogued the legislature shortly after its Sunday shopping legislation had passed, but the disorder that had plagued the first session revealed itself early in the second, when the opposition again interrupted the proceedings of the House. The first delay occurred out of protest against a scandal involving Solicitor General Joan Smith. Earlier in the year, Smith received a call in the middle of the night from a young girl, who expressed concern for the safety of her brother. While Smith attempted to reassure the girl that the police would look after the matter, the girl insisted that the situation was of the utmost urgency and required her intervention. Smith decided that the best course of action would be to go to the police station herself to express concern about the safety of the girl's brother and to urge the police to investigate the matter (Mellor 1989). When the details of the solicitor general's actions were made public, the opposition immediately demanded that she resign since it was deemed inappropriate for a solicitor general, responsible for policing, to intervene on behalf of an individual citizen, regardless of the purity of the intent.

Once the House resumed normal proceedings, NDP member Peter Kormos rose on a point of privilege and suggested that the premier "deliberately misled me and he deliberately misled the House." The Speaker interrupted him, asking him to withdraw his comments since, under the rules of parliamentary procedure, "a member cannot accuse another member of deliberately uttering a falsehood." Defiantly, he reiterated his claims, insisting that "the Premier lied to the House" (Kormos 1989). When Kormos refused to withdraw his comments, Edighoffer told the Assembly that he "had no choice but to name the member" (referring to the term used to describe disciplinary action taken against members who violate the rules) and to call upon the Sergeant-at-Arms to remove Kormos from the legislature for the balance of the day (Edighoffer 1989b). New Democrat Dave Cooke raised a point of order to argue that the words used by Kormos, although unparliamentary, were true and, therefore, should be ruled as being in order (Cooke 1989a). When the Speaker refused to change his decision, Cooke stood in the House to challenge it on the basis that it was in violation of the procedures of the House.

After consulting with the Clerk, the Speaker ruled that there was, indeed, precedent for challenging the Speaker on a decision to remove a member from the House for unparliamentary language, and therefore he called for a vote to be held. The New Democrats, knowing full well that their case had little standing and no chance of being upheld in the majority Liberal legislature, once again vacated their seats and allowed the division bells to ring. This time, they allowed the bells to ring for six days, until 6 June, before returning to their seats to vote on the Speaker's ruling, but only after Solicitor General Smith had announced her resignation from Cabinet. Even the Tories, who were as committed as the NDP to seeing to it that Smith resign her Cabinet seat, refused to join in the obstructionist tactics, instead voting with the government to uphold Edighoffer's decision to name Kormos. The NDP, despite losing the vote, had managed to delay the proceedings of the legislature for nearly a week and a half to protest the premier's refusal to ask Smith to step down. It was the second such delay that they had provoked in the span of thirteen months, and it would not be the last.

The NDP again obstructed the proceedings of the House in protest against the highly contentious Bill 162, the Workers' Compensation Amendment Act (Bill 162, 1988). As a means of delaying the passage of this bill, the NDP once again resorted to reading full petitions on to the record when the bill was at committee stage. Its reasoning was to extend the length of time the bill would spend in committee before it could be reported to the legislature for further consideration. After it became apparent that the opposition was prepared to use every tool at its disposal to stop the bill from proceeding beyond committee stage, the government imposed closure on the committee and ordered the bill sent back to the legislature so that members could adopt the recommendations of the report. During the debate, the NDP attempted to delay proceedings again by reading several petitions on to the record and further stood in their positions to speak for extended periods of time. The New Democrats extended the debate on the bill from 4:05 p.m. through the night until 9:45 a.m. the following day, during which time Shelley Martel spoke for three hours and fifteen minutes, the third-longest speech given during debates in the history of the legislature up to that time (Mellor 1989).

As a means of ensuring that the opposition could not further stall the debate, on 18 July the government again moved time allocation. Government House Leader Sean Conway called the move a "last resort" and a necessary means of dealing with an "obstructionist" opposition. "If two years in this job has taught me anything, it has taught me something about how the NDP in opposition, and on occasion with its friends to the right in the Conservative Party, can move from opposition to obstruction." Conway continued his justification of the motion, arguing that the government had introduced the bill more than thirteen months earlier and had allowed significant time for public consultation, and seven days of debate, involving twenty-two members from all sides of the House. The NDP, he conceded, "has opposed this with all its vigour and with all its passion. I think it is fair to say it has been a difference almost on first principles" (Conway 1989b).

NDP MPP Bob Mackenzie argued that the government had been resolute, even before bringing the bill forward, that few, if any, changes would be made to it. Thus, while there were extensive hearings, these amounted to "window dressing," to pacify public opposition. He argued that "almost from day one the minister responsible for Bill 162 has made it clear that the bill will pass basically as it is. Indeed, he was talking to our critic and did not really want to enter into the public hearings we had." He continued, "Not only were vitally interested parties denied a voice," but, during the committee hearings, "there was no response at all from the Liberal members of the committee. It was as though they were struck dumb, as though the fix was in and everybody knew it" (Mackenzie 1989).

Furthermore, Mackenzie blamed the need to resort to "closure" on the personal dynamics established by the Government House Leader in his interactions with the opposition. He accused Conway of being "incompetent" in his "my way or no way" approach to House governance. House Leaders meetings, he continued, were "always confrontational," and "so the opposition has felt that the only way to articulate their opposition clearly was with "use of the rules or the use of the bells." According to the NDP, then, the central problem with the decorum in the legislature had less to do with an obstructionist opposition than with a Government House Leader who refused to make compromises and who lacked the personal relationship skills to carry out the fragile task of all-party negotiations. Conway, Mackenzie argued, had "brought about the most unhealthy, nasty, personal and divisive House that is literally operating on invective and personal animosity. … I think the government House leader should be replaced as a first step to restoring any civility in this House" (Mackenzie 1989).

Further Restrictions on Debate: The Standing Orders Reforms of 1989

In response to the unravelling of House decorum, Conway announced a series of changes to the Standing Orders in late July; they were designed to both close the procedural loopholes that had allowed for the opposition obstructionist tactics and improve the general atmosphere of the House. The changes were significant in that they established fixed time restrictions on several of the procedures that had traditionally been left to negotiation among the parties in the legislature. The most fundamental changes were the following:

- If division occurred, division bells would ring for a maximum of five minutes.
- The period for petitions was restricted to a maximum of fifteen minutes per day.
- Motions to extend debate might be proposed by a Minister of the Crown without notice, although such motions might not extend beyond midnight.
- Challenges to Speakers' rulings were eliminated.
- The Chief Whip of any party was allowed to delay a vote until the following sessional day.
- A new parliamentary calendar was established, which created an average of one hundred annual sitting days per year.
- The ability of the opposition to introduce motions for special debates was eliminated, but replaced with five Opposition Days per session, during which the opposition would be granted the power to control the agenda of the House. (Conway 1989c)

The reforms to the Standing Orders established procedures that made it even more difficult than before for the opposition to delay government initiatives. Whereas the previous format had given the opposition parties flexibility to negotiate for additional time to debate issues of fundamental concern to them, the new procedures made such compromises from the government far less likely since they removed the majority of avenues left to interfere with the process. Conway argued that the government thought that changes were necessary: "We were facing a pattern of obstructionism that was really making this place somewhat less effective and less efficient than the people of Ontario expect it to be." The reforms would bring an end to the "endless ringing of bells, the mindless reading of petitions, the challenges of the Speaker's rulings to precipitate bell-ringing, [and] emergency debates," which had been "coming fast and furious" over the previous fourteen months (Conway 1989c).

The opposition parties were unanimous that amendments to the Standing Orders were necessary. Michael Breaugh expressed the sentiment of many MPPs when he said that changes "were long overdue" and would have the support of New Democrats in the House (Breaugh 1989). Although the opposition did not support the increased rigidity of House protocols, it appreciated the concessions the government had made by making the Speaker electable by the whole House and by granting the opposition parties specific Opposition Days to control the House agenda and bring forward its own legislation.

NDP MPP Dave Cooke explained that, with both the Sunday shopping bills and the Workers' Compensation Amendment Act, the opposition had been "really backed into a corner," and so it followed that "that is why those tactics were used." He added, "We were going to use every rule that was at our disposal to stop that legislation and to hold the government accountable. That was our responsibility, that was our job and that is exactly what we did." He explained that his party was now "happy that these rule changes are going to reform the system," but he was also pleased that it had been able to use "outdated" rules to hold the government to account on two pieces of legislation that it had considered to be unacceptable. "In many ways," he said, "we killed two birds with one stone" (Cooke 1989b).

The new Standing Orders came into effect on the day the legislature returned from summer recess. The House ran considerably more smoothly during the fall months because the structured approach to parliamentary governance provided by the new Standing Orders ensured the advancement of the government's program without obstruction from the opposition. The first Opposition Day in the history of the Queen's Park was held on 17 October 1989, when the NDP introduced a motion to debate the government's proposed auto insurance reforms (Sibenik 1989). For the time being, all three parties were content with the new rules of the Assembly. This period of armistice, however, was to be short-lived.

The 1990 Auto Insurance Controversy: The New Standing Orders Put to the Test

The atmosphere of reciprocity in the legislature descended into rancour once again as the fall turned to winter. The Liberals introduced a controversial auto insurance reform bill, which replaced the right to sue of persons injured in automobile accidents with a market-based, no-fault insurance system of payment. The NDP argued that the plan was bound to result in higher premiums for Ontarians and amounted to a publicly funded scheme of subsidization for the insurance industry. The Liberal government hoped to have the bill passed by late spring so that the new insurance system could be up and running by the fall. The NDP, however, had every intention of delaying the government's timetable by dragging the bill through the committee stage for as long as possible.

On 20 December 1989, new Government House Leader Christopher Ward introduced a routine motion to schedule committee business during the holiday break. Traditionally, these motions provide a sketch of the committee meeting schedule during the period of adjournment, often with provisions that the committee will report to the legislature at some fixed date once the House has been recalled. Such motions, however, are almost always agreed upon beforehand and so are merely pro forma votes in the legislature. In an unprecedented manoeuvre that attempted to undercut the NDP's desire to drag the bill through committee, Ward brought forward a motion to set a fixed date for the Committee on General Government to report to the House. The motion required that the committee meet for "a maximum of five weeks," in various places around Ontario, and that the bill be "reported to the House on 19 March 1990." In the event that the committee failed to report the bill to the legislature by the specified date, "the bill shall be deemed to be passed by the committee and shall be deemed to be reported to the House and the report shall be deemed to be received and adopted by the House" (Ward 1989).

The opposition was predictably outraged by the government's decision to limit the consideration that the bill would be given at committee stage, arguing that it constituted a form of closure without the inconvenience of a formal time allocation motion. Ward's motion, NDP MPP Dave Cooke argued, had the effect of "totally prejudging anything that might happen in the standing committee on general government on insurance." He argued that the motion was "antidemocratic" and represented the first time that the government had ever brought in closure on committee proceedings before a committee had even begun its work. "What the Liberals are really saying now," Cooke declared, "is that it is all going to be a public relations exercise and that anything the public has to say will not be listened to by this government" (Cooke 1989c). Ward argued that the motion did not prejudge the committee, but that the committee would bring the legislation back on the first day the House returned from break, and he promised that the government would provide time at the Committee of the Whole "to continue the discussion if the need arises." "We do not have the luxury," he continued, "to talk this out for a year and a half unless the drivers of this province are quite willing to accept increases in the neighbourhood of 30 percent for the coming year" (Ward 1989).

New Democrat Richard Johnston maintained that the abuse of a routine motion to stifle debate on a highly contentious article of legislation struck at the very heart of the democratic process in Ontario. He recounted that recent years had witnessed a trend by the executive to evade the legislature in the name of efficiency. He warned the Assembly,

> This is a very dangerous road to go down. The evolution in our parliamentary democracy should be slow and considered. It should not be precipitous and only meeting the needs of the executive council … There is the danger of looking at democracy and democratic institutions like this with an efficiency model rather than a democratic-procedure-and-rights-based model in mind. The more we swing into the presumption that the needs of the executive council are what this place must serve fundamentally, and not the needs of representation and the people as a whole, the greater the danger is to our democracy. (Johnston 1989)

Soon after the motion was brought forward in the legislature, the three House Leaders agreed to extend the filing date of the committee report by one week. This short extension of the committee's work demonstrated the leverage that the new Standing Orders had given the government since it could now set a fixed House schedule without being concerned that the opposition might obstruct proceedings.

Despite its promise to allow a robust debate on Bill 68, the government moved time allocation, on 3 April 1990, just a week after the committee had been ordered to return its report to the legislature. Ward told the House it was with "great regret" that the government felt compelled to proceed with the motion, but, "after having spent some 28 days, over 107 hours, discussing this matter, I do not believe the rights of the minority have been offended or abrogated in any way" (Ward 1990). NDP House Leader Dave Cooke argued that the motion should be ruled out of order because "the government now treats time allocation motions, even though they are not provided for in our standing orders, as routine." He claimed that continuing this method of House governance would set a precedent, empowering the majority to use time allocation as a method of invoking closure "as often as it feels like using it" (Cooke 1990).

Although the changes made to the Standing Orders the previous July had established limits on the methods available to delay the proceedings of the House, the opposition began searching for procedural manoeuvres not covered by the Standing Orders to extend debate on Bill 68. New Democrat Peter Kormos, a self-described "student of tradition and decorum," recognized that although the procedural rules limited the time for petitions, motions, and ringing the division bells, no such restrictions had been placed on the Orders of the Day (Kormos 1990a). According to House procedure, when the Orders of the Day were called, any debate that had not finished the previous day was to resume by recognizing the speaker who had held the floor when debate had adjourned. This meant that if Kormos could hold the floor until the House adjourned, he would be the first speaker called for debate the following day and could theoretically continue speaking each day until he was forced to stand down.

Kormos's filibuster began on 3 April on the debate scheduled for the time allocation motion. Every day for nearly a month, Kormos rose to speak at the beginning of the Orders of the Day and held the floor until adjournment. Because the time allocation motion did not stipulate a limit on the debate over the actual motion itself, the government was powerless to require him to stand down. On 26 April, after he had managed to delay the bill for more than three weeks, the government brought forward a motion, without notice, to extend the sitting of the House past midnight to force him to continue speaking until he was no longer able to physically do so. Kormos began his speech at 4:00 p.m. that afternoon and held the floor throughout the night, ultimately reading letters and faxes from constituents on to the record. So determined was he to hold the floor that he began taking requests for letters from constituents by using the live broadcast of the proceedings to advertise for more calls. He reached out to constituents watching at home: "The phone number to call is 965-1224. I need your calls. If that line is busy, people can call 965-1239. Of course, the area code is here in Toronto, area code 416" (Kormos 1990b). At just after 9:00

a.m. on 27 April, after Kormos had spoken for seventeen consecutive hours, the longest speech by a single member in the legislature's history ended when he stood down. Upon doing so, he stated,

> So I tell you, Mr. Speaker, I am tired … I could go on until one o'clock, two o'clock, or four or five. I could go on through to midnight tonight, I am sure of that, because my passion for the rights of drivers and taxpayers and, oh yes, innocent injured victims in this province is strong enough and has been reinforced by those hundreds and thousands of people phoning in and writing letters pleading for some decency and for some democracy here at Queen's Park. My passion is that strong. But do you know what, Mr. Speaker? I am fearful that the Liberals here do not listen. I am fearful that the Liberals do not care. I am fearful that the bonds between the Liberal Party in Ontario and the auto insurance industry are simply too strong to let the Liberals do what is right and do what is decent. At that, there is going to be an election in 1990, maybe before, probably after, Bill 68 gets rammed through, but we will let the electorate decide, I tell you that. (Kormos 1990b)

It was symbolic that what would turn out to be the last weeks of the final parliamentary session in the Peterson mandate saw an opposition filibuster hold up government business longer than any other in the province's history up to that point. While Kormos did not stop the passage of Bill 68, he had exercised his right as a member to use the means at his disposal to hold up the proceedings of the legislature, and he had exposed a loophole in the government's new Standing Orders. Ironically, after the New Democrats won the general election just a few months later, they brought in changes to the Standing Orders to restrict similar opposition tactics.

Conclusion

The Peterson era will almost undoubtedly be recorded by history as both a time of immense transition in Ontario politics and an interregnum period brought about by the relaxation of the crisis conditions that had characterized the final years of the Davis government. It is impossible to speculate whether the Peterson government's approach would have differed markedly had economic conditions not allowed them to implement policy at a pace that was consistent with the relatively slow democratic process.

The evidence shows that it has been the most radical governments in Ontario that have resorted to the most extreme measures to insulate their decisions from the legislative process. Given that the Peterson Liberals ran a largely moderate, pragmatic government during a time of economic growth, there was little need for them to establish a procedural model for speed or to marginalize decisions emanating from the parliamentary process. Instead, they were able to make good on some of their promises to restore trust in the parliamentary chamber following the tumultuous final few years of the Davis era. The decisions to televise legislative proceedings and to appoint an integrity commissioner were important steps in improving government accountability.

The democratic renaissance of this period should not be overstated, however. The Peterson era can be viewed as one in which certain trends established under Davis, such as time allocation, were reinforced and, in some cases, strengthened. The government used time allocation on four occasions – one more than the Davis government had – and enacted new Standing Orders in 1989 that significantly diminished opposition leverage to hold the government to account by delaying the passage of legislation. There was, however, a central difference between its approach to time allocation and the approach of governments that came both before and after: while the Davis, Rae, Harris, Eves, McGuinty, Wynne, and Ford governments used time allocation proactively, to implement their agendas, the Peterson government used it most often only as a last resort, as a method of breaking parliamentary gridlock brought about by an activist opposition.

The Peterson years were also something of a coming of age for the opposition parties. The accord between the NDP and Liberals marked a watershed moment in Ontario's politics. Not only had two opposition parties toppled the longest-serving government in the British Commonwealth, giving them the capacity to influence policy, but they had also altered the province's entire political landscape. The days of the clubhouse atmosphere at Queen's Park, in which the stakeholders understood their role as government member or opposition, were consigned to the past, replaced by a highly competitive dynamic in which all three parties would have opportunities to govern over the decade to follow. This produced a fractured and partisan legislature, and it began to reveal itself in Peterson's second mandate, as the opposition resorted to obstructionist tactics.

The decade, which had begun with Bill Davis proclaiming the "realities of March 19th," closed with Peter Kormos's month-long filibuster, underscoring how profoundly the dynamics of the legislature had changed. Queen's Park, despite its reputation as a dull and obstinate political Assembly, experienced an awakening, as the opposition parties began to assert themselves. These were undoubtedly the halcyon days for the opposition in Ontario; they were, however, to be short-lived. Within a few years, the Rae and Harris governments would take steps to remove all opportunities for the opposition to exercise their parliamentary right to obstruct House business in protest against the government's agenda.

7 "Democracy under Siege": The NDP's Neoliberal Turn and the Decline of Parliament at Queen's Park, 1990–1995

Introduction

History will doubtless record the Ontario general election of 1990 as producing one of the most surprising electoral results in Canadian history. By electing the NDP under Bob Rae, the public elevated to government a party whose raison d'être had traditionally been to oppose the existing structures of political and economic power. In opposition, the New Democrats had long functioned as the conscience of the legislature, taking strong, principled stances against government initiatives that, in their view, undermined the public interest, the rights of workers, and marginalized groups. In its first Speech from the Throne, the new government promised to earn "the trust and respect" of citizens by opening Queen's Park "to those who have never before had an effective voice in the corridors of power." In its pursuit of restoring a sense of "integrity" at Queen's Park, the New Democrats promised to hold the executive branch accountable to the electorate by establishing the highest standards of conduct and to "guard against institutional arrogance and the abuse of power wherever they exist" (Alexander 1990).

However, soon after the election, the Ontario economy sunk into its worst recession since the 1930s. Between 1990 and 1991, Ontario's gross domestic product fell by almost 1 per cent, as the province adjusted to the consequences of the 1987 Canada–United States Free Trade Agreement (Statistics Canada 2015b). Hundreds of small manufacturing companies in the province closed during this period, and more than three hundred thousand industrial-sector employees lost their jobs in the process (Rae 1997). By 1992, unemployment levels had risen to 10.8 per cent, despite the government's initial efforts to encourage job creation using traditional Keynesian stimulus measures.

The economy finally stopped its downward spiral in the middle of 1992, but it would be two years before the province's GDP rebounded to 1990 levels (Statistics Canada 2016). It would take even longer for companies to begin hiring again, as the unemployment rate increased in 1993 and fell to only 9.7 per cent by 1994 (Statistics Canada 2015b). The problem of economic decline was coupled with a policy of restraint at the federal level. In its 1991 budget, the Mulroney government imposed a series of restrictions on its social transfers to Ontario, which further eroded the Rae government's capacity to address the unemployment problem without resorting to historic levels of deficit financing.

In the Rae government's first budget, introduced on 29 April 1991, Finance Minister Floyd Laughren, who had been given the tongue-in-cheek moniker "Pink Floyd" by the *Toronto Sun*, sought to "pick up the slack in federal funding for social, health and educational programs" by increasing spending. To address the recession, the NDP would allow the deficit to rise to a record $9.7 billion over the next fiscal year. Whereas the federal government had "abdicated its responsibility to promote economic growth during hard times," Laughren stated that "allowing the deficit to rise to this level this year is the most responsible choice we could make, given the economic and fiscal conditions we inherited as a new government" (Laughren 1991).

Laughren told the legislature that "we had a choice to make this year – to fight the deficit or fight the recession. We are proud to be fighting the recession" (Laughren 1991). The government remained primarily focused on using the state to stimulate the economy as well as to offer skills training to some 250,000 workers displaced by the recession. However, by early 1992, as the economy continued to spiral downward and Treasury projections indicated that the annual deficit could come in above $20 billion, the Rae government's tone on fiscal restraint shifted markedly. Early in the New Year, Rae went on television to appeal directly to Ontarians that he was now of the view that "public sector restraint had to be the order of the day." This could be achieved within a vision of social democracy, he argued, so long as it was balanced with significant public- and private-sector investment in employment-generating policies (Rae 1997, 233).

So it was that, in April 1992, Floyd Laughren presented what has become known as the "three-legged-stool" budget; it focused on three central priorities: a jobs plan, spending on human services such as health care and education, and deficit reduction. The government would reduce total spending by more than $3 billion from its 1991 budget, with the cuts spread across fifteen separate ministries (Laughren 1992).

While the 1992 budget mixed Keynesianism with neoliberal policy solutions, by the time of the 1993 budget, the Rae government had become fully committed to the logic of fiscal restraint. During his 1993 budget speech, Laughren (1993) boasted that, for the first time since 1942, Ontario government spending would decline from one fiscal year to the next. The NDP would cut the costs of running programs by 4.3 per cent from 1992 levels and reduce the size of government by 5,000 employees from 1991 levels.

Laughren (1993) warned that without putting the brakes on debt levels, "even assuming that international bankers would lend us the money, our interest costs would take off." The necessary savings were to be achieved by finding efficiencies in the bureaucracy, by eliminating jobs, and by negotiating new contracts with public-sector employees. When the government was unable to reach a settlement with public-sector workers through negotiation, it simply legislated a new contract with a wage freeze, granting significant powers to Cabinet to enforce its terms through Order in Council.

The NDP era, then, can be understood only through the lens of the dramatic shift in policy that occurred at the beginning of 1992. During that time, the government abandoned Keynesian economic solutions to the recession, instead turning to a policy of aggressive fiscal retrenchment and neoliberal state restructuring to bring the deficit under control.

The NDP's shift is an ideal example of the contradictions confronted by governments – particularly social democratic ones – during the age of neoliberalism. Early efforts to govern according to an interventionist model were scrapped when the economy did not recover as quickly as the government had hoped and the deficit continued to grow. Forced to confront an aggressive business lobby and right-wing media that sought to portray the NDP as fiscally irresponsible, the Rae government sought a Third Way approach that could help it to both confront the recession and quash these concerns. This need to make up for lost time led the NDP to adopt a parliamentary strategy whereby, over the next three years, it imposed unprecedented restrictions on debate in the legislature by formalizing time allocation and misusing procedures, such as omnibus bills, to move its restraint agenda through the House as quickly as possible.

Some of the instances during which the NDP applied time allocation in its early mandate can be attributed to a highly partisan and contentious atmosphere in the legislature, which necessitated government intervention to break an impasse. However, in the second half of its mandate, it began to use such tactics indiscriminately to rush its unpopular restraint program through the legislature and grant itself the authority to impose spending restraint upon the public sector.

The government had already devoted a year and a half to attempting to spend its way out of the recession, so its change in thinking required carrying out significant and unpopular changes in short order. The deliberative nature of the parliamentary process meant that if the government were to initiate the public-sector restructuring necessary to bring the deficit under control, it required procedural mechanisms that could expedite its legislation through the Assembly. In putting those in place, however, the New Democrats set several new precedents, which undermined the rights of the legislative branch at the expense of the executive and ultimately prepared the ground for the Common Sense Revolution (CSR) in 1995.

Imposing Fiscal Restraint from the Centre

The NDP came to power amid considerable optimism within the labour community that the election of the first decidedly pro-labour party in the province's post-war history would result in a number of long-awaited social democratic policy reforms and continue the labour peace established under the Peterson government. Despite the fact that the NDP had legislated some measures to protect and extend labour rights early in its mandate, by 1993 it had become apparent that its restraint agenda would conflict with the interests of the province's public-sector unions. Early that year, Rae (1997) began to discuss with Cabinet the need to take dramatic steps to cut public-sector costs. To trim salaries to a more sustainable level, he speculated that his government might have to eliminate as many as 40,000 jobs. Since giving layoff notices to such a large number of employees was not consistent with his, or his party's, belief system, Rae did what would become his hallmark as premier – he sought political shelter in a compromise solution that ultimately satisfied no one. He proposed what he called a "Social Contract," in which the government would spare the majority of public-sector jobs, but achieve savings by forcing the unions to consent to a wage freeze and requiring employees to take a certain number of unpaid days per year. These became known as "Rae Days." As Rae himself put it, "better a Rae Day – or two or ten – in the context of a long-term job than no job at all" (ibid., 252).

In April 1993, the Rae government assembled public-sector union representatives for joint negotiations on the framework of the Social Contract (Rae 1997, 245). However, the negotiations did not prove fruitful, and the unions refused to accept either the wage freeze or the government's proposed furlough days. In turn, Rae made the decision that if an agreement could not be reached by the end of May, his government would take the precedent-setting step of using legislation to force the Social Contract on public-sector employees without their negotiated consent. Indeed, the only comparable precedent in Ontario's legislative history was the Davis Tories' 1982 Inflation Restraint Act, which Rae and the NDP had fought so ardently to stop.

On 14 June 1993, the NDP introduced Bill 48, the Social Contract Act. The bill was designed to "achieve significant savings in public sector expenditures in a fair and equitable manner" and to encourage "efficiency and productivity savings" by cutting more than $2 billion from the public sector, spanning eight ministries (Bill 48, 1993). The bill also empowered Cabinet to impose a wage freeze of up to three years and/or up to three unpaid furlough days per year in pursuit of this objective without having to ratify such decisions in the legislature. Liberal MPP Greg Sorbara argued that the authority granted to the minister of finance had essentially placed "arbitrary powers … in his hands, where he can make decisions on behalf of 900,000 workers as to what he thinks is right or wrong in Ontario" (Sorbara 1993).

In keeping with its devotion to fiscal discipline, the government followed up the Social Contract with legislation designed to reorganize the health care sector. In 1993, it commissioned a Hospital Restructuring Committee to search for cost savings in the sector. Previously confidential Cabinet documents prepared by the committee show that the government sought advice from private-sector management consultants about how to improve the administrative structure of Ontario's health care system. The committee considered a number of changes, including the amalgamation and reorganization of hospital management structures in various communities, changes to the dispute-resolution process with health care workers, the contracting out of certain services, a growth in the use of home care services, and a reduction in staff across the health care sector (Ontario. Administration Institute Hospital Restructuring Committee 1994).

This planning process resulted in Bill 50, the Expenditure Control Plan Statute Law Amendment Act, which gave Minister of Health Ruth Grier sweeping powers to control the restructuring process. Bill 50 authorized the minister to determine the number of times doctors were permitted to bill the province for specific treatments for individuals and to rule that doctors should not be paid for services they had provided that were determined to be unnecessary. Perhaps most significantly, the bill also authorized the Executive Council to suspend the government's normal contractual obligations to health care workers and to refer them to arbitration when a negotiated contractual settlement could not be arrived at. This provision gave Cabinet the power to achieve its fiscal targets by overriding the collectively bargained reimbursement structures for health care practitioners (Bill 50, 1993).

Minister Grier claimed that such measures were necessary to harness rising salary costs in the health care sector, which were acting as a significant drain on the provincial Treasury. She explained, "If we keep spending as though the sky were the limit, we will not have a universal health care system to pass on to our children and our children's children, because the system would become unsustainable" (Grier 1993). Liberal MPP Barbara Sullivan, however, argued that Bill 50 undermined the principle of parliamentary democracy by granting the health minister "draconian powers to impose massive cuts on medical services, and hence, patient care" (Sullivan 1993).

The government's relationship with the province's public-sector unions had become so poisoned that the NDP had little choice but to use the political shell provided by delegated legislation to enable ministers to make cuts without having to engage in contractual negotiations or, if negotiations were successful, to bring the cuts back to the legislature for ratification. This was a tactic to which both the Harris and McGuinty governments would turn in the future to force contractual terms upon the public sector and to make politically contentious cuts to core government services.

Regulation functioned as a crucial vehicle through which the neoliberal state took shape in Ontario. For the New Democrats, using their executive prerogative was born not out of any philosophical antagonism to the deliberative democratic process, but out of the recognition that, without it, they could not deliver change at the speed required to bring the deficit under control during their mandate. The government maintained that the only way to reliably achieve the savings required was to establish centralized managerial control and to use the power of the provincial executive to enforce unpopular decisions. As the years went by, the New Democrats became increasingly comfortable with this notion, despite its obvious contradictions to their traditional beliefs.

The Introduction of the Omnibus Bill

The ambitious nature of the government's deficit-reduction program required large-scale changes to the province's fiscal structure. Meanwhile, there was urgent demand within the Premier's Office and the Ministry of Finance to cut costs as soon as possible. Neither objective, however, was particularly well suited for the often slow and considered nature of the legislative process, which was designed to encourage public debate and deliberation. The NDP made the decision to overcome this obstacle by bundling several of its most ambitious reforms into omnibus bills, which would allow it to introduce a number of loosely affiliated bills at the same time, while allowing the opposition the time to debate only a single bill. Although omnibus bills were common in the legislature's history, they had generally been used to package a number of closely related housekeeping measures into the same bill to avoid having to introduce several different pieces of legislation to effect minor changes to the law.

It is no coincidence that the Rae government's shift towards the use of omnibus legislation in the spring of 1993 occurred at the same time as both its turn towards neoliberal policy solutions and its preoccupation with restructuring the state apparatus. Omnibus legislation proved to be an alluring parliamentary tactic for a party seeking to undertake complex and multi-faceted changes in a short space of time, as the New Democrats were. The majority of the omnibus bills they proposed did possess a common theme, in that they sought to reform the government or other state institutions to improve their efficiency and to reduce their costs to the Treasury. These changes often occurred across several ministries, affecting numerous pieces of legislation. Had the government provided full time for debate on each bill, passing each of the proposed reforms individually would have absorbed the majority of its agenda; but by packaging multiple bills together, it was able to implement changes quickly and with minimal political consequence. The use of omnibus legislation also gave the government the strategic advantage of burying controversial policies within legislation that contained otherwise popular measures, thus downplaying its more controversial elements.

The government's first misuse of omnibus legislation occurred on 17 May 1993, when it introduced the Capital Investment Plan Act. The bill amended seven acts and made significant changes to several ministries by establishing four new Crown corporations: the Ontario Financing Authority, the Ontario Transportation Capital Corporation, the Ontario Realty Corporation, and the Ontario Clean Water Agency (Bill 17, 1993). The Ontario Realty Corporation, for example, was designed to obscure the extent of the province's debt load by empowering the government to transfer publicly owned assets such as land, buildings, and resources to the corporation, allowing it to count the funds received as revenue. While the corporation had the right to keep these assets and sell them back to the government, it was also granted the authority to seek private-sector buyers for public assets at the minister's discretion. Establishing the Crown corporations enabled the government to move more than three thousand employees off its payroll and onto the budgets of the newly formed corporations, thereby allowing it to claim that it had taken steps to reduce the size of the public service.

Although Bill 17 arguably contained a number of similarities as part of a government-wide retrenchment program – for instance, it created the four Crown corporations, all of which were designed to help the government reduce its deficit – the introduction of legislation that made so many fundamental changes to the architecture of the state without having first received the tacit or explicit approval of the opposition was without precedent in the history of the legislature. Parliamentary tradition stipulated that changes of such magnitude should have been separated and considered as four individual bills, each of which would have to be allocated time for debate on its own merits. In hindsight, Bill 17 proved to be one of the most significant pieces of legislation in the province's history, not because of the policies it implemented – important though they were – but because it was the proverbial canary in the coalmine for what lay ahead in Ontario's immediate future. The blueprint it established would become one of the essential procedural mechanisms through which the New Democrats would seek to reform the public sector.

The government again brought forward omnibus legislation in June 1993 to implement other aspects of its budgetary policy. The Expenditure Reduction and Non-Tax Revenues Statute Law Amendment Act dealt with revenue-generating policies. It made amendments to a number of bills, including the Corporations Information Act, the Small Business Development Corporations Act, the Health Insurance Act, the Ontario Drug Benefit Act, the Game and Fish Act, and the Public Lands Act (Bill 81, 1993). One issue that drew particular criticism was the government's decision to amend the Ontario Drug

Benefit Act to grant Cabinet the power to impose user fees on the purchase of pharmaceutical products. The opposition argued that a change that would require patients to pay additional fees on the purchase of drugs deserved to be considered as a single bill and given considerable time for debate and public consultation, rather than being bundled into a package with miscellaneous legislation that, among other provisions, imposed royalties on commercial fishing and additional hydro charges for developers. After consulting with the opposition parties, the government agreed to withdraw its "severe and heavy handed" bill and unbundle it into separate pieces of legislation (Wilson 1993).

Any hope that the goodwill expressed with the withdrawal of Bill 81 in December 1993 would carry over to the following year was dashed when the House returned from recess and the NDP introduced another omnibus budget-implementation bill. The Budget Measures Act (Bill 160, 1994) amended sixteen separate pieces of legislation, ranging from reforms in education to corporate taxation. Liberal MPP Murray Elston lamented that there were elements of the budget that his party would have willingly supported, but when they were bundled with various other issues that his party opposed, members could not give it their support:

> Why wouldn't we be dealing with some of the things on the Game and Fish Act? Why do we have to hide it under the cloak of this omnibus bill? What about the Ontario home ownership plan? Good news for a lot of people, a well-received portion of this year's budget, why does it have to be in this omnibus bill? (Elston 1994)

Similarly, Liberal MPP Eleanor Caplan argued that, with its third significant omnibus bill in a year, the government had begun to exhibit a "command-and-control method of governing," which was "tremendously undemocratic." She warned that the NDP had established

> the enormous precedent which I predict will be used by future governments because the precedent has been set and established to deal with budgetary matters flowing from the provincial budget in one piece of omnibus legislation, I believe democracy and the precedents of this House are such that we will look back on this day and see this precedent as not having been a positive one. (E. Caplan 1994)

Caplan's warning proved prophetic. Within a year, the Harris government would be in office, and the omnibus bill would prove to be the most important legislative tool available to it in implementing its neoliberalization plan.

Later the same month, the government introduced the Planning and Development Municipal Statute Law Amendment Act, which amended parts of more than twenty pieces of legislation (Grandmaître 1994). The NDP made the case that these changes were necessary to streamline the approval processes of urban planning and to implement major planks in the government's fiscal-restraint agenda, which were of the utmost urgency. When opposition members expressed their desire that the bill be unbundled and debated as several pieces of legislation, the government invoked time allocation. Jim Bradley summarized his reaction to the government's tactics:

> I think this is regrettable for democracy, because it again places in the hands of those who are not elected, the people who cannot be accessed by the general public very easily, much more power and less power in the hands of democratically elected politicians. We're the only people they can get at. We are the ones who have to be reassessed and either elected or not elected at election time. That does not happen with those who are in the civil service; that does not happen with those who work for the Premier's office or who are political appointees in ministers' offices; in other words, people who have had in several governments many powers and I think in this government even more powers because of the changes to the rules that were made at the behest of Mr. Rae. (Bradley 1994a)

Any doubt that the use of omnibus legislation had become a customary element of NDP procedure was eliminated when, on 6 June 1994, the government introduced the Statute Law Amendment Act, a massive bill designed to make "moderate but real improvements in service to the public and improvements in the administration of government and its programs" (Bill 175, 1994). Bill 175 amended over one hundred pieces of legislation, across fourteen ministries, and repealed seven acts entirely. While the government claimed that most of the changes were minor and involved only matters of housekeeping, the amendments ranged from allowing alcoholic beverages to be sold in provincial parks, to the payment of driver's licences by credit card, to the harmonization of federal and provincial food-grading systems – all in the name of improving government efficiency.

Progressive Conservative MPP David Tilson claimed that his privileges as a member had been violated by the omnibus bill since its format did not afford him the same opportunity to debate the various provisions that would have been available to him had the government presented the bill in fourteen pieces of legislation, one for each ministry it affected. He argued that the opposition critics for each ministry under omnibus legislation would be limited to just thirty minutes to deal with all the changes proposed. While omnibus bills had been ruled in order with House procedure in the past, he asked the Speaker to consider that Bill 175 "goes beyond the generally accepted form of legislation and is using an omnibus format that is inconsistent with the practice of omnibus bills." Furthermore, the bill did not meet the standard set by parliamentary precedent, in which omnibus legislation was required to feature "one purpose that ties together all the proposed amendments and therefore renders the bill intelligibly for parliamentary purposes." In Bill 175, he argued, "the range and scope … are not related in any meaningful way" (Tilson 1994).

It is often assumed that the Harris government was responsible for pioneering the massive omnibus bill as a tool to marginalize the legislature. This assumption is no doubt rooted in the fact that the Harris government often used the omnibus bill prodigiously, far eclipsing any bill introduced by the New Democrats. However, the precedent was established in the late spring of 1993, when the Rae government, consumed with making up for lost time in bringing the deficit under control, sought to bundle its legislation to move it through the legislature in short order. It was these first few bills, brought forward by the New Democrats in 1993 and 1994, that put the notion of the omnibus bill as a series of unrelated measures to the procedural test and entrenched it as practice at Queen's Park.

The Normalization of Time Allocation at Queen's Park

A Chaotic First Year

Despite having been the catalyst of the tumultuous atmosphere that had hung over Queen's Park during the Peterson era, the New Democrats pledged that they would reach across the aisle to establish an effective and democratic working relationship with the opposition to bring a semblance of order and decorum back to the legislature. To be sure, there was considerable optimism that the New Democrats, who had long served as the democratic conscience of the legislature, and who had stood in steadfast opposition to attempts by both Liberal and Conservative governments to circumvent the will of the House, would reverse the use of procedural trends to marginalize the legislature that had taken hold at Queen's Park during the 1980s.

In the early months of the NDP's mandate, the House Leaders met on several occasions in the recognition that it was in the interests of all three parties to foster a more functional procedural environment in the legislature. Although they managed to forge a temporary truce, it was undone shortly after the legislature returned from winter recess in early 1991 by the opposition's resistance to one of the government's signature legislative initiatives, Bill 4, the Residential Rent Regulation Amendment Act. Tension quickly emerged between the starkly opposite views of the social democratic New Democrats and those of Mike Harris, the leader of the Progressive Conservatives, who had moved his party towards a more fundamentalist interpretation of economic liberalism (McDonald 2005). When the Rae government attempted to move Bill 4 through the House using normal procedural channels, the Tories took pains to block its passage.

Making good on their commitment to facilitate better relations among the three parties, the New Democrats first sought to break the impasse by hosting a series of meetings of the House Leaders. When the Progressive Conservatives refused to allow the bill to pass without significant amendments, which would have reconfigured its entire intent, the NDP made the decision to proceed with a time allocation motion to ensure that the bill would pass. By bringing down the guillotine, the NDP broke one of its fundamental promises, just months into its first mandate. Bill 4 received ten hours and thirty-three minutes of debate in the Committee of the Whole and eight hours and thirty-six minutes of debate on second reading (Eves 1991). In a candid speech to the legislature, Government House Leader Shelley Martel explained that the government felt it had little choice but to call for time allocation given the intransigence of the Progressive Conservatives. She described the most recent House Leaders meeting:

> It was clearly told to me that the government would have to do what the government had to do. That was a pretty clear signal to me, and I think everyone around the table understood what that meant. What it meant very clearly was that the issue would be forced and we would have to bring in a time allocation motion. (S. Martel 1991a)

The NDP was unapologetic. Dave Cooke, the minister of municipal affairs and housing – who, as former house leader for the NDP in opposition, had fought numerous battles against the Liberals when they had attempted to use time allocation – argued that since the Tories had "said from day one they are opposed to Bill 4," the government was left with "no alternative" but to bring down the hammer of time allocation to move the bill through the legislature. Now, in a considerable departure from his earlier position, Cooke told the Assembly that the government had "an agenda to protect tenants and we as a government are determined to do that. The Conservative Party is trying to prevent that from happening and that is why we have had to bring in time allocation today" (Cooke 1991). In response, Progressive Conservative MPP Ernie Eves identified the absurdity of Cooke's comment given his previous position on the issue. "My, how times have changed," he said, "the former House leader of the New Democratic Party, now the Minister of Housing, standing up and talking about defending time allocations" (Eves 1991).

Liberal MPP Yvonne O'Neill argued that the use of time allocation on so controversial a bill, without giving additional time for deliberation and public consultation, undermined her privileges as a member and the spirit of the democratic process.

> I take this motion as being arrogant. It is a sad commentary on what I know and many know as a bad bill. It is an abuse of majority government. We are limiting debate on a bill that is not fair. It is retroactive. It has had incomplete public hearings. More people have been turned away from expressing a viewpoint on this

> bill than were received, and in every instance this bill is controversial. It has been the focus of two major marches to this legislature, the only bill that has received that kind of attention in this province, so we are shooting down debate from the floor of this legislature, while we are still listening to and discussing the very first amendment presented by my party. I feel this is an infringement of my rights as a member of this legislature. The NDP government is acting exactly like the Mulroney government, "it is either our way or the byway." (O'Neill 1991)

The time allocation on Bill 4 was significant for two reasons. First, it signified a breakdown in the short-lived pledge for cooperation among the three parties from which the 35th Parliament never recovered. Second, it represented the first time that the NDP, the party that had stood steadfastly against time allocation on so many occasions over the previous decade, eagerly endorsed its use. The surprise was not merely that the government used this procedural tactic, but that it did so using the same arguments, and following the same logic, as the Liberals and Progressive Conservatives had done before them.

It is not an overstatement to suggest that Bill 4 heralded the moment at which time allocation became entrenched in House procedure. While it had arguably become customary long before this, the NDP had always opposed it, and this had enabled it to claim the moral high ground as the gatekeepers of parliamentary democracy. However, having adopted time allocation so brazenly in this instance, it joined the other two parties in establishing a recent history of bringing forward and using time allocation as a tactic for implementing its legislative program.

Any pretension of collegiality that may have remained after the NDP's first use of time allocation was eliminated when Floyd Laughren introduced his first budget in April 1991. In protest against the Keynesian-style stimulus measures it sought to impose, the Progressive Conservatives once again took to a series of parliamentary tactics to delay the routine proceedings of the House. On 6 May, they engaged in obstructionist tactics, the audacity of which had precedent only in the actions of the New Democrats themselves during the Peterson government. During Members' Statements, Tory MPP Norm Sterling (1991) rose on a point of order to voice his displeasure with the government's budget. Although he was repeatedly rebuffed by the Speaker, who ruled that his arguments did not constitute points of order, he rose three more times throughout the day as a method of stalling proceedings.

Later the same day, Progressive Conservative leader Mike Harris rose in the legislature to introduce a private member's bill, Bill 95, the Zebra Mussels Act. While the Standing Orders provided that the introduction of bills had to allow the member, the Speaker, and the Clerk to each read the title of the bill on to the record in both English and French, they included no restriction on how long the title might be. So it was that when Harris introduced Bill 95, its title included the name of every lake, river, and stream in the province, which he proceeded to read on to the record for the rest of the day (Harris 1991). Although the reading of the bill was then dispensed with, Harris had succeeded in making his point about the budget by stalling normal proceedings for the entire afternoon. Indeed, as shown in chapter ten, the Zebra Mussels Act would return to the legislature in 2018 as a tactic used by the opposition New Democrats to protest the actions of a Progressive Conservative government under the leadership of Doug Ford.

The Tories continued to delay the proceedings of the House in the days to follow. Beginning on 7 May, they sought to exploit another loophole in the Standing Orders by bringing forward repetitive motions to adjourn debate and adjourn the House without first giving notice to the government. Since there was no provision in the Standing Orders for how many motions to adjourn members could bring forward in a given sessional day, Conservative members continued to rise to move adjournment, requiring time-consuming votes on division. Although the NDP was able to use its majority to defeat each motion, the Tories succeeded in absorbing a considerable amount of the time scheduled for the budget debate. In the first two weeks of May, the opposition introduced eight routine motions to adjourn debate and eight motions to adjourn House business. Additionally, it introduced twenty-one private members' public bills, many of which dealt with the same issues, and rose on nineteen mostly superfluous points of order on matters related to the failure of the government to respond to written questions in a timely fashion under Standing Order 95(d) (Warner 1991).

On 13 May, Government House Leader Shelly Martel argued on a point of order that the opposition tactics constituted "an abuse of process and of democracy" because Mike Harris had already made it clear that he would not support the budget under any circumstances. She claimed that while the government had attempted to extend an olive branch by offering an extension of debate in committee, Harris had called the premier a "dictator" and argued that, given the NDP's majority, such a debate would be superfluous. Martel implored the Speaker to use his "inherent authority to prevent such abuses of process from bringing the work of the House to a standstill" since the interruption of proceedings had "nothing to do with bringing out alternative points of view on the budget" (S. Martel 1991b). Tory MPP Donald Cousens argued that the government was attempting to "bring its power into focus, using the Chair against the opposition to achieve the government's ends." He also pointed to the deep irony of the government's position, given that it had been the initiator of the majority of the delay tactics in the legislature's recent history. He quipped,

> It would be absolutely hilarious if it were not necessarily so sad, the fact that the government, when it was in opposition, used every device and technique possible

> to try to draw attention to the issues and in so doing was able to articulate a concern that otherwise it felt could not be expressed. (Cousens 1991)

After hearing submissions from the government and opposition, Speaker Dave Warner ruled that Martel's request that he intervene to resolve the impasse was "incompatible with not only the nature of the office of the Speaker but also the idea of parliamentary democracy." In short, he ruled that so long as there remained an opportunity for the House Leaders to negotiate a settlement, this route should be explored rather than asking him to exercise his rarely used discretionary authority to put a stop to the opposition's delay tactics (Warner 1991).

While the parties were ultimately able to come to an arrangement that saw the budget pass within the government's time constraints, Warner's ruling marked a watershed moment in the history of legislative procedure at Queen's Park. The New Democrats, having lost on this point of order, prepared to bring forward amendments to the Standing Orders to ensure that future attempts to obstruct their agenda could not occur without contravening the rules of the House. The resulting reforms to the Standing Orders would permanently reshape procedure at the Ontario Legislature.

Civility returned to the legislature for the balance of the year, but in the spring of 1992, the Progressive Conservatives once again refused to cooperate with several of the NDP's signature pieces of legislation. The Tories were unwilling to negotiate time limitations for debate on the Credit Unions and Caisses Populaires Act (Bill 143, 1994), which would implement a Waste Management Authority to seek out locations for new landfill sites in the Greater Toronto Area. In response, the NDP proceeded with the second time allocation motion of their mandate on 16 April 1992 (S. Martel 1992).

Less than three weeks later, the government attempted to invoke closure without notice during third reading of Bill 86, the Gasoline Tax Amendment Act, after being frustrated in its deliberations with the opposition. NDP member Ed Phillip (1992) rose in the House to move that "the question now be put" on third reading of the bill, given the "very urgent business this House has to deal with on a number of matters." Deputy Speaker Gilles Morin, who served as a member of the Liberal Party, was in the Speaker's chair at the time of Phillip's request for closure and elected to use his discretionary authority to disallow the request. Morin told the House, "I feel there hasn't been sufficient debate on this third reading; therefore, the debate will continue" (Morin 1992).

Although the NDP could not challenge the Speaker's ruling, some members used their time during third reading to express their discontent. For instance, Gilles Bisson, New Democrat MPP for Cochrane North, argued that the urgency of the economic crisis required that the business of the House move forward:

> We're in the middle of the worst recession since the 1930s. To have the opposition stall, deter and try to slow down every piece of legislation that we're putting through for their own political means is not appreciated on the part of the people of this province … We have the right and we have the responsibility to govern this province over the next four years. The quicker the opposition can realize that, the quicker we can get to the business of this House and deal with the issues that affect the people of this province, day by day. (Bisson 1992)

After the Speaker rendered his decision, the NDP had little choice but to continue to debate the bill for the balance of the evening, as the House schedule directed. While it was able to work out an arrangement with the opposition to end debate on Bill 86, the arbitrariness of Morin's decision did not sit well with the government. It seemed to have become obvious that change was necessary to blunt opposition efforts to stall its agenda.

Formalizing Time Allocation: The 1992 Standing Orders Reforms

What followed from the tumultuous first twenty months of the Rae government was the implementation of the most restrictive amendments to the Standing Orders in the legislature's 125-year history. There can be little question that the amendments announced on 25 June 1992 were a seminal moment for procedure at the legislature. While the reforms under the Peterson government had restricted the time allocated in the House for petitions and ringing the division bells, they had largely kept with the convention that important decisions regarding the legislative schedule were left to deliberation among the House Leaders. The changes implemented by the NDP, however, went far beyond this convention, taking power away from the House Leaders by establishing formal time limits on all aspects of routine proceedings in the legislature.

The amendments set definite time limits of thirty minutes on all speeches in the House, unless otherwise agreed to by the Assembly, with the exception that, during debate on second or third reading of a bill, a debate on the Speech from the Throne, or a budget, interim supply, or any other substantive government motion, the first member for each party was permitted to speak for up to ninety minutes. In light of Mike Harris's attempts to exploit this loophole in the Standing Orders to delay proceedings in May 1991, the reforms also established a time limit of thirty minutes for the Introduction of Bills (Manikel 1992).

Additionally, the Standing Orders made, for the first time, specific provisions for time allocation. Whereas one of the central criticisms of the first time allocations moved during the 1980s was that such motions were not formally provided for in the Standing Orders, the NDP resolved this problem once and for all by entrenching them as a part of House procedure and establishing rules for their use. The new Standing Orders allowed a Minister of the Crown or the Government House Leader to move time allocation on any government bill or substantive government motion so long as notice had been filed with the Clerk before 5:30 p.m. the previous evening. When any time allocation motion was the first order of the day, it was incumbent upon the Speaker to put the question before the House, without further debate, at the end of that sessional day (Manikel 1992). This particular provision had its roots in Peter Kormos's infamous filibuster on the Peterson government's auto insurance reforms. As a concession to the opposition, the government allowed that three full days of debate must be held on a motion for time allocation on second reading of a bill or any substantive government motion. Perhaps most importantly, the government included a provision that prohibited the Speaker from overruling any time allocation motion as being out of order (ibid.).

In short, the changes to the Standing Orders granted the government full control over the proceedings of the House by ensuring that each bill would pass within the new time limitations. While the House Leaders would continue to negotiate the time set out for debates, they would now be required to do so within the framework of those limitations. The tradition since 1975 at Queen's Park that House business should be set through negotiation among the House Leaders, on the principle that all parties should have input into the process, was now relegated to the history books. From this moment forward, the government of the day had the right to pass any piece of legislation without having to placate the opposition at any stage of the process. In the event that the opposition attempted to stall the passage of a bill, the government now held the formal right to bring forward a motion of time allocation, which the Speaker was powerless to object to.

Government House Leader Dave Cooke (1992) argued that the new Standing Orders were necessary to "modernize the rules in the legislature." In light of the increased use of obstructionist tactics by the opposition, the reforms were needed to "bring in some changes to the rules that will allow the government of the day to get its legislative agenda through the House." In his speech on the changes, Liberal House Leader Steve Mahoney made his position clear: his party had not consented to the amendments, as the New Democrats had claimed in their initial attempt to provide the illusion of all-party agreement.

> I want to set the record straight and tell you there was no deal on the part of the official opposition, the Liberal Party. What there was in essence was capitulation, facing the reality that the government, with its large majority, really had us in a position where we were backed up against the wall, backed into a corner, no tomorrow, all those clichés that forced us to say, "Well, I guess you're going to shove this down our throat and I guess we're just going to have to live it."

> The reason there was no deal or no agreement, even through all the negotiations the government House leader referred to with regard to the opposition House leader and the House leader for the third party, is that the word "draconian" would not do justice to some of the amendments. (Mahoney 1992)

Mahoney argued that while his party disputed the time limits placed on speeches, it was particularly concerned about the decision to formalize time allocations and eliminate the Speaker's prerogative to disallow them. In a moment of prescience, given what was to come only three years later, after Mike Harris had been elected as premier, Mahoney warned the legislature of the implications of the new time allocation rules:

> If a government does not abuse it, the implication may not be that great. But what about a government that does abuse it? This government may say, "Well, gee, we wouldn't do that." What if – and I would ask members in the opposition to think about this – we wound up with some very radical right-wing government, maybe 20 years from now, that might decide it's going to ram through its legislation and its agenda and to heck with the members of the opposition? This will give them the power to do it. (Mahoney 1992)

For Mahoney, the changes were a far too drastic step. He argued that the time limits placed on speeches functioned as a form of time allocation and that new rules surrounding the establishment of both mechanisms were merely superfluous. The two reforms, he said, acted as a "double hammer" that was "totally unnecessary and simply shows that this government is afraid to debate the issues that are of such significance at any length beyond the controls it's putting in place" (Mahoney 1992). Liberal MPP Greg Sorbara concurred with Mahoney's sentiments:

> What's happened here is that the government, the state, the executive, the cabinet, the power of the state has been increased and the power of the opposition, the power of the minority, has been reduced. I want to just tell you, I think the last thing we need in this great province is a further augmentation and a further centralization of the power of the state. (Sorbara 1992a)

Perhaps most tellingly, New Democrat Peter Kormos spoke out against his own government's reforms. In a speech to the House, he declared that he could not in good conscience support the new Standing Orders, calling them a "dangerous assault on what this institution should be." He warned that while the opposition's obstructionist tactics might make such reforms provocative, government backbenchers should beware of making hasty decisions. "I'm incredibly concerned," he said, "that what we're seeing here is a silencing of backbenchers, a silencing of opposition members, and I'm confident that democracy will not necessarily be well served" (Kormos 1992).

The government put the new Standing Orders into effect just two weeks after the reforms had been passed by the House, when it brought forward a time allocation motion on Bill 40, the Labour Relations Amendment Act (Bill 40, 1992). Under the motion, the bill would receive five weeks of public consultations during the summer and two days for both the Committee of the Whole and third reading after the House had been recalled in the fall (Cooke 1992). The opposition decried the use of time allocation on a highly contentious piece of legislation. Long-time MPP Sean Conway argued:

> It is absolutely unprecedented that this or any government in this jurisdiction would introduce a bill of this kind on the 4th of June 1992 and expect to have that bill given Royal Assent on or about Thanksgiving of the same year. That is mind-boggling. My friends, particularly the Treasurer, know that. (Conway 1992)

Tory House Leader Ernie Eves, however, had resigned himself to the reality that executive dominance had become the model in Ontario. He lamented,

> I don't believe in Tinkerbell ... I can remember Bill Davis's government ramming through legislation without amendment, I can remember David Peterson's government ramming through legislation without amendment and now I have lived through Bob Rae's government ramming through legislation without amendment. That is the way the place operates. (Eves 1992)

The new Standing Orders also received the first test of their legitimacy when, on 17 July, the government introduced a motion for time allocation on third reading of Bill 150, which had begun the previous day. The NDP employed a new provision in the Standing Orders that allowed it to bring forward a bill to vote on third reading after only two days of debate. The difficulty, however, was that while the government had satisfied this condition, Progressive Conservative MPP Norm Sterling, whose speech had been cut short by the motion, had not yet completed the ninety minutes allotted to him in the Standing Orders. In this respect, the new provisions seemed to contradict one another. Liberal MPP Greg Sorbara argued, on a point of order, that the attempt by the government to bring about a vote without first allowing Sterling to complete his time constituted closure rather than a time allocation motion and should be ruled out of order. He argued that this tactic was "the most serious assault on our right to debate legislation ever presented in this House," and he pleaded with the Speaker to "reflect on this issue, to sleep on this issue, to read the precedents of the House" (Sorbara 1992b).

The following day, Speaker Warner (1992) ruled that the time allocation motion was in order since, under the new Standing Orders, the government's satisfaction of the provision requiring two days' debate was sufficient to call for a vote the following day. While the motion did indeed cut Sterling's speech short, the time limitations set out in the new rules were merely maximum thresholds; therefore, they did not preclude the government from truncating them through time allocation any more than if the parties were to come to a unanimous agreement to yield the balance of their time. Fundamentally, however, Warner's decision reaffirmed the extraordinary powers granted to the government by the Standing Orders reforms. The government now had full control over the legislative process, and by abolishing the prerogative of the Speaker to overrule motions of time allocation, it had eliminated any check on its power. If the first months of 1992 were any indication, the government had implemented the new rules not as a safeguard, but rather as a routine part of its strategy for House governance.

Time Allocation Trends at Queen's Park

The use of time allocation by the NDP may be crudely divided into two periods. The first, throughout 1991, saw the government use time allocation as a last resort to thwart efforts by an obstructionist opposition to stall its social democratic policy agenda. The second began in 1992 with the adoption of the new Standing Orders, after which the government began to use time allocation with an increased frequency. This trend was also consistent with the government's shift towards a politics of restraint, but with a central difference. While the government used time allocation during the first period reluctantly and to break parliamentary deadlock until the new Standing Orders had been passed, after that time it began to bring forward time allocation motions pre-emptively, and often without provocation, as a means of fast-tracking its restraint agenda through the legislature. The new Standing Orders, by formalizing the practice of time allocation, eliminating the right of the Speaker to overrule time allocation motions, and establishing limits on each aspect of the sessional day, created an environment in which the Rae government could be assured that it would be able to implement its deficit-reduction strategies without interference. Time allocation, then, looms as an indispensable part of the story of the government's implementation of fiscal discipline measures.

Although the government brought forward time allocation motions on three occasions in 1992, it was not until 1993, when it passed time allocation an unprecedented eight times, that the full impact of the new Standing Orders were felt. The most controversial bill subjected to time allocation that year was the Social Contract (Bill 48, 1993). The government's desire to fast-track Bill 48 led it to bring forward a time allocation motion, despite having never given the bill a chance to be reviewed in committee or to be discussed at public hearings, and with only one day at Committee of the Whole. Although the government had originally promised to use the new Standing Orders only when all other contingencies had been exhausted, it was now moving pre-emptively to stifle debate on a controversial and precedent-setting piece of legislation that would affect more than one million public-sector workers. It justified its decision to truncate debate on the premise that the Social Contract was emergency legislation, and it demanded immediate implementation to bring the province's budgetary crisis under control. The Chair of the Management Board of Cabinet, Brian Charlton, who introduced the motion, claimed that it was the government's responsibility

> to ensure that this legislation is amended and passed as quickly as possible to deal with so that those parties to this legislation, those that will be impacted by this legislation, whether the employers or employees, will fully understand the context in which either a negotiation and a settlement will be reached or an imposition will be imposed. (B. Charlton 1993)

MPP Dennis Drainville, a former New Democrat who had left the party to sit as an independent member because of the government's increasingly anti-democratic tendencies, said he felt betrayed by Rae's initial promise to the NDP caucus that time allocation motions under the new Standing Orders would be deployed only "carefully and judiciously." Instead, he argued, the government had made time allocation routine on every controversial bill before the House, often restricting debate on sensitive and contentious issues before reasonable debate could occur. With regards to the Social Contract, he argued,

> We would think that commensurate with the importance of this bill, we would have a government that would afford the legislature and the members of this legislature the amount of time that they need to go through this legislation and to talk about this legislation and put forward substantive amendments that would help to change this legislation and make it better.
>
> What in fact we see is that, as usual, the government is trying to destroy the democratic process. They are not indeed allowing adequate debate on Bill 48. They are not allowing for public hearings. They are in effect not even allowing the people of the province the opportunity to have this looked at through the eyes of the public …
>
> Indeed, what we see in this House continually is that the government is pushing through legislation which is going to have a very major effect on people,

> legislation that is going to affect what people make, what people's seniority is going to be like in the future, what kind of collective agreements they are part of. They are in fact taking away the very process of law that defends those people and gives them an opportunity of being protected in their jobs and in their earnings.
>
> What do we have then? We have a government that cannot be trusted, we have a government that cannot be believed in terms of the kinds of priorities it puts out there, but more than that, we have a government that has believed in a total lack of faith in the parliamentary system and how that system can work in this place between all the parties. (Drainville 1993)

In 1993, the government began to change its rhetoric surrounding the use of time allocation. While opposition interference with legislative initiatives remained its central justification, under the new Standing Orders it could no longer reasonably claim that impasse was its primary rationale. Now, the government's language emphasized the *urgency* of passing certain seminal bills as a means of carrying out its agenda and bringing the deficit under control. This shift in political discourse, however, was crucial because it indicated that time allocation was no longer a last-resort measure, but a means to an end. By 1993, time allocation had become part of the NDP strategy, guaranteeing that its agenda would be implemented within the aggressive time frame it had set out. From this point forward, time allocation would become a conventional part of business at Queen's Park, regardless of which party was in power.

As table 7.1 shows, the legislature saw an unprecedented increase in the use of time allocation. While it had been brought forward only a handful of times before, the Rae government began to make prodigious use of it, applying it to 21.6 per cent of the total government bills that received royal assent during its mandate.

In 1994, the government continued to use time allocation to pursue its restructuring agenda. It used it to ensure the passage of Bill 143, which

Table 7.1. Time allocation motions to government bills passed, 1981–1995

Parliament	Date	Number of government bills passed	Number of time allocation motions	Percentage of time allocation motions to government bills passed, %
32nd Parliament PC	1981–5	292	3	1.0
33rd Parliament LIB	1985–7	129	1	0.8
34th Parliament LIB	1987–90	183	3	1.7
35th Parliament NDP	**1990–5**	**97**	**21**	**21.6**

Note: The bolded row indicates the Rae government.

transferred several important powers to the Regional Municipality of Ottawa-Carleton as a means of maximizing government efficiency in the Ottawa area. The bill was rushed through the legislature, despite widespread public concern about the transfer of local democratic control in the suburban municipalities to a regional body with increased powers. The government also fast-tracked the Tobacco Control Act and the Labour Relations Act, using time allocation to ensure that the bills received royal assent before the House adjourned for the summer on 23 June 1994.

The legislature remained on summer recess until 31 October, a period of more than four months. When it resumed, the NDP invoked time allocation in an effort to pass the final major initiatives of its mandate before calling an election. As though to reaffirm the extent to which the use of the guillotine had become routine under the Rae government, the NDP moved time allocation three more times during the fall, despite the fact that the legislature sat for only twenty days. The opposition argued that if these bills were of such significance, the House ought to have sat for a sufficient period to debate them properly, rather than compressing them into a twenty-day time period and using time allocation to rush them into law. Jim Bradley proclaimed,

> Democracy is under siege in the Legislative Assembly of Ontario. After imposing draconian new rules that severely limit the ability of opposition members and government backbenchers to carry out their responsibilities by restricting the amount of time MPPs are permitted to speak, and giving ministers new powers to determine the length of debates, this government has now also restricted the parliamentary calendar and has reduced the number of days this House normally sits. (Bradley 1994b)

Perhaps appropriately, the final moments of the Rae government's mandate in the legislature was spent giving royal assent to Bills 163, 165, and 173, each of which the government used time allocation to pass. The legislature sat for the final time on 8 December, after which Rae advised the lieutenant-governor to prorogue the House. He waited until 28 April 1995 before calling an election for 8 June. In his government's final year in office, the legislature had sat for only twenty days, an unprecedented silencing of the democratic process at Queen's Park. Bob Runciman summarized the general sentiment towards the NDP's approach to House governance during that final year by observing that "it would appear they don't want to face the heat or the critical scrutiny that they'd be forced to face if the House is sitting. They have no real agenda" (Runciman 1994).

The government was by now trailing badly in the polls, and it appeared to have given up hope that its diminished prospects of remaining in office would be aided by facing the perpetual scrutiny of the opposition in the legislature.

It seemed to have simply elected to shut down the House in hopes that its fortunes might somehow be reversed if it could shield itself from criticism. Rather than engage in democratic debate on an election platform, the government returned to the House for just three weeks to tie up loose ends and time-allocate those bills that the opposition objected to so that House business would be finished by the first week of December. While time allocation was a convenient method for an unpopular government to avoid exposing itself to further criticism, its disregard for the parliamentary process set a precedent for future governments: they could use it as an escape hatch when the political scrutiny became too much to face.

Conclusion

There was rich symbolism in the fact that the legislature sat for only twenty total days during the Rae government's final year in office. This was a government that, by halfway through its mandate, had deviated from many of the most fundamental principles that had defined the NDP for decades. Not only had the party abandoned its Keynesian roots, but it had also taken the most aggressive steps towards neoliberalization in the history of the province. Furthermore, in its haste to implement the large-scale changes necessary to achieve its deficit-reduction goals, the government sought to make up for time lost during the first years of its mandate by forcing its neoliberal reforms through the legislature at a precipitous pace, undermining the principle of parliamentary debate to an unprecedented degree. The economic crisis facing the province became the catalyst that allowed the Rae government to justify all forms of parliamentary tactics to implement its agenda.

By the end of the government's mandate, time allocation had become a central part of regular proceedings in the legislature, having been enshrined in the Assembly's Standing Orders. Furthermore, although it had been used on only six occasions before the NDP's election in 1990, the New Democrats brought it forward on an unprecedented twenty-one occasions during its four and a half years in office. It is somewhat ironic that the party, which had, in opposition, fiercely spurned both the use of parliamentary tactics to expedite the passage of legislation and the adoption of neoliberal policies, left behind a legacy of having severely undermined the legislature's capacity to hold the executive to account in its pursuit of deficit reduction. The language of "crisis" used by the Rae government to justify its use of such tactics was similar to the discourse employed by the Davis government during the inflation-restraint crisis a decade earlier.

The same principles that Bob Rae had vehemently opposed as undemocratic when he was in opposition, he later defended as premier as being necessary to bring the province's deficit under control. Thus, when the Progressive

Conservatives came to power after the 1995 election, the path had already largely been cleared by the New Democrats. In pursuit of the rapid implementation of the CSR, the Harris government did not have to invent any new legislative precedents. The precedents of omnibus legislation and time allocation left behind by the Rae government enabled the Harris Tories to merely dig deeper into the ground that had already been prepared for them by the NDP.

8 Revolution at the Ontario Legislature: The Harris/Eves Era, 1995–2003

Introduction

At a crucial point in the 1995 general election, Progressive Conservative leader Mike Harris made a campaign stump speech, standing in front of a large sign that read, "Welfare, Ontario. Population: 1,000,000." With this enormous prop as his background for the assembled cameras to record, Harris admonished the Liberal and New Democratic governments for spending a decade overtaxing ordinary working people, while providing income for more than one million Ontarians to stay at home and receive social assistance. Although the math was dubious, the claim found a receptive audience in a deficit- and recession-weary province in search of a panacea (Ibbitson 1997).

Running on a platform they called the "Common Sense Revolution" (CSR), the Progressive Conservatives provided Ontarians with a convenient scapegoat for the cloud of economic malaise that hung over the province, and promised to restore economic competitiveness. It was on these grounds that the Harris government sought to legitimize its radical agenda. It was elected for, and would work for the benefit of, the taxpayers who had elected it to solve the crisis of overspending that, it claimed, had brought about the historically large deficits witnessed during the Rae era.

Actualizing a radical reform agenda would prove a difficult proposition, however. In practical terms, parliamentary procedures obstructed the government from doing what it considered to be its obligation – to fulfil its mandate by implementing the reforms set out in the CSR and to better serve the taxpayers and consumers of Ontario. While it is true that many of the tactics the Harris government used to insulate its agenda from public opposition had been previously tested by other governments, the scale, extent, and speed with which it used them were without precedent in the history of the Ontario Legislature. This is the period during which the central features of neoliberal parliamentarism in Ontario took form, as the Tories resorted to unprecedented norm-breaking to push legislation through the House, all the while establishing a new standard for what would constitute "normal" rules for governing the legislature.

In its effort to implement its restructuring initiatives, the government was confronted with two problems. First, it had to find a way to move its radical reforms through a hostile legislature. This would prove to be a significant challenge since the legislative process was designed to encourage slow and deliberate consideration of issues to counter precisely the kind of radicalism the Tories proposed. The government could anticipate that the opposition parties would use every means at their disposal to undermine its efforts. It could be certain that they would demand extensive public consultations, committee hearings, and time apportioned for debate in the legislature on the most controversial measures, all of which meant that each initiative could take months to pass. Second, even once it managed to move its agenda through the legislature, the government would still have to deal with a path-dependent public service and community efforts to undermine its plans at the implementation stage.

In response to these challenges, the Harris government developed a dual strategy. First, to pre-empt efforts by the opposition to block its agenda, it adopted an approach to Parliament that was "built for speed" (Loreto 1997, 101). It established its legislative agenda by following the example of the NDP, which had introduced the concept of packaging unrelated reform measures into large omnibus bills, which were subject only to the time restrictions of debate for a single bill. Using the omnibus bill format would allow the government to combine several of its restructuring initiatives into one bill, which, if time-allocated, could be rammed through the legislature and made law in a matter of weeks.

This process began in the fall of 1995 with the introduction of the Savings and Restructuring Act, which amended or eliminated dozens of unrelated bills and regulations under the umbrella of a single piece of legislation (Bill 26, 1996). The purpose of Bill 26 was to overwhelm the opponents of the government's reform agenda with so many changes at once that they had little chance to build public support against any one of them. The omnibus bill became a crucial political instrument in the Harris government's policy-implementation effort. In the first two years of its mandate, the government established new procedures for the use of omnibus acts and time allocation, and it rewrote the Standing Orders to severely restrict the time provided for the opposition to debate legislation.

The government's second problem was that, to ensure that its legislation would be passed by the legislature, it needed to streamline managerial control over the implementation and consolidation of its neoliberalization agenda. To do this, it made prodigious use of its regulatory powers to give itself the authority to supervise and direct the restructuring process without interference.

This included granting Cabinet the authority to manage many of the reforms through delegated legislation – in some cases, suspending the authority of democratically elected school board trustees and municipal councillors. By the end of its two mandates, the Progressive Conservatives had pushed the constitutional limits of nearly every possible procedural instrument and established a new culture at Queen's Park that had few precedents outside wartime in a Canadian Parliament.

It is probable that a neoliberalization process on the scale carried out by the Harris government in the first two years of its mandate could not have been achieved without reconstituting the traditional rules of Parliament. Omnibus legislation and time allocation were essential ingredients in the government's implementation plan because they allowed it to subvert traditional parliamentary processes. Having moved its reforms through the legislature, the government could then focus on the consolidation and administrative-implementation phase of its agenda.

Right-Wing Populism and the Common Sense Revolution

Daniele Albertazzi and Duncan McDonnell define *populism* as "an ideology which pits a virtuous and homogeneous people against a set of elites and dangerous 'others' who are together depicted as depriving (or attempting to deprive) the sovereign people of their rights, values, prosperity, identity and voice" (Albertazzi and McDonnell 2008, 3). The CSR was constructed on the ideological grounds that the undeserving poor were receiving more than their fair share under the rule of the Toronto cultural elites, who did not understand the *true* interests of the people. The Tories based their capacity to represent the interests of "the people" on the grounds that Mike Harris had spent the four years before the 1995 election touring the province, spending time in church basements and coffee shops, where he came to understand the public's desire to see the size of government and the tax burden reduced. The Tories used this imagery to validate Harris's divide-and-conquer approach by presenting the illusion that they were representing the will of the people, rather than an elite-driven process of fiscal austerity.

Gillian Hart (2013) has argued that populism is the politics that emerges from a population that has become increasingly vengeful. This was the approach the Progressive Conservatives used to justify further marginalizing the most disadvantaged members of society, whom they portrayed as a drain on the system and the cause of rising taxes and declining standards of living. Stefan Kipfer and Parastou Saberi argue that "populisms from above," like the CSR, "thrive on intensifying, instead of containing, political antagonism" (2014, 130). Changing attitudes towards politics and institutions were clearly articulated in the CSR campaign platform, which baldly stated that the party would seek to "reinvent" the way government functioned by making it "work for the people" since "the political system itself stands in the way of making many of the changes we need right now" (Pond 2005, 176). Politicians were framed as self-interested and corrupt, and the entire activity of politics was delegitimized as something counterproductive and antithetical to the interests of society.

Brought forward in 1996, the Fewer Politicians Act highlighted this anti-parliamentarism. The bill reduced the number of seats in the legislature from 130 to 103 for the next election, thereby aligning provincial electoral boundaries with their federal counterparts. The government made the case that the bill was being brought forward to reduce the number of politicians and the size of government. Although even optimistic government estimates expected total savings to amount to little more than $11 million, the bill's stated intent was "to achieve savings by reducing the number of Ontario's provincial electoral districts" (Bill 81, 1996). While introducing the bill in the legislature, House Leader David Johnson argued that it was a product of consultations that the party had held with the public, who told them that "government was too big, and government was too costly." Reducing the size of the legislature would make government "clearer, more effective, more efficient, more understandable and more workable." Bill 81 marked "another step to reducing the size and the cost of the government, to do better with less" (Johnson 1996).

The Harris government's approach to populism, then, demonstrated the influence of Hayekian thought on the right-wing characterization of parliamentary governance. It believed that "unrepresentative interest groups" wielded such influence over the policymaking process that they had "plunged parliamentary democracy in Canada into a legitimation crisis" (Pond 2005, 177). The action of political dialogue was reimagined as another systemic inefficiency to be streamlined and made to operate in a more rational manner, one that responded more directly to the demands of the marketplace.

This view was expressed by Progressive Conservative MPP Steve Gilchrist, who noted in debate on the bill that changes were made necessary by the misguided nature of the previous Rae government, whose "mismanagement and fiscal irresponsibility leave us no choice but to examine every possible avenue of new operational efficiencies and ways of making the taxpayers' dollars go farthest." Reducing the number of seats in the legislature responded to the concerns of voters, who demanded that the government "find ways to save on frivolous duplication, find ways to end the pyramid-building, find ways to end the justification of all the empires that have been built up in the civil service, arm's-length agencies and the like" (Gilchrist 1996). The "political dimension" of legislative governance needed to be undermined to increase efficiency and to avoid what Milton and Rose Friedman called a "vast bureaucracy" that was "largely devoted to shuffling papers rather than to serving people" (Friedman and Friedman 1980, 107).

Another bill demonstrated a similar intolerance for alternative approaches to policy, seeking once again to permanently insulate reforms from the reach of an unrestrained legislature. In the spirit of Buchanan's neoliberal constitutionalism, the Balanced Budget and Taxpayer Protection Act required that provincial governments present a balanced budget for each fiscal year beginning in 2001–2; special exceptions were to be made only in the case of "extraordinary circumstances," such as war or a natural disaster. The bill also contained a "taxpayer protection" provision, which required that a public referendum be held before any future tax increases could be passed (Bill 99, 1998).

As David Pond recognized in his article on the legislative approaches used by the Harris government, under the Taxpayer Protection Act, "only the electorate, and not the legislature, could legitimize a government decision to raise taxes" (Pond 2005, 179). The bill's purpose was to remove control over the capacity to raise revenues through taxation from future governments that did not share the Progressive Conservatives' market-based understanding of the role of political institutions. The chief purpose of the bill was to appeal to the idea of direct democracy, while at the same time entrenching neoliberal principles in the law, making it politically difficult for any future government to repeal them. (These provisions were repealed by the Liberals in 2004, when the legislature passed the Fiscal Transparency and Accountability Act. However, so as not to stray too far from the ideas of fiscal prudence, the act allowed for "short-term" deficits so long as Cabinet designed a fiscal "recovery plan" for a balanced budget in the near future [ibid., 188].)

The Progressive Conservatives repackaged their "neoliberal hostility" to the public service as an anti-parliamentarism in which legitimate efforts to scrutinize the executive branch were increasingly framed as being contrary to the taxpayer interest (Pond 2005, 176). This form of populism necessarily rejects institutional accountability measures because they undermine the flexibility of the state to respond to the taxpayer interest and are beholden to special interests. This resulting vacuum is filled by a strong executive, which wields considerable control over the affairs of the legislative process.

The Role of Regulation in Neoliberal Restructuring

During any other period in Ontario's history, undertaking any *one* of the major reforms planned by the CSR would have absorbed much of the government's political capital. The Premier's Office was aware that the radical reforms the Tory government planned would necessitate an entirely different strategy if it were to retain the political capital to carry them out. Staffers spent the summer months of 1995 devising a policy-implementation scheme that would minimize the damage that the inevitable conflicts with labour and other activist organizations would do to the government's popularity. The government decided to bring forward its major reforms in the first two years of its mandate, presenting controversial policy to the public in large bundles that made it difficult for public and political opposition to coalesce around a single issue before another significant reform was brought forward (Ibbitson 1997). It would then use whatever means were necessary to move its policies through the legislature at breakneck speed. This approach proved far more effective as a public relations strategy than the traditional method of releasing a constant, slow drip of controversial measures over a lengthier period.

The government's first, most aggressive attempt to restructure the province's finances was Bill 26, the Savings and Restructuring Act, a massive omnibus bill that was without precedent in terms of either the size or the scope of the reforms being undertaken. Its stated purpose was to "achieve fiscal savings and promote economic prosperity through public-sector restructuring, streamlining and efficiency and to implement other aspects of the government's economic agenda" (Bill 26, 1996). Foreshadowing a strategy that would become a hallmark of the Harris Conservatives, the bill granted the Executive Council sweeping powers to fundamentally reshape the structure of government by Order in Council. But its most significant power granted the minister of health the authority to amalgamate or close any hospital, and to terminate any service in the province, without having to consult either the legislature or the public. This included the power to "refuse applications for appointment and reappointment to the medical staff, revoke existing appointments and cancel or substantially alter the privileges of any physician on the medical staff" (ibid.).

Bill 26 also permitted the minister to "reduce, suspend, withhold or terminate funding to a hospital if the minister considers it in the public interest to do so." Where hospitals were unable to balance their budgets, or exhibited what, in the minister's opinion, constituted financial "mismanagement," he or she was empowered to appoint a hospital supervisor with "the exclusive right to exercise all the powers of the board and, where the hospital is owned or operated by a corporation, of the corporation, its officers and the members of the corporation." This considerable power, to appoint a financial czar with absolute power to undertake the financial restructuring of public institutions, was a trend that the government would return to numerous times over the next several years.

The Savings and Restructuring Act also contained provisions to grant considerable powers to the minister of municipal affairs and housing to undertake the process of "disentanglement" between the province and its municipalities. The bill authorized the minister to take disciplinary measures against any local government that did not comply with the government's demand for deficit reduction by exercising its authority to arbitrarily withhold municipal grants. Through this process, the province could achieve two goals. The first was to grant the minister the power to restructure local governance structures to ensure that they were able to accommodate the considerable number of hard services that it intended to download to the municipal tax base. The second was to give the minister the ability to attach conditions to grants and to exact discipline where the government deemed it necessary. This had the effect of forcing municipalities to make cuts to the hard services the government would thrust upon them because they would need to maintain a balanced budget. In this way, the government hoped to trim billions from the provincial deficit. Bill 26 granted czar-like powers to Cabinet, which could demand conformity with the government's fiscal targets; this was a crucial, strategic arrow in the government's quiver, one it would return to on several occasions in the years to come.

The Harris government's restructuring plan, while couched in the language of increased local control, was fundamentally about centralizing power as a means of controlling costs. Downloading services accomplished two important goals in this respect. First, writing provisions into legislation allowed the government to influence key elements of the disentanglement process through regulation, thereby exerting control over providing these services by disciplining any local governments that did not comply with their mandate. Although municipalities would be responsible for dispensing these services and would have the capacity to make some administrative decisions, Queen's Park retained control over the financial framework. The cuts to many of these core services were to be made by the municipalities themselves under the supervision of the province, giving the Harris government the added benefit of being insulated from the political consequences of these decisions.

Second, downloading core services allowed the province to upload education, giving it more control over the highly decentralized public school system, which had previously been the domain of dozens of different, often ungovernable boards. Centralizing control allowed the province to control costs by negotiating with teachers directly, setting policies, and changing curriculum – all the while reducing the role of democratically elected school boards to that of provincial technocrats with little agenda-setting power.

Centralizing Education

The government fulfilled its commitment to seize control of education from the school boards through the Fewer School Boards Act. Bill 104 (1997) ushered in dramatic changes to the province's education system, largely through a heavy-handed concentration of power in the executive branch. In total, the government reduced the number of school boards across the province from 164 to 72 and the number of trustees from more than 1,900 to nearly 700 (Snobelen 1997). The bill also reduced the composition of all boards in Ontario to between five and twelve trustees and up to a maximum of twenty-two for the Metropolitan Toronto School Board, which had responsibility for more than three hundred thousand students (ibid.; MacLellan 2009). Minister of Education John Snobelen argued that the bill was necessary to "streamline the way education in Ontario is financed and governed" because school boards had "demonstrated little control over their spending habits" (Snobelen 1997).

The Fewer School Boards Act granted Cabinet increased power to use Orders in Council to reconfigure school boards by regulating their composition, decision-making processes, election guidelines, and geographical boundaries. The bill authorized the minister of education to unilaterally change school board boundaries by regulation as a method of reducing the total number of boards and trustees in the province. It also established an Education Improvement Commission, which, like the Hospital Restructuring Committee established by the Savings and Restructuring Act, was authorized to supervise the transition to the new system of education governance in the province. Like that commission, its counterpart was accountable only to Cabinet and was required to follow any directions issued by the minister. Its responsibilities ranged from reviewing budgets and ensuring compliance with ministry mandates to requiring the production of documents and information for audits or disciplinary measures dispensed to non-compliant local governments.

Most striking of all, the Fewer School Boards Act contained two extraordinary provisions that were without precedent in Ontario's modern history. The first held that no court was permitted to review or question the directives of the commission. Theoretically, this meant that the commission would have free rein to violate any law, or the rights of individuals, without repercussion through the justice system. Recognizing that this clause was certainly unconstitutional, the government eventually amended the legislation to remove it. Second, the bill contained a provision, often referred to as a "Henry VIII clause," after the sixteenth-century king's effort to grant himself the authority to govern by proclamation. Section 349(2) stipulated that "in the event of a conflict between a regulation made under this part and a provision of this act or of any other act or regulation, the regulation made under this part prevails." This extraordinary power would ensure that the government could make any unforeseen adjustments to its transition plan by regulation, even if doing so was in violation of regulations passed under the authority of other statutes.

Although the government eventually repealed this provision, it did so only after an alliance of teachers' unions took action against the bill. In his decision, Justice Campbell ruled that it was premature to render a decision on the use of such powers unless or until the government made an attempt to use them. While there was precedent for the use of such provisions being upheld by the Supreme Court, that had been under emergency circumstances, during the First World War. At that time, the federal House of Commons had passed the War Measures Act, which included such a clause so that the government could react quickly in the event of changing circumstances in association with the war effort.

In his ruling, Justice Campbell condemned the government for resorting to the use of such extreme measures.

> It is one thing to confer this extraordinary power if it is actually needed for some urgent and immediate action to protect an explicitly identified public interest. It is quite another thing to hand it out with the daily rations of government power, unlimited as to any explicit legal purpose for which it may be exercised. (*Ontario Public School Boards' Association v. Ontario [Attorney General]* 1997)

Campbell maintained that the use of this power was "constitutionally suspect" in peacetime circumstances

> because it confers upon the government the unprotected authority to pull itself up by its own legal bootstraps and override arbitrarily, with no further advice from the Legislative Assembly, and no right to be heard by those who may be adversely affected by the change, the very legislative instrument from which the government derives its original authority. (*Ontario Public School Boards' Association v. Ontario [Attorney General]* 1997)

Despite this setback, the Harris government had demonstrated that it would use all means at its disposal to give itself the sweeping powers necessary to undertake a swift and comprehensive restructuring program. Furthermore, it had shown its contempt for democratic institutions, which it viewed primarily as impediments to implementing its agenda to serve the taxpayers' interests.

The second major initiative in the Harris government's education reform platform was the Education Quality Improvement Act, a massive omnibus bill that both centralized control over education policy in Cabinet and gave the Executive Council the power to unilaterally cut education expenses by more than $1 billion (Bill 160, 1997). The legislation also included a provision to remove the rights of teachers to negotiate the terms of their working conditions, such as preparation time, class sizes, and total hours spent in the classroom.

Instead, the power to make determinations regarding these aspects of teachers' working conditions was removed from the public realm entirely and placed at the discretion of the minister of education. Under section 11(7) of the bill, the minister could make regulations regarding the length of the school year, instructional time within the year, the number of days allocated for exams, and the number of vacation days that would be permitted. Furthermore, section 127.1 removed principals and vice-principals entirely from the realm of collective bargaining. The power to designate the terms and conditions of their work would instead be transferred to Cabinet and set out through regulation.

As a means of enforcing the essential features of its education restructuring program, in its second mandate the government introduced Bill 74, the Education Accountability Act (Bill 74, 2000). The bill permitted the minister of education to discard the terms of existing collective agreements with teachers to enforce new provisions for instructional time. High school teachers were required to teach seven rather than eight classes during the school year in addition to assuming increased responsibilities for extracurricular, counselling, and administrative duties, which had previously been exercised by staff members specifically designated to these tasks. The government's intention was to cut expenses by forcing existing staff to give up preparation and administrative time, thereby reducing the number of paid administrative and teaching positions.

Bill 74 imposed the threat of sanction upon any school board that did not follow the regulations of the minister of education. Section 230 empowered the minister to direct an investigation of boards when he or she had "concerns relating to the boards' compliance with certain legal requirements" set out by the ministry. In the event that the investigator's report disclosed evidence of non-compliance, Bill 74 granted the minister the authority to direct the boards to address the non-compliance immediately. Should a board continue to fail in its compliance with these terms, the minister was empowered to take full control over it.

The government followed through on its threats to take over three school boards in 2002, when boards in Toronto, Ottawa, and Hamilton were unable to balance their budgets. In each instance, the government appointed an emergency economic supervisor to oversee a restructuring process to return the board to a fiscal surplus. This process involved the complete suspension of the democratically elected school board's power throughout the supervisor's mandate. In all three cases, the supervisors initiated cost reductions through a mix of austerity measures, ranging from teacher layoffs to school closures.

Municipal Restructuring

As part of its reconfiguration of municipal government, the Harris government announced in December 1996 that it planned to force the amalgamation of the boroughs of Metropolitan Toronto with the introduction of Bill 103, the City of Toronto Act (Bill 103, 1997). The bill dissolved the cities of Toronto, York, East York, North York, Etobicoke, and Scarborough to create a newly amalgamated City of Toronto. The new city would be divided into forty-four wards, with a city council consisting of one member from each ward. Arguably the most remarkable section of the bill was a clause that transferred political power, from its introduction in the legislature until the new city came into existence on 1 January 1998, to a Cabinet-appointed board of trustees, which was empowered to oversee the financial affairs of each of the affected municipalities. Bill 103 granted this board the power to direct, supervise, and, where necessary, overrule all decisions of the old city councils. The board would additionally have the authority to make appointments to boards and commissions, hire and fire city employees, direct the privatization or reorganization of municipal services, and impose deadlines for compliance with its directives.

In forcing this amalgamation, the province took the extraordinary step of dissolving the existing municipal councils comprising the province's largest city and replacing them with an interim financial authority, accountable to Cabinet, that would oversee the restructuring process. The commission was granted full supervisory power over financial transactions to ensure that, in the words of Minister of Housing and Municipal Affairs Al Leach, "municipal expenditures and municipal assets, assets that belong to the people, are safeguarded during this time of change." Leach issued an ominous warning to those communities that might disregard the orders made by the transition committee:

> We've also heard some politicians say that the advice of the board of trustees does not have to be recognized and that they have no legal right to do their job until the legislation is passed. That's technically correct. However, as the trustees' right to examine municipal decisions will be retroactive to the day this legislation was introduced, it is in everyone's interests to cooperate with them. (Leach 1997a)

Liberal MPP Mike Colle called the appointment of the transitional supervisory body "unprecedented" and a contravention of the basic principles of democracy:

> Here's a duly elected local government, supported by grass-roots organizations and neighbourhoods, essentially dictated to by an imposed trusteeship that under law has no jurisdiction, but this minister somehow tried to intimate that these people had power when the bill hadn't even gone to second reading. (Colle 1997a)

Despite ample polling data revealing widespread discontent with the restructuring plan, the government intended to usher the bill through the legislature with little public consultation. Critics charged that the decision to amalgamate Toronto would erode the local responsiveness that could be provided only by councillors serving smaller, more geographically specific locations. To tear these municipalities apart would be to silence many whose voices would be lost in the expansive new "megacity." The government, however, rationalized its decision to amalgamate Toronto as an enhancement of democracy.

Al Leach argued that the new arrangement would bring greater accountability:

> Today, with so much duplication and overlap, taxpayers have no idea who is accountable for what in their neighbourhood. Under the provisions of the new City of Toronto Act, people will have a very clear idea of who is responsible and who is accountable. This act is not just about efficiency and cost saving. It's also about making government truly representative, truly accountable and truly responsible to the people who elect it, and that's what democracy really means. (Leach 1997a)

The following day, he continued his speech, adding that amalgamation would decrease the government's size:

> It will reduce the number of politicians from 106 to 45, and services will be delivered at a price that we can afford. A unified Toronto will have a better chance of bringing investment into the GTA and it will give us greater clout in the international arena. (Leach 1997b)

At issue here was that the Progressive Conservatives and their critics held fundamentally different views of what constituted good government. From the government's viewpoint, good government was defined by an ideal of effective fiscal management and responsiveness to taxpayers. The new Toronto was to be "more streamlined, more accountable and more efficient" and, therefore, more deeply obligated to serve the taxpayers' interest than a more decentralized structure (Leach 1997b). From the opposite perspective, the role of government was to improve the well-being of the community, which locally elected councillors were more readily able to do than those belonging to a large, metropolitan city council.

To take but one example, the minister of housing and municipal affairs used the power provided to him in the bill to override a decision by the East York City Council, which had voted to explore the idea of gifting certain buildings in the community to non-profit housing agencies in anticipation that they would be privatized by the transitional committee. In the legislature, Al Leach raised this as an example of why the government needed a transitional team with such extensive power:

> If there was ever a doubt about whether that power was necessary, it disappeared on December 16. That's the day when East York council voted to explore options for giving away public property to a non-profit foundation, giving away buildings built and paid for by the taxpayers of East York. Having a board of trustees that can watch over issues like that is definitely in the public interest. (Leach 1997a)

For the Progressive Conservatives, accountability meant preserving taxpayers' money, even when that included governing by fiat to overrule the authority of a democratically elected council.

The megacity issue also laid bare a further contradiction at the heart of the government's view of Parliament. When the government was approached by the soon-to-be-amalgamated municipalities about holding a plebiscite to determine the issue, it rejected the idea outright. While Al Leach admitted that "referendums have their place," he argued that "in some cases there are more effective ways to gain public input. With respect to one Toronto, we believe the best way is through the legislative process and committee hearings" (Leach 1997a). He made these claims even though the government had already tried to fast-track Bill 103 through the legislature with minimal public consultations, only to be restrained by opposition resistance.

A plebiscite was indeed held, and when the results were tallied in early 1997, they revealed that roughly 76 per cent of Metro residents opposed amalgamation (Wildman 1997c). Despite the overwhelming victory for the No forces, the Conservative government ignored the results and charged ahead with its plans, ultimately time-allocating the bill to secure its passage by the end of April 1997. It was clear that, despite the government's rhetoric, its primary concern was with restructuring at the expense of public consultation and openness.

Shortly after winning its second mandate, the Harris government set out to restructure four other metropolitan areas using the same justification as for the City of Toronto Act. Before doing so, however, it tasked four Cabinet-appointed special advisers to review each municipality for possible amalgamation. Unsurprisingly, the advisers' findings provided local variations on the same theme: each metropolitan area should be restructured to reduce overlap and operating costs through a process of local amalgamation, which would streamline and simplify the delivery of services. The advisers' findings were enshrined in Bill 25, the Fewer Municipal Politicians Act, introduced in December 1999, which empowered the province to dissolve certain municipalities in the Ottawa-Carleton, Haldimand-Norfolk, Hamilton, and Sudbury areas by amalgamating them into larger metropolitan areas (Bill 25, 2000). The number of municipalities in those four areas was reduced from thirty-five to five, while the number of total politicians was cut from 254 down to 64 (Clement 1999).

The Fewer Municipal Politicians Act enacted many of the essential features of the City of Toronto Act, including the imposition of a transitional supervisory committee, which was granted full and immediate power to carry out financial transactions. As was the case in Toronto, existing municipal councils were stripped of their authority to make financial transactions without the committee's approval. Again, the transitional committee was empowered to make regulations pertaining to all activities of the councils and to set the budgets for each of the new municipalities for two entire fiscal cycles. In case this was not sufficient for the province to imprint its mandate on the newly created cities, Bill 25 also permitted the minister to change existing by-laws by regulation alone, granting it extraordinary authority to override the decisions of democratically elected councils, both past and present.

Perhaps most significantly, the Harris government once again included a Henry VIII clause in a bill. Section 37(2) provided that "in the event of a conflict between a regulation made under this act and a provision of this act or of another act or a regulation made under another act, the regulation made under this act prevails" (Bill 25, 2000). Liberal MPP Jim Bradley (1999) called the clause "repulsive" and "draconian to the greatest extent." In the end, the government decided to repeal the provision, a move that NDP MPP David Christopherson summarized this way:

> A clause like this surely would have been challenged constitutionally. I can't imagine a Supreme Court of Canada saying that this is acceptable. Obviously, the word got to this government. They had to pull this back or they'd have a major tiger by the tail. (Christopherson 2000)

Dubbed the "omnibus sledgehammer bill" by Liberal MPP Lyn McLeod, the Fewer Municipal Politicians Act was also significant omnibus legislation because it amended several bills in the process of creating the new municipalities (McLeod 1999). The opposition argued that the government ought to split the bill into four separate pieces of legislation to ensure that each would receive proper time for debate and could be dealt with according to its locally specific characteristics. The government, however, claimed that there was no need for separate bills since the special advisers had conducted public consultations and had taken local variables into consideration in their reports.

The government expressed a desire to have Bill 25, which it introduced on 6 December, passed before the House recessed for Christmas, without committee hearings or further consultation. It ultimately resorted to time allocation to ensure that the bill passed third reading on 20 December, only two weeks after it had been introduced. NDP MPP David Christopherson encapsulated the opposition's response to the government's actions:

> Let me also say to the minister that his comments – this whole business of accountability, and he's going to improve democracy – are so galling, absolutely galling in the face of a mammoth bill like this that in every likelihood is going to be rammed through this House in a matter of a few days: 167 pages affecting hundreds of thousands of people, and not one minute of committee hearings – never mind public hearings – to do the work that we do at committee, which is to go through these bills and make sure they're as good as they can be and to try

> to avoid major mistakes ... Don't talk to us about accountability. You're the ones who don't understand democracy. (Christopherson 1999)

In early 2000, the government brought forward Bill 62, the Direct Democracy through Municipal Referendums Act, which provided the new municipalities with a framework for holding referendums. Minister of Municipal Affairs and Housing Tony Clement maintained that the bill reaffirmed his party's longstanding commitment to openness and accountability. He reminded Ontarians that "the current premier of the province of Ontario, Mike Harris, has been advocating the greater use of direct democracy quite consistently since at least 1990" (Clement 2000). However, while Bill 62 provided the means for local governments to hold referendums affecting by-laws, zoning regulations, and other responsibilities that fell within the municipal sphere, it did not give them the ability to overturn the provincially mandated amalgamation schemes. The government claimed to support a spirit of openness and accountability, but only to matters related to technocratic governance. Where the amalgamations were concerned, it ignored plebiscite results, which overwhelmingly rejected the mergers, as it charged ahead with its plan.

The Omnibus Bill

Although the use of regulation was critical to the implementation of the Harris government's radical agenda, it is arguably the case that omnibus bills were the most important instrument in its legislative toolkit. From the beginning of its mandate, the government began using omnibus legislation to make numerous sweeping changes to provincial law. On 29 November 1995, little more than two months after its Speech from the Throne, it introduced the Savings and Restructuring Act, one of the most controversial pieces of legislation ever brought forward in the Ontario Legislature. The bill made twenty-six amendments to forty-four statutes and included seventeen separate schedules, most of which had no meaningful relationship to each other. Among other things, the "bully bill," as it was colloquially known, granted the government significant powers to impose and eliminate certain taxes, direct the closure of hospitals by regulation, amalgamate municipalities, and impose mandatory arbitration on public-sector employees (Bill 26, 1996).

Bill 26 was unique not merely in terms of the sweeping nature of the reforms proposed by a single bill but also in the unprecedented procedural tactics used by the government to ensure its swift passage through the legislature. Despite introducing a bill with numerous highly contentious and intricate changes to provincial law, the government told the opposition House Leaders that it intended to have it passed before the House recessed for Christmas break and that it would use time allocation to ensure that this occurred. This meant that the several-hundred-page bill, which made reforms to dozens of pieces of legislation, would receive no time in committee and a bare minimum of debate in the legislature.

Additionally, the government made the decision to introduce the Savings and Restructuring Act, without notice, on the same day as its fall economic statement so that it would be overshadowed by the massive cuts announced by Finance Minister Ernie Eves (Ibbitson 1997). The two opposition leaders were in a lockup, discussing the economic statement, when the bill was introduced. Leader of Her Majesty's Official Opposition Lyn McLeod argued that this constituted a breach of her privilege as a member. In a speech to the House, she said,

> To think that a government could present a bill of this nature without notice, without any indication of what would be in this bill; to do it at a time when we were, under the government's orchestration, in a lockup, unable to even be aware it was being introduced and so raise our concerns on first reading as we are required according to our responsibilities to do; to think that they could do that; to think that they could then expect that this kind of bill would be – not debated, because we will not have an opportunity for debate, but passed without debate, without consultation, without due consideration, before Christmas, is truly a breach of the privileges of every member of this House … It is an abuse of power of a kind that we have never encountered in this province before. It is an abuse – and I ask you to rule on this – of the privileges of the members of this House, because if this government can behave in this way, it takes away from us our ability and our duty to debate the issues that are of public interest. (McLeod 1995)

Describing the size and the scope of the reforms proposed in the bill, longtime Liberal MPP Sean Conway argued, "Never in my time has there been a bill that is so unprecedented in what it proposes to do" (Conway 1995). For him, the bill constituted a breach of privilege because it attempted to circumvent the legislative process by rushing numerous highly consequential reforms through the House with a bare minimum of debate. Conway replied to rebuttals from the Progressive Conservative benches that the results of the 1995 election granted those members the right to implement their mandate. He argued that although the government had

> clearly won a right to change the course of Ontario's public policy, they have not won the right, no government ought to have the right, ever, to proceed with such unilateralism, with such callous regard to an appropriate time for legislative scrutiny and public interest. (Conway 1995)

He continued, asking the government a rhetorical question: "When does revolution become dictatorship? It becomes dictatorship when this House is presented with, and passes on the nod, Bill 26" (Conway 1995).

A further concern with Bill 26 was that it was contained many of the features of a budget bill, while masquerading as a routine piece of legislation, since it authorized the government to amalgamate municipalities, implement new fees and taxes, and establish the apparatus necessary for deep spending cuts without being subject to the necessary requirements of the budgetary process. The opposition argued that if the government were free to pass significant and varied spending reforms without being subject to the rigours of the budgetary implementation process, it would set a precedent that could allow future governments to exploit this loophole by passing supply bills without receiving the confidence of the House.

Despite appeals from the opposition, the Speaker ruled that while he was concerned with the intent of Bill 26, it did not constitute a breach of privilege. On the question of whether the government had breached the privilege of the leaders of the opposition parties by keeping them in a lockup while the bill was being introduced in the legislature, and by introducing it without notice, the Speaker determined that the members' rights had not been violated since

> members are not, nor should they be, forced to enter a lockup. It is not a question of privilege since I must assume that the members agreed to attend the lockup even though they were aware that it would cover at least a portion of the time that the House would be sitting. (McLean 1995a)

Speaker Al McLean determined that he could not rule the bill out of order despite its unprecedented omnibus provisions. He contended that there existed

> no rules or precedents in this House or in other jurisdictions that give me the authority to rule Bill 26 out of order or to divide it. I can find no major difference between Bill 26 and omnibus bills that have confronted previous Speakers of the House of Commons. (McLean 1995a)

Instead, he encouraged the government and opposition parties to work together to "find solutions to the problem of the omnibus nature of this bill" (McLean 1995a). The Progressive Conservatives, however, were not interested in negotiating solutions with the opposition. Instead, they charged forward and pursued all avenues to ensure the bill's passage before the House recessed for Christmas.

McLean's decision charted the course for the Tories to continue to fast-track their legislative initiatives by introducing massive omnibus bills. While Bill 26 remains arguably the most controversial omnibus bill in the province's history, the Tories introduced several other bills that rivalled it in both their size and their implications for the province. One such piece of legislation, Bill 47, dealt with measures contained in the 1996 budget, but included other elements that had nothing to do with announcements made during the finance minister's budget address. For example, the bill included amendments to the Family Benefits Act, which were not even mentioned in the budget. By including these changes in its budget-measures legislation, however, the government was able to limit exposure to any debate that could be devoted to its controversial cuts to family allowances.

Omnibus legislation also played a critical role in the government's red-tape-reduction strategy. Shortly after taking office, the Cabinet appointed a Red Tape Review Commission, comprised of eleven Tory MPPs, to review opportunities for reducing regulatory burdens in the private sector and finding efficiencies within government. The report, released in January 1997, made 132 recommendations, which included the following: establishing a framework to facilitate the elimination of unnecessary laws or regulations, eliminating costs in the delivery of government programs, harmonizing the inter-jurisdictional relationship between Queen's Park and its municipalities, removing duplication among various levels of government, extending the overtime hours that employees were able to work in any given week, and streamlining the process for approving that overtime (Ontario. Red Tape Review Commission 1997).

Rather than bringing forward dozens of bills to deal with the separate amendments that the government claimed were necessary to streamline the public sector and scale back regulation, it instead used the omnibus bill to push numerous significant reforms through the House at once. In 1997, it brought forward Bills 115, 116, 117, 118, 119, 120, 121, and 122, each of which contained dozens of amendments to adopt the recommendations of the Red Tape Review Commission's report. While the government made a concession to the opposition by dividing the massive omnibus reforms into eight separate bills designated by ministry, each bill made numerous, mostly disconnected changes to the law and were rushed through the House on a time allocation motion.

Even in its second term, when it had achieved much of the major restructuring that it had set out to accomplish, the government continued to use omnibus legislation as a means of both saving time on its institutional reform agenda and minimizing the political damage that any of its reforms might do to the party's brand. Examples include transferring health services to municipalities (Services Improvement Act), empowering the minister of health to continue to direct hospital closures (Ministry of Health and Long-Term Care Amendment Act), providing tax credits for private schools (Responsible Choices for Growth and Accountability Act), implementing restrictions on teachers' labour rights as well as reconfiguring their work time (Education Improvement Act), and amalgamating municipalities (Fewer Politicians Act).

After being sworn in as premier in the spring of 2002, Ernie Eves became particularly reliant upon omnibus legislation, using it early in his mandate to pass the Post-Secondary Act, which packaged six separate acts into a single bill, and the Electricity Pricing Conservation Supply Act, designed to offer a variety of tax credits to incentivize businesses to invest in Ontario's newly privatized energy industry. In 2002, the Eves government also introduced Bill 179, the Government Efficiency Act, the largest bill introduced in the legislature since the Savings and Restructuring Act in 1995 (Bill 179, 2002). It was a massive omnibus bill: it was 247 pages long and addressed more than four hundred items, ranging from domestic violence to international interests in aircraft equipment, and encompassed fifteen ministries, while repealing fifteen separate acts (Martin 2002). One of its most controversial elements was a clause that removed the appointment of members of the Ontario Securities Commission from the scrutiny of the Government Agencies Committee of the legislature.

The importance of the omnibus bill to the Progressive Conservative government's policy-implementation strategy cannot be overstated. As evidenced by its introduction of the Savings and Restructuring Act only weeks into its first Parliament, the government saw the omnibus bill as a critical part of its strategy to accelerate its restructuring initiatives through the legislative branch. Taking this approach allowed it to begin the process of implementing its policies at the administrative level, while at the same time reducing the public exposure that its highly controversial measures would be subject to. This was a practice that it would return to on numerous occasions to actualize its major neoliberal reforms.

Although the use of the omnibus bill as a deliberate tactic to subvert parliamentary debate was a precedent that dated only to 1993, when the Rae government began using it, by the end of the Progressive Conservatives' second mandate just a decade later, it had become a common part of procedure at the Ontario Legislature.

The Decline of Parliamentary Procedure under the Progressive Conservatives

Establishing a New Precedent for Time Allocation

By the time the Harris government came to office in 1995, time allocation had become an established part of the business of the House. After having been used for the first time in the modern history of the legislature by the Davis government in 1982, it was applied with increasing frequency in the years that followed by all three parties in office when they were confronted with contentious political issues or an obstructionist opposition. The use of time allocation reached its heights during the mandate of the NDP, which used it on twenty-one occasions during its four-and-a-half years in office and established formal rules for its application in the legislature's Standing Orders.

The Harris government first resorted to time allocation during its battle with the opposition over the Savings and Restructuring Act. Its desire to have the massive omnibus bill passed before the House adjourned for the Christmas holidays was met with fierce hostility by the opposition, which called for a lengthy public consultation process and for the bill to be split into several separate pieces of legislation. In many ways, the act marked a watershed moment in the Ontario Legislature's procedural evolution and was a litmus test for the capacity of the province's institutions to keep an aggressively reformist Executive Council accountable to the legislature.

After Speaker Al McLean ruled that it was not in keeping with the practice of the Westminster system for him to either use discretionary power to intervene and force the opposition to split the Savings and Restructuring Act or disallow the government from using the instrument of time allocation on an omnibus bill, the opposition was left with little ammunition to compel the government to allow public hearings. However, Liberal MPP Alvin Curling made a decision to obstruct the passage of the bill.

On 6 December 1995, when Government House Leader Ernie Eves brought forward a normally routine motion for unanimous consent for the House to move to the Orders of the Day, the Liberals forced a vote on division by refusing to give their consent. When the Speaker called each member to rise and be counted for a divided vote, a number of Liberals, including Alvin Curling and fellow Liberal MPP Bernard Grandmaître, refused to stand and be counted. Under Standing Order 28(c), it was impermissible for a member to be in the House and refuse to vote on division over any matter. When the Liberal members refused a second request that they stand to be counted on division, Al McLean warned them:

> I'll ask once again that those who are opposed would rise. I have no alternative but to enforce the standing orders of this Legislature. If the members are not going to vote, then I will have to name the members. The rules of the House are very clear. (McLean 1995b)

When both Curling and Grandmaître continued to refuse to stand to vote, McLean proceeded to name them and ask the Sergeant-at-Arms to escort them from the House. Although Grandmaître left the chamber without incident, Curling refused to leave his seat, locking arms with fellow Liberal MPPs David Ramsay and Tony Ruprecht. In a show of solidarity, the remaining members of the Liberal caucus and the entire NDP caucus formed a circle around Curling to prevent the Sergeant-at-Arms from escorting him from the House.

While the Speaker reminded Curling that, according to Standing Order 15(d), any member who disobeyed an order of the Speaker could be subject to suspension for the balance of the parliamentary session, Curling continued to resist, remaining in his seat despite McLean's warnings and repeated requests to follow his orders. Unable to remove Curling without first breaking through the ring of opposition MPPs surrounding him, the Speaker was forced to recess the House. Curling remained in his seat throughout the evening and into the night, refusing to leave until he received an assurance from the government that it would allow public consultations.

Curling finally vacated his seat the following morning at 10:11 a.m., at which time it was too late for the legislature to begin another sessional day. After the eighteen-hour delay, the government had little choice but to simply adjourn the House for the weekend. The government, recognizing that Curling's actions had created a precedent for other opposition members to engage in similar tactics, made the decision to concede to opposition demands for public consultations in order to work out an arrangement for the bill's unobstructed passage by the end of January 1996.

A new time allocation motion was brought forward in the House the following week, requiring that the House return early from the Christmas holidays to debate and pass the Savings and Restructuring Act no later than 29 January. The opposition, having come to an agreement with the government, did not contest the motion. While Curling was unable to ultimately stop the passage of Bill 26, he managed to achieve the important concession that the government would delay its timetable by more than a month in order to conduct public consultations and allow additional debate in the legislature.

The consequence of Curling's obstruction of proceedings was also to nurture a temporary culture of cooperation among the House Leaders in spite of the opposition's deep hostility to the government's reform agenda and the tactics it was using to achieve its objectives. Despite the government's desire to rush its legislation through the House, it was able to reach consensus with the opposition to set a parliamentary calendar for the passage of all its legislation through to the end of 1996 without resorting to time allocation. This spirit of reciprocity, however, ended in January 1997, when the government recalled the House two months earlier than it had initially planned to announce a series of significant reforms. In what would later become known as "Megaweek," the Tories brought forward several complex bills, all designed to implement its disentanglement agenda.

The government announced a total of $6.4 billion in transfers to the municipalities so that they could assume responsibility for welfare, child care, nursing homes, transit, public health, and subsidized housing. In turn, the province took responsibility for $5.4 billion in education financing (W. Walker 1997). The opposition decried this announcement of the most fundamental restructuring of the Ontario government in modern history, in a single week, as an attempt to overwhelm the public with the scale and complexity of the changes.

In an op-ed article in the *Toronto Star*, Liberal leader Dalton McGuinty claimed that the Megaweek announcements were intentionally "designed to confuse." "Each of the complex announcements could have been made a few weeks apart, giving people a chance to study, digest and debate them before they were finalized" (McGuinty 1997). With its Megaweek initiatives, the government again resorted to its strategy of managing controversial reforms by inundating the public with numerous significant and complicated reforms at one time so as to obfuscate their implications and minimize the amount of scrutiny they would be subject to. This is a tactic to which they would return time and again.

The Opposition's Last Stand: The Filibuster of 1997

Without question, the most controversial initiative brought before the House in the winter of 1997 was the City of Toronto Act (Bill 103, 1997). Although the bill was introduced in December 1996, it was brought forward for second reading during Megaweek. The Conservatives sought to use the controversy created by their decision to amalgamate Toronto to bury the most controversial elements of their disentanglement program. From the outset, the government declared its desire to pass the bill by the early spring without permitting public consultations. On 19 January 1997, Government House Leader David Johnson brought forward the second time allocation motion of the government's mandate, and the first in over a year, on the bill. The motion required that the committee report to the House no later than 6 March, that debate in the Committee of the Whole be limited to one hour, and that third reading be limited to a single sessional day. Under the conditions of the motion, the government could have the City of Toronto Act passed by the second week of March.

The opposition argued that the bill should not go forward until all the plebiscites throughout Toronto's six municipalities had been held and after extensive public consultations. Liberal MPP Joe Cordiano argued that the government

> deemed the time we are taking to democratically debate matters of such grave importance to this province as a waste of taxpayers' time and money because it doesn't conform to their tight schedule to get everything rammed through this legislature. (Cordiano 1997)

On 2 April 1997, the government brought forward the City of Toronto Act for the consideration of the Committee of the Whole House. The New Democrats were resolved to once again obstruct proceedings because they had been unsuccessful in their efforts to have the government either consider the rejection of the amalgamation by the residents of the six communities affected by the bill or allow public consultations.

The first sign that 2 April was to be unlike any other in the legislature's history occurred immediately after Prayers, which opened the sessional day. NDP member Frances Lankin (1997) rose on a point of order to ask the Speaker whether it would be permissible for the Committee of the Whole House to extend past the one hour permitted by the time allocation motion in the event that the opposition were to bring forward amendments that went beyond the time set out for it. In response, Speaker Chris Stockwell ruled that while time allocation motions dictated the way that a bill was to be considered at various stages of the process, the decision as to whether the House would proceed to third reading was solely at his discretion. In short, he ruled that the NDP would be permitted to go beyond the allotted one hour if, at his discretion, the amendments were relevant to the bill (Stockwell 1997a).

Stockwell's decision set the stage for a showdown that stalled the business of the legislature for more than two weeks and established a new precedent for filibusters at Queen's Park. Once the Committee of the Whole had commenced, the NDP announced its intention to introduce over thirteen thousand amendments to the bill. The vast majority of them were minor variations on the NDP's request that the community have the opportunity to hold public hearings on Bill 103. However, instead of proceeding with a single amendment to this effect, the New Democrats introduced an amendment for each street, avenue, road, boulevard, lane, and crescent in the affected municipalities. Each motion was a variation of the following, with only the street named changed:

NDP motion, Subsection 24(4):

I move that Section 24 of the bill be amended by adding the following subsection:

Public consultation

(4) Despite Subsection (1), no regulation that may affect the residents of Abbotsfield Gate living in the urban area shall be made unless the following conditions have first been satisfied:

1. The minister has given notice of the proposed regulation, in a manner that will come to the attention of the residents of Abbotsfield Gate living in the urban area.
2. The minister has considered all written submissions made by members of the public that his office received within 30 days after the notice was given.
3. If 10 or more persons requested a public hearing within 30 days after the notice was given, a public hearing has been held and the minister has considered all oral submissions made at the hearing.

> 4. The minister shall give three weeks' notice of a public hearing, in the same manner as the notice under paragraph 1.
> 5. The notice under paragraph 1 shall,
>   i. include a copy of the proposed regulation,
>   ii. tell members of the public where and how to obtain, without charge, a copy of this act together with background material,
>   iii. advise members of the public of their rights under paragraphs 2, 3 and 4,
>   iv. advise members of the public where their written submissions and requests for a public hearing should be sent. (Churley 1997)

Unless the Speaker ruled the filibuster as being out of order, all thirteen thousand motions would have to be read on to the record and ultimately voted upon by the legislature. To work through the thousands of streets in the Toronto area, it was feared, could take months of twenty-four-hour-per-day sittings. As expected, Government House Leader David Johnson rose on his own point of order to argue that the amendments were out of order on the grounds that they were "in the spirit of mockery" of the procedures of the House (Johnson 1997a).

In constructing the government's argument about the vexatious nature of the amendments alone, however, Johnson had made a crucial mistake. As NDP MPP Tony Silipo pointed out, parliamentary precedent dictated that in order for an amendment to be ruled out of order on "frivolous" grounds, it must be demonstrated that "it attempts to alter the objective of the legislation." Silipo made the case that while the amendments would require considerable time to work through, the request for public hearings was germane to the bill itself and in no way altered its central objective. The amendments would merely establish, he argued, "a series of actions that would have to be taken by the minister, but to do that in a way that still respects and reflects the intent of the legislation" (Silipo 1997).

In his ruling, Stockwell agreed with the NDP's contention that the motions were not in and of themselves "frivolous and vexatious." Instead, he stated that while he could not rule on the thousands of additional motions since he had not yet seen them, before him appeared to be "motions put by honourable members, honourable" (Stockwell 1997a).

The introduction of the thousands of NDP amendments began at approximately 7:00 p.m. on 2 April. Members took to shift work as the legislature sat around the clock for the next several days. At the same time, Premier Mike Harris left for a vacation at Whistler Ski Resort to wait out the filibuster (Crone 1997). On 6 April, Stockwell ruled on a government point of order, appealing to the Speaker to use his discretionary powers to end the filibuster, which, he argued, had proved to be a misuse of parliamentary privilege and contrary to the spirit of the House. By this time, the House had reached the letter *E* in the list of Toronto-area street names, but it still had more than five thousand names left to read on to the record, and three thousand additional NDP amendments, as well as deferred votes on each amendment (ibid.). NDP leader Howard Hampton warned, "We will be here for a very long time. I think we're still close to 40 days and 40 nights" (Hampton, quoted in ibid.).

Stockwell found that there was precedent to reduce the redundancy by simply reading the name of the street on to the record rather than forcing both the member who introduced the amendment and the Clerk to read it in its entirety; but he ruled against a government request to have similar amendments voted on as a single block. He also ruled that there remained insufficient grounds to put an end to the amendments and allowed them to continue. He maintained that the Assembly found itself in the midst of "exceptional circumstances" and, as a result, urged the House Leaders to negotiate a settlement if they desired to put an end to the filibuster before it ran its natural course (Chris Stockwell, quoted in Crone 1997). While the government had offered the opposition two weeks of public hearings to break the stalemate, the NDP rejected this attempt at conciliation, asking instead that the government allow a binding referendum on amalgamation (ibid.).

The filibuster included its share of bizarre moments. In one instance, when the deputy chair of the Committee of the Whole asked for an oral vote on one of the motions, Progressive Conservative members seemingly forgot to announce their objection to one of the amendments (Morin 1997). As a result, the motion passed, and the residents of Cafon Court in Etobicoke were temporarily granted the right to public hearings on the amalgamation. A subsequent amendment overturned the original amendment, but the situation spoke to the remarkable circumstances in which the Assembly found itself in the midst of twenty-four-hour-per-day sessions. On another occasion, Peter Kormos rose on a point of privilege to further extend the filibuster by reading from Hansard the lyrics to a song he had recited in the legislature earlier that year.

> We're gonna clean out the Eves, chase off the thieves,
> tell Mike Harris where to go.
> We're gonna flush 'em down the drain,
> pull the Leach from our veins, and free Ontario.
> 'Cause Johnson's a weenie and so is Palladini,
> and Mike keeps Harrissing the poor.
> We're gonna send all those dopes back to the slopes,
> and free Ontario.
> And when we kick out their butts, we'll cut all the cuts,
> and tell them, megacity, no.

We're going to break off our chains,
pull the Leach from our veins, and free Ontario.
'Cause Johnson's a weenie and so is Palladini,
they all keep Harrissing the poor.
We're gonna send all those dinks back to the links,
and free Ontario. (Kormos 1997)

Swallowing the bait, Minister Tony Clement (1997) raised a point of order for Kormos's use of "unparliamentary" language in reference to Ministers of the Crown, bringing to a halt the introduction of motions while the members debated the point and a decision was rendered. Ultimately, the deputy chair of the Committee of the Whole ruled that Kormos's language was in order since he was quoting his own words in Hansard, although the lyrics had been written by someone else. More importantly, however, Kormos had succeeded in briefly extending the filibuster by agitating government members.

The spectacle dragged on through the week of 2 April and into the following week. Finally, on 11 April, the NDP agreed to end the filibuster in exchange for an additional two weeks of debate before the bill would be put forward for third reading. The government, however, would neither hold public hearings nor recognize the plebiscite results from the six affected municipalities. Shortly after 9:00 p.m. on 11 April, after more than eight days and three hours, the Assembly voted to adopt the report from the Committee of the Whole House, thus ending the longest sessional day in the province's history. While the NDP was not able to force the government's hand to hold public hearings, Kormos argued that the filibuster "brought a little bit of democracy back to the chamber" (Peter Kormos, quoted in Ferguson 1997).

The New Democrats were successful at holding up the government's entire agenda for two weeks, but their tactics also cast a permanent pall over any spirit of cooperation that had existed. From this point on, the government began preparations to change the Standing Orders so that they could time-allocate bills without interference and block any opposition attempts to delay its legislative agenda. At the end of the marathon filibuster, Al Leach warned, "Clearly the floodgates are now open. We'll have to look at changing the rules" (Leach, quoted in *Ottawa Citizen* 1997).

The End of the Filibuster at Queen's Park: The 1997 Standing Orders Reform

The day after the City of Toronto Act passed third reading, the government brought forward a time allocation motion to "discharge" the Fewer School Boards Act immediately from the Committee of the Whole House, without debate, to avoid the prospect that the NDP might once again introduce thousands of amendments. As a result, the bill was moved to third reading (Johnson 1997b). The opposition raised objections about this tactic on the grounds that the motion "violates a very fundamental right of all members of the House to move amendments to public bills" (Wildman 1997a). However, Speaker Chris Stockwell found that the time allocation was consistent with the protocol of the Assembly because, once adopted by the House, time allocation motions functioned as temporary Standing Orders at the various stages of a bill. He explained his decision this way:

> To look at it another way, the House adopts its standing orders by motion. If such a decision of the House were final and unchangeable, then the House would be powerless to revise its own standing orders in the future. (Stockwell 1997b)

While the government was able to use time allocation to avoid another marathon filibuster, it indicated its intent to make changes to the Standing Orders. On 2 June 1997, the day of the Canadian federal election, Tory MPP John Baird held a press conference to announce a series of changes to the Standing Orders. The opposition argued that the government had chosen the day of the election to attempt to bury news of the most restrictive changes to the Standing Orders in the legislature's history. The Conservatives refuted this, claiming that the reforms were designed to improve the efficiency of the legislature, but, in practice, they removed all plausible mechanisms by which the opposition could delay the proceedings of the House. The changes, introduced in the legislature on 16 June, included the following:

- Reduced the speaking time on all bills and motions from ninety minutes to forty minutes for leadoff speeches. Follow-up speeches were limited to twenty minutes rather than the thirty minutes that members had previously been granted. After five hours of debate, speakers were limited to just ten minutes.
- Allowed the Speaker to continue with the regular business of the House in the event that a member refused to leave his or her seat after being named by the Speaker.
- Allowed chairs in committees and the Committee of the Whole House to group votes on amendments, to dispense with reading amendments of any kind, and to establish filing deadlines for amendments.
- Permitted the Speaker to deem adjournment procedures to be concluded at 6:25 p.m. and allow the government to introduce a motion without notice for an evening session from 6:30 to 9:30 p.m., which would count as an additional sessional day.
- Authorized the Speaker to rule out of order any motion that he or she deemed to have been moved with the intention of causing delay in the proceedings of the House.

- Granted the House Leader the option to provide a previously mandatory business statement for the upcoming week.
- Limited motions for interim supply to a single sessional day of debate rather than the several days they had traditionally received.
- Permitted government bills introduced during the final two weeks of a parliamentary session to immediately proceed to second reading.
- Reduced all standing committees to nine members.
- Allowed the Speaker to refuse to adjust voting times and adjournment times if a delay occurred as a result of unforeseen circumstances.
- Required any point of privilege not directly related to the business of the day to receive a minimum one-and-a-half-hours' notice. The Speaker was granted the authority to deny a request for a point of privilege that violated this principle. Such rulings were not subject to debate.
- Forbade members from interrupting the Speaker when he or she had risen to speak, was rendering a ruling, or placing a question before the House. (Decker 1997)

The rules were to be applied retroactively so that any bill that was then before the House would be subject to the new procedures. The government maintained that they improved the legislature's accountability to the public, who expected politicians to focus on policy implementation rather than obstructionist tactics. In addition, it claimed that the reductions in speaking time were designed after the Standing Orders at the federal House of Commons and addressed the "concern that the time is restricted and many members are not allowed or do not have the opportunity to participate in the debate of this House" (Johnson 1997c).

Liberal MPP Jim Bradley retorted that the federal House had more than three times the members of the Ontario Legislature and that if the government took issue with providing opportunity for members to speak, it should "allocate more time" for them to do so (Bradley 1997a). He claimed that the drastic, extreme changes to the Standing Orders were designed primarily "to make it more convenient for the advisers, the unelected whiz kids, the people who have little regard for those of us who are elected, to get their way, and to get their way more quickly. It has nothing to do with anything else and people in this province should know that. … Democracy is best served," he argued,

> when there is a strong and influential opposition, with the tools to be able to slow down and, on very rare occasions, halt the government for a short period of time to allow it to reconsider, to allow it to reflect, to allow it to make changes to its own legislative initiatives. (Bradley 1997a)

Furthermore, the new Standing Orders would function to "diminish the role of members of this House. This legislature, if this motion passes, will be a much more insignificant place than it has been for many years since I've been in the House" (Bradley 1997a). NDP MPP Bud Wildman contended that new House rules were "not about democracy," but rather "the kind of efficiency that makes it possible for the government to deal with issues quickly without proper debate." The amended Standing Orders, he claimed, made it possible "for any government, this government or any future government, to bring in the most controversial legislation and have it passed before the public even knows about it. That's not democratic. You might as well just rule by decree" (Wildman 1997b).

The NDP filibuster and the reforms to the Standing Orders that followed marked a shift in the relationship between the government and the opposition parties. The new Standing Orders skewed the balance of power even more significantly in the government's favour by eliminating virtually any mechanism through which the opposition might threaten to obstruct proceedings. Stripped of this capacity to hold up the business of the House, the opposition had little to offer the government besides agreeing to stand down on the highly structured time allotments provided for debate on certain bills in exchange for lengthier debates on other items. In the wake of the filibuster on the City of Toronto Act, the Tories attached time allocation motions to fourteen individual bills in just seven months before proroguing the House, revealing the extent to which the spirit of cooperation between the House Leaders had been irreparably damaged by the government's heavy-handed approach to the Megaweek legislation and the opposition's obstructionist reply.

The most contentious time allocation motion brought forward by the government during this period was to a package of six bills concerned with reducing red tape, which the opposition derisively named "the omnibus six-pack" (Colle 1997b). As the result of the report by the Red Tape Reduction Commission, the government introduced six omnibus bills dealing with dozens of individual reforms to the structure of government. While the bills passed second reading in June 1996, they had been temporarily shelved once the government had become preoccupied with its disentanglement agenda. As the parliamentary session drew to a close in December 1997, the government attempted to have all six bills treated as a single piece of legislation during its various stages. In short, the government was attempting to pass six bills, with the time for debate that would normally be given to a single bill, on legislation that was already contentious due to its omnibus status.

There were two relevant precedents for this approach in the recent history of the legislature. First, the NDP had brought forward a time allocation motion, with numerous bills attached to it, in 1992; however, it had been the result of an all-party agreement, whereas the opposition remained vehemently opposed to the omnibus six-pack. Second, Bills 113 and 114, the Sunday shopping legislation, had been passed in tandem under the Peterson government, but that time allocation motion was subject to more than sixty hours of debate (Wildman 1997d). The opposition argued that the omnibus six-pack set a highly dangerous precedent, which "will allow the government then to simply, at the end of the session, bring in as much legislation as it wishes and with one fell swoop pass that legislation with a minimum of debate in this House, with a minimum of consideration" (Bradley 1997b). NDP MPP Gilles Bisson (1997) issued an ominous warning to the government: "Be careful. The precedent you're setting here you may one day have to live with." His words would prove to be prophetic. Packaging multiple bills together in a single time allocation motion became the preferred tactic of the Liberal government a decade later, to the immense frustration of the Progressive Conservative opposition.

If it can be said that time allocation became habituated under the NDP, then one can characterize it as being entrenched as a customary matter of House business in the post-1997 period of the Progressive Conservatives' mandate. Even the Rae government, which had established the standard for time allocation, had invoked it only twenty-one times relative to the ninety-seven bills it had passed during its time in office. The first Harris mandate, meanwhile, attached time allocation motions to thirty-five of the bills it passed. Thus, while it used time allocation more than any other government in the province's history, it applied it to only approximately 30 per cent of its legislative initiatives. In its second mandate, however, it used time allocation on more than 60 per cent of the bills it passed. (See table 8.1.)

This trend is, in part, attributable to the erosion, after the NDP filibuster, of an early commitment between the government and the opposition to cooperate on the government's agenda; but it can also be explained by an increased disregard for the legislative process as a whole. By 1997, the government seemed

Table 8.1. Time allocation motions to government bills passed, 1981–2003

Parliament	Date	Number of government bills passed	Number of time allocation motions	Percentage of time allocation motions to government bills passed, %
32nd Parliament PC	1981–5	292	3	1.0
33rd Parliament LIB	1985–7	129	1	0.8
34th Parliament LIB	1987–90	183	3	1.7
35th Parliament NDP	1990–5	97	21	21.6
36th Parliament PC	**1995–9**	**118**	**35**	**29.7**
37th Parliament PC	**1999–2003**	**111**	**67**	**60.4**

Note: The bolded rows indicate the Harris and Eves governments.

emboldened in its view that the legislature served as an impediment to its reform agenda; it thought that democracy was better served when the elected party had a free hand to implement its agenda without interference from an obstructionist opposition. This prodigious use of time allocation continued after Ernie Eves succeeded Mike Harris as premier in April 2002.

By the end of the Harris and, later, the Eves governments' tenures in power, the use of time allocation had become so commonplace that the opposition hardly bothered to oppose it during debate. While opposition members would rise to speak when debate had been set aside for time allocation motions, most often they would make only vague reference to the motion itself before using the balance of their time to speak to the bill in question. During the final sessional day of the 37th Parliament, for example, the opposition spent its time during debate on a time allocation motion paying tributes to members who planned to retire at the end of the session. As Peter Kormos (2003a) observed, it was "befitting" that the last moments of the 37th Parliament were spent debating a time allocation motion. As the afternoon sitting of 26 June drew to a close, the legislature passed the government's final time allocation motion with hardly so much as a groan from the opposition members. By the end of the Tory mandate, time allocation had become such an integral part of the fabric of legislative governance that meaningful resistance had long since ceased to be anything more than an exercise in futility.

Spectacle over Substance: The Magna Budget

There is arguably no better illustration of the Progressive Conservative government's contempt for the legislative process than its unprecedented decision to introduce the 2003 budget at a Magna International auto parts factory in Brampton, while the legislature was prorogued. On 12 March, as members were preparing to return for the spring session, set to begin on 17 March, Premier Eves called upon the lieutenant-governor and asked him to prorogue the legislature indefinitely. Moments after the request was granted, Finance Minister Janet Ecker held a press conference outside the legislature, in which she announced the government's plans: "We have completed our pre-budget consultations, we have listened to the people and we intend to deliver our budget at a yet-to-be-disclosed location outside the legislature and while the legislature is not in session" (Ecker, quoted in Conway 2003). This announcement broke with the long-standing tradition in the Westminster system that supply bills first be introduced in Parliament.

The government argued that although the House was prorogued, it was imperative that the budget be presented on time. This reasoning, however, conveniently ignored the fact that both the choice to prorogue and the decision to hold the budget announcement outside the legislature were made by the government within two weeks of each other – and in the absence of a political crisis that might justify introducing a budget during parliamentary intersession.

The event itself was unlike any the province had ever seen. Ecker delivered the budget speech to an audience of mostly party loyalists. When she had finished, a large screen featured testimonials from other Cabinet ministers, who praised the government's approach and its featured program announcements. Ecker also fielded scripted questions from citizens, most of which avoided controversial interpretations of the government's economic plan.

Minister of Energy John Baird contended that the government's unique approach to introducing the budget reflected the "evolving role of Parliament." He claimed that it sought to recognize the "huge influence of mass communications" by emphasizing the production quality of the event.

> No longer is there a 24-hour news cycle; there is in fact a news cycle that demands instant reaction, almost to the hour, if not the minute … This challenges Parliament's role, and that's not a reflection on either opposition party or on the government. (Baird 2003)

Besides the violation of parliamentary tradition, introducing the budget at the Magna International facility raised questions about whether the government was in a conflict of interest, given that its chairman, Frank Stronach, was a financial supporter of the Ontario Progressive Conservatives and that former premier Mike Harris was on the company's board of directors (Mallan 2003). Liberal MPP Michael Bryant contended that the event was a partisan political ploy designed to reward its largest financial donors. "This confirms the worst – this is not about outreach to the people, this is about payback to noted supporters of the PC party" (Bryant, quoted in Mallan 2003). NDP leader Howard Hampton echoed Bryant's sentiments, claiming that "the government is supposed to be in the democracy business, not in the auto parts business. This is truly one more gift to one of the closest corporate friends" (Hampton, quoted in ibid.).

When the legislature returned in May, the opposition protested to the Speaker that the government had acted in contempt of Parliament by holding the budget announcement outside the House. Liberal MPP Sean Conway argued that the government's actions constituted "an offence against the authority and the dignity of Parliament" (Conway 2003).

The government countered that there had been precedent for holding the announcement outside the legislature. In 1988, Finance Minister Bob Nixon had been unable to introduce the budget in the legislature due to a filibuster by the NDP, which was occupying the business of the House. While he had eventually introduced the budget in the House, he was unable to deliver his speech until the filibuster had ended, and he subsequently had to announce its essential details outside the legislative chamber. However, the difference between the two occasions is that, in 1988, the Liberal government had been restricted from making its budget speech by extenuating circumstances specific to the proceedings of the legislature, whereas, in 2003, the Eves government made a conscious choice not to deliver its budget in the House. In his decision, Speaker Gary Carr chastised the government for its approach:

> Parliamentary democracy is not vindicated by the government conducting a generally one-sided public relations event on the budget well in advance of members having an opportunity to hold the government to account for the budget in this chamber. A mature parliamentary democracy is not a docile, esoteric or one-way communications vehicle; it is a dynamic, interactive and representative institution that allows the government of the day to propose and defend its policies – financial and otherwise. It also allows the opposition to scrutinize and hold the government to account for those policies. It is an open, working and relevant system of scrutiny and accountability. I have a lingering unease about the road we are going down, and my sense is that the House and the general public have the same unease. (Carr 2003)

Carr ruled that "the 2003 budget process has raised too many questions for the House not to reflect on them," and he found that a *prima facie* case of contempt had indeed been established (Carr 2003). He referred the matter to the Assembly to decide what to do. In the days following the ruling, Sean Conway introduced a motion to confirm the Speaker's ruling that the government was in contempt of Parliament and to resolve that all future budgets must be presented in the legislature first. Although the motion was ultimately voted down by the Tory majority, the opposition had managed to embarrass the government, which was also pilloried by the press, for its attempt to circumvent the parliamentary process. With only a few weeks left to sit before dissolution, the opposition had at last found cause to hold the government responsible for contempt of Parliament. It was, however, a small victory.

Conclusion

The argument presented in this chapter is that the contemporaneous occurrence of radical neoliberal restructuring and aggressive tactics to circumvent the legislature are not coincidental. By establishing a state of permanent crisis in the legislature, the Harris government was able to sufficiently insulate the restructuring processes from public control to guarantee that they would be actualized without democratic interference. A restructuring process of this magnitude could not have been carried out with such rapidity, or on such a scale, without the suspension of the traditional processes of the legislature.

The use of legal provisions to implement a form of technocratic control over virtually any interest that might oppose it – doctors, unions, municipalities, community interest groups, teachers, to name a few – was not only an important variable in actualizing the CSR agenda, but an indispensable component of the restructuring process.

When the Progressive Conservatives' mandate ended in 2003, they left the legislative chamber a fundamentally different place than they had found it. While the government's first mandate had been characterized by a feverish restructuring program, by the time its second had begun, most of the major changes it had proposed in the CSR had been implemented. The post-1999 period was characterized by the consolidation of both the radicalism of its first mandate and its approach to Parliament. Having already established new precedents in nearly every area, the government began to stifle debate even more indiscriminately than before, using time allocation and omnibus legislation more as a matter of convenience and custom than for a discernible political cause.

The misuse of the legislative process became normalized during this period, as governments began to use legislative provisions, once reserved for emergency circumstances, as a customary part of House procedure. This was expressed most clearly during the years of the Eves government, during which time the Tories used time allocation on nearly two-thirds of the legislation passed by the House. While the Liberal government that followed it vowed to refrain from using the same tactics, it predictably found it to its benefit to follow the precedent that had been set for it by the Tories.

The impact of the CSR, then, was not merely to restructure the Ontario state but also to fundamentally alter the functioning of its political branch. One of the overlooked aspects of the Harris legacy is the extent to which it changed the customs of the legislative branch to easily accommodate new waves of neoliberal reforms. This is the torch it passed to the McGuinty Liberals.

9 Consolidating a Revolution: The Liberal Years, 2003–2018

Introduction

In his final work, *The Double Vision*, literary and social theorist Northrop Frye claimed that "nothing in any revolutionary situation is of any importance except preserving it" (Frye 1991, 9). For Frye, then, the true test of a revolution was defined not by the moment of rebellion itself, but by its ability to transcend the old order and sustain itself as a revolutionary force. It was this period of consolidation, after the dust from the revolutionary moment had begun to settle, that determined the ability of a social movement to entrench itself as a new, historical pattern.

Although the McGuinty government promised a departure from the unvarnished, free market fundamentalism of the Harris and Eves Progressive Conservatives, it adopted a Third Way approach to public policy that fused "prudent financial management" with a devotion to fostering "social inclusion." Such policies have commonly appealed to social democrats and those on the centre-left because they have been presented as transcending ideological divisions entirely, in favour of an approach that is more pragmatic than the "old," leftist party platforms, yet more humane than the free market orthodoxies of the neoliberal radicals (Coulter 2009, 191).

Neoliberalism was "repackaged" in a "softer, kinder" manner, maintaining a commitment to efficiency, competition, fiscal prudence, while at the same time adopting the language of inclusion (Coulter 2009, 201). The Liberal approach was to make "progressive nods to the importance of universality and commitments to make certain public investments, bundled with neoliberal rhetoric about tough choices, cutbacks to the budgets of 15 ministries, and warnings about additional service reductions" (196).

The ascendency of the McGuinty Liberals to government did not lead to a "rupture" with the principles of the CSR, then, but instead "served to sustain that project" (Evans 2007, n.p.). Their first years in office were characterized by "rescinded promises that quietly consolidated and extended the earlier core of Harris's project" (Fanelli and Thomas 2011, 149). The Liberals offered a sanitized version of neoliberalism, reinvesting in core public services such as health and education, while at the same time leaving in place many of the Harris-era reforms to the welfare and taxation systems (Fanelli 2018). Carlo Fanelli argued that their time in office was ultimately "never about a wholesale repudiation of the CSR, but rather about deepening and extending it in ways that were more palatable to a public increasingly fed up with the uncompromising and aggressive style of their Conservative predecessors" (ibid.).

Consequently, the legacy of the Harris government "lives on" in Ontario, "having been politically embedded in policy and structures" (Evans 2007, n.p.). Examples include the privatization of key public services, such as the partial sell-off of equity in Hydro One, and the privatization of services previously offered under the Ontario Health Insurance Plan, such as physical rehabilitation (Fanelli and Thomas 2011). By the end of the Liberal era in 2018, Ontario ranked last in Canada in per capita program spending and had the second-lowest corporate tax rates in North America (Fanelli 2018).

The story of the Liberal years, then, is one of *consolidation* – both of the policies of the CSR and in its approach to parliamentary governance. Although the Liberal government did not pursue an aggressive neoliberal restructuring strategy – most of this work had already been done during the Harris/Eves era – the McGuinty and Wynne governments maintained the aggressive use of parliamentary tactics to move their legislation through the House. The result was that they left in place, with only a few modifications, the Standing Orders and major parliamentary practices passed down to them from the Progressive Conservatives.

While previous governments had typically used mechanisms such as time allocation and omnibus legislation to usher contentious or contested legislation through the Assembly under the spectre of a crisis, the Liberals began to use these techniques more broadly and indiscriminately. The story of the Liberal era, then, is one in which the Harris-era approaches to parliamentary governance were consolidated and customized as conventional practice at Queen's Park.

Democratic Renewal at Queen's Park?

At the outset of its first mandate, the McGuinty government pledged to rehabilitate the role of the legislature in Ontario after eight years of neglect at the hands of the Progressive Conservatives. Premier McGuinty appointed one of his senior Cabinet ministers, Michael Bryant, to serve as minister of democratic renewal as well as attorney general. In this role, Bryant would be accountable for implementing new procedures to re-establish the principle of the supremacy of Parliament. Shortly after taking office, Bryant (2003) pledged in the legislature that the Liberals would "treat our institutions with the respect they deserve" by ensuring that the executive branch was accountable to Parliament.

One of the issues that tested the Liberal government's commitment to its promise for democratic renewal occurred in the wake of the 2003 election, when the NDP returned to the legislature with only seven seats, one short of recognized party status. Though the number of seats necessary for recognized party status is arbitrary, it is a critical issue in the legislature because it provides parties with a variety of fundamental rights, the absence of which makes the job of holding the government to account considerably more difficult. Parties that do not reach the eight-seat threshold are not eligible for critical opposition research and staff funding. They are also ineligible for certain House privileges, such as a regular turn in Question Period and a place on the standing committees of the legislature, and they are excluded from debates in which time is to be equally divided among the parties.

Although it was a political adversary of the Liberals, the NDP had been a consistent presence in the legislature since the 1960s, had received more than five hundred thousand votes in the election, and were firmly part of the province's three-major-party political culture. Having fallen only one seat short of recognized party status, the NDP argued that the government ought to ensure that the voices of constituents in the ridings where it had been elected were heard, and that a plurality of perspectives were heard in the legislature, by granting it formal status.

Initially, McGuinty refused to make any concessions, requiring NDP representatives to sit as independent members of the legislature until they had acquired enough seats to achieve the threshold for recognized party status and maintaining, "There was a rule in place … We'll respect that rule" (Dalton McGuinty, quoted in Mackie 2003). As a result, the NDP leader's office had to lay off staff, and party leader Howard Hampton was evicted from his office (McGrath 2018b). Additionally, when New Democrats rose to ask questions during Question Period, they were identified only by their name, not their party name. This led to the spectacle of New Democrat MPP Marilyn Churley applying to formally change her surname to "Churley-NDP" so that the Speaker would have no choice but to refer to her using her party's name (Mackie 2003).

With a big majority government, the Liberals had members spill over to the other side of the House. They were given front-bench seats on the other side, while the New Democrats were seated at the back, as though to reinforce their subordinate status (McGrath 2018b).

The government ultimately reached an agreement with the NDP that saw its members receive turns during Question Period and some funding for staff (McGrath 2018b). It received recognized party status in 2004, when Andrea Horwath won a by-election in Hamilton Centre, but the precedent had been set. This is an issue that the Liberals would confront themselves in 2018, when they failed to reach the threshold for recognized party status in the legislature and were forced to appeal to the Ford government, in the same way as the NDP had done in 2003.

The most significant changes the government enacted to improve the responsiveness of the executive to the legislature were enshrined in the Executive Council Amendment Act, introduced in December 2003. The bill required Cabinet ministers to attend Question Period for at least two-thirds of the days the House was in session, with fines of up to $500 per day if they failed to attend for reasons deemed by the premier to be unacceptable. Furthermore, the bill required the premier to file a status report at the end of each session, updating the public on ministers' attendance records (Bill 17, 2004).

Besides the obvious problem that the justifications for missing Question Period were to be left to the discretion of the premier, the bill did little to alter the essential relationship between the executive and legislative branches since it left in place the procedural framework used by the Tories to subvert the Assembly. Despite the government's haughty rhetoric on the issue of accountability, it failed to implement a counterforce to the executive's power that would act as a disincentive for it to circumvent the legislature.

Another central plank in the government's plan to renew accountability was to improve budgetary and fiscal transparency after it discovered a $5.6 billion deficit, despite claims from the Eves government during the election campaign that it had maintained a balanced budget. As its first order of business in the new Parliament, the government introduced the Fiscal Transparency and Accountability Act, which required increased transparency of its fiscal outlook by ensuring that information about the province's economic complexion was readily available to the public (Bill 2, 2004). However, the bill also included provisions that appeared strikingly similar to the neoliberal philosophy of the Harris/Eves era. It required the government to "maintain a prudent ratio of provincial debt to Ontario's gross domestic product" and to provide a recovery plan specifying a process for achieving fiscal equilibrium if, in any year, the government ran a deficit. The act foreshadowed much of what was to come under the Liberal government: it promised accountability but was simultaneously entrenching the market logic of neoliberalism in the central nervous system of the province's finance ministry.

While the Liberals promised to change the way government operated, it became clear within a short period that little would change. The substantive changes made by the Harris government, establishing restrictive rules on parliamentary debate, were left in place, and it was not long before the McGuinty government began using many of the same strategies in earnest.

The Use of Regulation in Liberal Ontario

The conclusion of the era of major restructuring in Ontario brought with it a temporary end to the widespread misuse of the executive's regulatory powers witnessed during the Harris years. However, what is most striking about the Liberal record is, as the government shifted to a policy of fiscal austerity in the years following the Great Recession of 2008, the extent to which it began employing the tactics used by the Progressive Conservatives. Under pressure to reduce the deficit, the government sought the shelter of its regulatory powers to enforce its decisions. By its third mandate, during which it was confronted with a highly fractured and obstructionist minority Parliament, it came to the realization that it required a political approach that could insulate its restraint agenda from the political forces that sought to undermine it. The result was the most prodigious use of regulatory powers since the Harris years.

Although Dalton McGuinty often proclaimed himself to be the "education premier," it was in the education sector that his Cabinet intervened most forcefully to restrain the growth of public spending (Marchese 2004). In its 2012 budget, the government demanded a two-year wage freeze from all public-sector employees and threatened that if the public-sector unions did not comply, it would use legislation to force them to do so. McGuinty called upon public-sector workers to support the wage freeze on the grounds that the fiscal crisis of the state required collective action. The government adopted a policy of negotiating only within the parameters of what Education Minister Laurel Broten (2012) called "the province's fiscal reality."

In a different parlance, from this point on, no public-sector salary increases would be forthcoming until the province managed to bring its budget back into balance. "We're all in this together," McGuinty said, while appealing to teachers to be "part of the solution" by agreeing to the austerity measures without causing the government to resort to legislation to enforce the pay freeze (Dalton McGuinty, quoted in Howlett 2012). Broten claimed, "If Ontario does not take strong action, the deficit will grow, which would mean unsustainable levels of debt. We cannot allow that to happen. We will not allow that to happen" (Broten 2012). What she neglected to mention, however, was that the government's 2010 Open Ontario plan had slashed corporate tax rates from 14 per cent to 11.5 per cent, depriving the Treasury of crucial revenue in the midst of a recession. Following in the example of the Progressive Conservatives, the Liberals were seeking to replace the revenue lost through tax cuts by forcing restraint upon public-sector employees.

The government's first showdown over the wage freeze with the unions came at the end of August 2012, when the contracts of the province's elementary school teachers were set to expire. Although the unions reached out to the province during the summer, the government took a hard line on its request for a wage freeze. In response, the teachers threatened to strike when their contracts expired at the beginning of the school year if the government refused to change its demands. With both sides entrenched in their respective positions, Dalton McGuinty advised Lieutenant-Governor David Onley to recall the legislature from summer recess during the last week of August to follow through with his threat to legislate contractual terms upon those unions that failed to comply with the wage freeze.

On 27 August, the Liberals introduced Bill 115, the Putting Students First Act, which functioned as a pre-emptive piece of back-to-work legislation. The sweeping powers it granted to the minister of education were comparable to the most extreme uses of its executive authority exercised during the Mike Harris years. The bill placed an outright ban on teachers' strikes in Ontario and imposed a twenty-four-month "restraint period" for salaries, thus undermining the right of unions to collectively bargain for teachers' wages. Most significant, however, was the extraordinary discretionary authority it granted to the minister of education. The minister was granted broad, regulatory powers to impose new collective agreements on teachers' unions, require parties to negotiate new collective agreements, prohibit or end any strikes or lockouts, and require employees to reimburse any money paid to them by a school board that had acted in contravention of the wage-restraint conditions (Bill 115, 2012).

The bill raised immediate and widespread concern that the power granted to Cabinet to unilaterally impose contracts and end strikes violated the constitutionally protected right to free collective bargaining. Sam Hammond, president of the Elementary Teachers' Federation of Ontario, claimed that Bill 115 went "far beyond any wage restraint or back-to-work legislation ever enacted in Ontario" (Hammond, quoted in Leslie 2012).

Recognizing that the response to the powers granted to the minister would be unpopular, the government included a provision under section 9 of the bill that prohibited the Ontario Labour Relations Board, any arbitrator, or any arbitration board from holding an inquiry into the bill to determine whether it was constitutionally valid and/or in violation of the Ontario Human Rights Code. This unprecedented clause was included as a means of insulating ministerial authority from the scrutiny of public institutions designed to protect citizens from the abuse of power.

In October 2012, four public-sector unions filed legal action against the government for violating their collective bargaining rights. Perhaps most interesting about this suit was that it cited a case from 2002 in British Columbia, where the government had introduced similar legislation. In 2011, parts of that legislation had been overturned, in large part because the BC government had failed to adequately consult with the province's teachers' unions beforehand (Nesbitt 2012). Liberal MPP Dipika Damerla (2012) expressed confidence that the Putting Students First Act would hold up to a court challenge given that the BC bill had been overturned not on its merits, but because of inadequate consultation with the unions. The Liberals, on the other hand, had permitted the unions to engage in negotiations over the summer, within the parameters of its mandated wage freeze.

Premier Dalton McGuinty echoed this view, suggesting that his government had "a tremendous amount of confidence in the position that we have taken, and the law that we have adopted here in Ontario through working in concert with the opposition in the legislature" (McGuinty, quoted in Leslie 2012). His view was not entirely accurate, however. While the Liberals did ultimately receive the support of the Progressive Conservatives, whose leader, Tim Hudak, had long pressured the Liberals to enact an across-the-board public-sector wage freeze, the NDP was vehement in its opposition. Furthermore, the government used its regulatory powers to shield its austerity measures from public institutions that might overturn them. By placing these powers in the hands of the education minister, the government could eliminate potential obstructions to their restraint program. Ultimately, the opposition members would be proven correct in their criticisms. A 2016 decision by the Ontario Superior Court of Justice ruled Bill 115 unconstitutional on the grounds that it violated the collective bargaining rights of teachers. The Court determined that the "process engaged in was fundamentally flawed" given that it "could not, by its design, provide meaningful collective bargaining (*OPSEU et al. v. Ontario* 2016, 43).

The day after the government brought forward Bill 115 in the legislature, Education Minister Laurel Broten also announced that it was appointing a financial supervisor to oversee the affairs of the Windsor-Essex Catholic District School Board. While the board had posted a $2.4 million surplus in its 2012 budget, a report prepared by Deloitte and Touche LLP claimed that there could be a $3 million variance in the board's accounting. Additionally, five of the board's previous six budgets had run a deficit. The report stated that the board had "an inability to meet its financial management obligations under the Education Act" because of a number of factors, including "an inability to develop accurate budgets, inadequate financial management and an absence of budgetary control" (Lajoie 2012).

Appointed under the terms of the Harris-era austerity legislation – Bill 160, the Budget Measures Act – the financial supervisor was authorized to suspend the authority of the democratically elected school board in Windsor-Essex in order to restructure its finances and bring it out of deficit by following the recommendations set out in the report by Deloitte and Touche. The supervisor was granted full power to make the cuts necessary for an indefinite period, without interference from the school board, whose authority was effectively neutered until the minister declared the supervisor's tenure to be complete. Broten justified granting the supervisor such considerable powers on the grounds that "the board's actions have called into question their ability to manage their financial affairs … I want this board to have stability and solid financial controls in place so that it can focus on its main job of improving student achievement" (Laurel Broten, quoted in Lajoie 2012). Although the Liberals had promised a more conciliatory approach to negotiations with the public sector than its predecessors, its shift towards a policy of public-sector austerity in the wake of the global financial crisis of 2008 led it to embrace, as other governments had before it, the use of its executive authority as a means of enforcing a wage freeze on the Ontario public service.

The Use of Omnibus Legislation during the Liberal Era

On 6 December 1999, at the height of the controversy over the Harris government's Bill 25 (the Fewer Municipal Politicians Act), Leader of Her Majesty's Loyal Opposition Dalton McGuinty had told the legislature,

> This omnibus, megabill approach to legislation makes for bad legislation … We will not buy into that sort of approach by supporting this bill. We will not set a precedent that gives the government the green light to continue to ram omnibus bills down our throats. We want the bill split to allow separate votes on each piece of legislation. (McGuinty 1999)

As opposition leader, McGuinty had made it clear that the mechanism of omnibus legislation corrupted the parliamentary process. However, once in government, he followed the trail blazed by the NDP and the Progressive Conservatives, using this tactic on several important initiatives throughout his nine years as premier. While the Liberals largely steered clear of the enormous bills involving several seminal reforms that had characterized the Harris era, the omnibus bill was a no less important procedural tool than it had been at that time.

Liberal omnibus bills tended to take two forms. First, following the example set by the Tories, the Liberals introduced a number of bills with broad, disconnected themes dealing with government efficiency. During their eight years in power, the Progressive Conservatives had habitually brought forward red-tape-reduction legislation, which packaged together mostly minor, loosely associated reforms designed to reduce regulatory burdens on business and improve government efficiency. Although the Liberals avoided using the term "red tape," preferring more politically neutral phrases such as "regulatory modernization," the bills they brought forward were virtually indistinguishable from the majority of the Tories' red-tape-reduction legislation.

The first of these bills, the Ministry of Consumer and Business Services Act, was an attempt to roll back regulations in areas long lobbied for by business, but that the Tories had failed to address before losing the 2003 election. Passed in November 2004, the bill amended twenty-four statutes, making mostly minor changes to regulatory provisions. Peter Kormos summarized the omnibus bill's central purpose to reduce regulations as

> a dusty old piece, a hodgepodge of dusty old Tory amendments that have been sitting on the shelf for Lord knows how long, well past their expiration date. In a stricter regime around consumer protection, this expired date, shelved item would have been discarded. (Kormos 2004)

The most significant red-tape-reduction bill brought forward by the Liberals was the Open for Business Act, a signature piece of legislation passed during the government's turn to fiscal austerity during the spring of 2010. The bill made changes to ten ministries, amending legislation to streamline registration and review processes, eliminate excessive regulations, and establish processes to reduce bureaucratic backlogs. It granted discretionary power to employment officers to clear up a backlog of more than fourteen thousand employment-standards claims. It also attempted to address a shortage of engineers in the province by eliminating the requirement that a person have Canadian citizenship before being able to work as an engineer in Ontario (Bill 68, 2010). Although members of the opposition argued that the bill should be split into several pieces of legislation, given that it dealt with a variety of important changes to the law in Ontario that warranted debate and public hearings independent from the omnibus legislation, it was time-allocated and received royal assent in the fall of 2010.

Liberal omnibus bills tended to take a second form as well. The Liberal government made a habit of packaging dozens of reforms into its budget-implementation bills. It had often been the case that the initiatives written into omnibus legislation had had nothing to do with a budget or fiscal policy, but were included as part of a government's desire to hasten a bill's implementation and reduce its exposure to debate.

The most comprehensive bill passed during the McGuinty era was Bill 55, the Strong Action for Ontario Act. This 2012 budget-measures bill enacted a variety of austerity measures announced by Finance Minister Dwight Duncan in his spring budget speech. The bill was, in part, a product of the unique political circumstances of the spring of 2012. The Liberal minority government found itself in the difficult situation of trying to navigate restraint measures through a legislature in which the Progressive Conservatives, led by Tim Hudak, upheld an unofficial policy to oppose virtually all Liberal initiatives, regardless of their content, while the New Democrats remained naturally opposed to a policy of austerity. The Liberals made support for their budget-implementation bill a necessary condition for agreeing to NDP leader Andrea Horwath's demands during budget negotiations. Once it had secured the support of the New Democrats, the government recognized that it had been presented with an opportunity to pass several of its legislative initiatives, which had been stalled in the minority legislature, under the umbrella of its budget-measures bill.

The outcome of this political deadlock was a bill that was the province's largest since the Harris era. The Strong Action for Ontario Act amended fifty pieces of legislation and totalled 327 pages. It included a commitment to implement a two-year wage freeze on public-sector employees; mechanisms to ensure restrictions on public-sector-executive salaries; tax increases on the wealthiest Ontarians; a plan to sell off parts of the provincially owned rail service, Ontario Northland; an expansion of the mandate of the minister of natural resources to delegate certain responsibilities to the private sector; an allowance for the self-regulation of a number of industrial activities; and procedures to amalgamate smaller school boards across the province. There were numerous other reforms (Bill 55, 2012).

Michael Prue claimed that the bill was "Harperesque," referencing the federal Conservative government's tendency to use large omnibus bills to hide unpopular measures. For Prue, the government's intent with Bill 55 was to bury its less publicized austerity measures in the text of a 327-page bill in order to give members as little time as possible to digest their implications. He told the legislature that even the NDP's research team had had trouble reading through the bill before it was brought forward for second reading:

> It's taken a while for them to get through the tome – this is a tome; it's at least an inch thick of little tiny minutiae and details. But if you get into the environment, what you're going to see is that the laws to amend the environment and all the administration by the Ministry of Natural Resources – it's all in there – are all being amended without discussion, being hidden in a type of omnibus bill. (Prue 2012)

The opposition argued that Bill 55 ought to be split into several distinct pieces of legislation; however, by 2012, omnibus bills had become a well-established procedural mechanism of the legislature. While the opposition considered the use of such legislation lamentable, only a few members made more than passing reference to the omnibus nature of the bill during their debate time, preferring instead to focus on discussing the merits of its content. To underscore this point, despite its opposition to the largest omnibus bill in more than a decade, the NDP abstained from voting on the bill, allowing it to pass before summer recess.

During their time in office, the Liberals found the instrument of omnibus legislation simply too convenient a political tool to discount when attempting to pass controversial legislation. In using it, they maintained the practice of the Tories before them, entrenching it as a procedural custom. Peter Kormos summarized the menace of the Liberal omnibus strategy in his usual colourful way:

> It's not a healthy, not a good way to pass legislation. What inevitably happens is that it's like peeling back the layers of an onion: You think you've found the bad spot and sure enough, sure as God made little apples, you dig a little deeper and something else jumps out at you. (Kormos 2006)

The attitude of the Liberal government towards omnibus legislation was perhaps best expressed by Liberal member David Zimmer, who explained to the legislature that omnibus bills had been a part of the legislative tradition since 1994 and had become established as a parliamentary custom since that time. Indeed, he argued that omnibus bills had "become a regular feature of the Ontario Legislature, and this approach has become a model for several other Canadian jurisdictions as well. In short, they are a necessary element of good government" (Zimmer 2006). The Liberal era, then, can be characterized as a period of continuity in the use of the omnibus bill as a method of "greasing the skids" for the government's parliamentary agenda.

The Continuation of Harris-Era Practices: Parliamentary Governance under Liberal Rule

The Use of Time Allocation, 2003–2018

By the time the Liberals came to office, time allocation was long established as a custom of the legislature. For his part, Dalton McGuinty had devoted tremendous energy, both as opposition leader and during the 2003 election campaign, to opposing the Conservatives' autocratic approach to Parliament. In a 1997 speech to the legislature opposing the Harris government's continued misuse of its regulatory powers at the expense of Parliament, McGuinty pleaded with members to remember the importance of their roles.

> The Premier and the cabinet do not make the laws; we do, all of us here do … I say very directly to the backbenchers of the government: Don't let the train drivers in the Premier's office railroad you into going against the best interests of the people you were elected to represent. Don't forget those who sent you, and don't forget what you were sent to do. (McGuinty 1997)

Given his strong criticism of the practices of the Harris and Eves governments, there was considerable optimism that the Liberals would institute significant changes to Parliament to restore democracy to the legislative chamber. Indeed, in their inaugural Speech from the Throne, they pledged to "bring an open, honest, and transparent approach to government" and to "give all members an opportunity to do more on behalf of their constituents" by enhancing the roles that backbench and opposition members of government played in the daily proceedings of the legislature (Bartleman 2003). However, after a short attempt at conciliation with the opposition, McGuinty adopted an approach to House governance that, by the end of his tenure as premier, placed him alongside Mike Harris and Ernie Eves as one of the most anti-parliamentary leaders in the legislature's modern history.

Time allocation was designed to break deadlock in an era during which there were no constraints on the opposition's ability to hold up House business. However, the reforms to the Standing Orders, made during the Rae and Harris governments, rendered time allocation unexceptional since they set out clear time limits for debate at each stage of a bill's progress through the legislature. Under the Progressive Conservatives and Liberals, time allocation became an oppressive force, used by majority governments to exert their authority to restrict debate. The Liberals initially tried to avoid using time allocation altogether. They hoped to bring back the custom of setting the parliamentary calendar collaboratively with the support of the opposition House Leaders (McGuinty 1997). When talks with the opposition failed to result in a collaborative working arrangement for the House schedule, the government was presented with a decision: it could take the time necessary to debate each of its primary legislative initiatives, or it could expedite the process significantly by breaking its promise to restore principle to the procedure of the legislature and invoking time allocation. Ultimately, following the same path as the NDP and Progressive Conservatives before them, the Liberals would find the shelter of time allocation too useful a political tool to pass up.

So it was that, less than a month after its Speech from the Throne, in which it had pledged to restore democracy to the legislative chambers, the McGuinty government brought forward a massive time allocation motion, encompassing three of its signature pieces of legislation – Bills 2, 4, and 5 – two government motions, and a motion by the official opposition. In an unprecedented manoeuvre, the government brought forward the time allocation motion without using Standing Order 46, which dealt with time allocation in the legislature. Citing a precedent from the British House of Commons, it simply proceeded with a regular House motion to impose time restrictions on these initiatives. Doing so allowed it to limit debate without having to publicly admit that it was breaking a promise by resorting to time allocation so early in its mandate.

House Leader Dwight Duncan argued that the motion was "not time allocation or what used to be called a guillotine motion." Rather,

> This is a motion to program a bill or, in the case of this, a series of bills and motions and special debates for the remainder of the fall sittings. It's designed to move the legislature forward in a way that allows all members a full opportunity to participate in the important work in front of us. (Duncan 2003)

Instead of the "draconian and heavy-handed nature of time allocation," Duncan said, the motion was the product of more than three weeks of consultation with the opposition, and it merely set out a "program" for the remainder of the current sitting of Parliament (Duncan 2003). The opposition argued that while the motion did reflect the outcome of several weeks of discussions, negotiations had reached an impasse. While there was precedent for proceeding in such a manner through unanimous consent, the opposition had not consented to the motion. Thus, the motion functioned in effectively the same manner as a time allocation motion by establishing limits for debate through the bludgeon of majority rule (Kormos 2003b).

From the opposition's perspective, the government's motion was merely a time allocation ploy masquerading as a housekeeping matter. Peter Kormos argued that it was "designed to curtail debate." The government was using the guise of consultation with opposition parties to use a heavy-handed tactic, which, he argued, "quite frankly makes Standing Order 46 redundant" (Kormos 2003b). While time allocation corrupted the essential foundations of parliamentary supremacy, circumventing the legislature's Standing Orders was an even more dangerous precedent to set. In his speech during debate on the motion, Kormos issued an ominous warning to neophyte members of the Liberal government: they should understand that real decision-making authority was not located in the legislative chamber, but rather in the executive branch. Regardless of the government's lofty rhetoric during its first few weeks in power, he claimed, the McGuinty Liberals were demonstrating that they were no different from any other government over the previous two decades in Ontario.

> Parliament is not about government; Parliament is where government comes to have its policies and its positions challenged and tested. Government occurs in the Premier's office, in cabinet office, not in Parliament … I have no hesitation in telling you that I think I understand why the deputy government House leader would support this motion, why these sorts of pacts are not uncommon in history. I mean this style of governing is entirely consistent and in tune with what the Tories did for eight years. I admonish you, don't take any real pleasure in the fact that the Conservatives support you enthusiastically in your efforts.

> It, in and of itself, is not a good sign of anything. As a matter of fact, it should be the red warning flag; it should cause you to hesitate, step back and reflect. (Kormos 2003b)

By 2004, time allocation had become a routine government tactic to limit debate and advance the Liberals' legislation through the House.

The Liberals would again use time allocation, on 10 June 2004, as a means of passing their 2004 budget-measures bill. This bill was particularly controversial since it implemented matters related to the government's Ontario Health Premium, an increase on income taxes to deal with the $5.6 billion deficit left by the Tories. On this occasion, the government used Standing Order 46 as opposed to the programming motion that it had passed during the fall sitting. From this point forward, having already crossed the time allocation threshold, the government used Standing Order 46 only to expedite the passage of a bill.

Rather than justify the decision on moral grounds, Dwight Duncan went on the attack, accusing the opposition of having originated the use of time allocation. He pointed out that this was the first of the ten bills passed by the legislature for which Standing Order 46 had been invoked, while the Harris and Eves governments of 1999–2003 had used time allocation for 61 per cent of the legislation it had passed. He also made a point of recalling that the NDP, "lest they think they are as pure as the driven snow … set the trend for the use of time allocation motions." Given that the McGuinty government was using Standing Order 46 for the first time, Duncan claimed that his party had the lowest percentage of bills time-allocated "since way back in the Bill Davis government. We're very proud of that" (Duncan 2004).

During the 2004 fall sitting, the government began to customize the use of time allocation. It again demonstrated a propensity to use it on more than one piece of legislation at one time when it introduced a motion to restrict debate on Bills 106 and 149. This trend became a hallmark of the Liberal governments of both Premiers Dalton McGuinty and Kathleen Wynne. During debate on the motion, Michael Prue argued that the government was breaking its promise to enhance the role of Parliament by restricting debate on an omnibus budget-measures bill and another bill, which made significant changes to the allocation of forestry licences in the province:

> I would tell you, the minister's interest and the government's interest at present is getting through two very controversial bills today. They have invoked closure for one of the first times in this legislative session and one of the first times in this new government's mandate. I am saddened, because these two bills are without a doubt the most controversial bills that have been brought forward in this Parliament. (Prue 2004)

Minister of Public Infrastructure Renewal David Caplan acknowledged that Bills 106 and 149 were "very important" budget bills, but he too resorted to attacking the opposition parties for their records on time allocation when in power. He told the legislature, "Our government will not treat this House with the disrespect that the previous government did. Time allocation will be used, but it will be used sparingly; only on major legislation that is time-sensitive" (D. Caplan 2004).

Among the most flagrant uses of time allocation to this point in the province's history was the government's decision, in February 2006, to use it to restrict all debate on a recent report of the Integrity Commissioner of Ontario. The report made accusations against the minister of transportation, Harinder Takhar, for an alleged conflict of interest: failing to maintain an arms-length relationship with a family business, while serving as a Minister of the Crown. However, when the report was due to be adopted in the House, the government brought forward a time allocation motion; it wanted to avoid further debate on Takhar's actions by disposing of the routine procedure that members debate the adoption of any report by an independent officer of the legislature. Government order 9 was tantamount to invoking closure:

> Pursuant to Standing Order 46 and notwithstanding any other standing order or special order of the House relating to government order 9, when government order 9 is next called, the Speaker shall put every question necessary to dispose of the motion without further debate or amendment; and That there shall be no deferral of any vote allowed pursuant to Standing Order 28(h); and That, in the case of any division, the members shall be called in once, all divisions taken in succession, and the division bell shall be limited to 10 minutes. (D. Caplan 2006)

Progressive Conservative MPP Toby Barrett told the legislature that he was "disappointed" with the premier's "lack of action with respect to the reckless behaviour of his appointed Minister of Transportation." He continued his condemnation of the government's actions:

> Rather than choking off debate and compromising the integrity of this legislature, I'm convinced that the premier should be seeking his minister's resignation. I'm concerned that the members opposite are forced to sully their own reputations defending the transgressions of their colleague, defending the transgressions of their premier. This Takhar mess, this scandal, is contributing to our democratic decline. This time allocation motion, coupled with last night's time allocation motion and this scandal of which we speak, is recklessly destroying democratic debate and the sense of honour and the sense of principle that should exist within this chamber. This is a price that I'm not willing to pay and in fact none of us should pay. (Barrett 2006)

Two months later, Premier McGuinty quietly shuffled Takhar out of the higher-profile transportation ministry and into a junior portfolio as minister of small business and entrepreneurship. While the Takhar issue was only a minor scandal, it was emblematic of the McGuinty government's approach to centralizing decision-making in the Premier's Office, as the primary forum of political accountability, at the expense of the function of Parliament.

While the government's use of time allocation in the first session of the 38th Parliament reflected its efforts to restore democracy to the legislative chamber, by the second session it was using time allocation at a rate that rivalled the Harris and Eves governments. Although it brought forward time allocation less often during the minority 40th Parliament, the majority 41st Parliament under the premiership of Kathleen Wynne saw time allocation used on more than 40 per cent of the government bills that had received royal assent. (See table 9.1.)

The 2011 general election, which returned the McGuinty Liberals to power with a minority government, brought a temporary chill in the routinization of time allocation since the government was no longer able to command a majority vote in the legislature. To underscore this point, during the first session of the minority Parliament, the government brought forward time allocation on just two occasions in the nearly eleven months before the House was prorogued. On the first occasion, the government brought forward a motion

Table 9.1. Time allocation motions to government bills passed, 1981–2018

Parliament	Date	Number of government bills passed	Number of time allocation motions	Percentage of time allocation motions to government bills passed, %
32nd Parliament PC	1981–5	292	3	1.0
33rd Parliament LIB	1985–7	129	1	0.8
34th Parliament LIB	1987–90	183	3	1.7
35th Parliament NDP	1990–5	97	21	21.6
36th Parliament PC	1995–9	118	35	29.7
37th Parliament PC	1999–2003	111	67	60.4
38th Parliament LIB	**2003–7**	**109**	**28**	**25.7**
39th Parliament LIB	**2007–11**	**94**	**41**	**43.6**
40th Parliament LIB	**2011–14**	**25**	**4**	**16.0**
41st Parliament LIB	**2014–18**	**93**	**39**	**41.9**

Note: The bolded rows indicate the McGuinty and Wynne governments.

with all-party support to fast-track a bill to restrict bullying in the province's schools. It was one of the rare instances of collegiality in an otherwise fragmented Parliament.

On the second occasion, the government applied time allocation to the Putting Students First Act. Government House Leader John Milloy brought forward the motion after eight and a half hours of debate on second reading, citing a need to move the bill to third reading since the school year had already begun. Milloy assured the House that he recognized the "seriousness" of resorting to time allocation on such an important legislation, but argued that "there is urgency that's associated with this" (Milloy 2012). The motion passed with the unanimous support of the Progressive Conservative caucus, which had long advocated for a public-sector wage freeze.

The significant decline in the incidences of time allocation during the minority period of 2011–14 was primarily the consequence of the political dynamics of the 40th Parliament. Throughout the first session, both the Progressive Conservatives and the NDP demonstrated an unwillingness to support the government's agenda. This is perhaps best reflected by the fact that the Liberals were able to pass only nine of their bills in those eleven months. Thus, the decline in the use of time allocation was not so much indicative of a reluctance on the part of the government to employ it as it was a symptom of its inability to acquire the necessary support from the opposition.

The ascendency of Kathleen Wynne to the leadership of the Liberal Party in February 2013 had little tangible impact on the parliamentary impasse that had plagued the final year of Dalton McGuinty's tenure as premier. Despite her effort to make overtures to the opposition, both the NDP and the Progressive Conservatives continued to oppose a majority of her government's legislative initiatives.

The Wynne government brought forward time allocation for the first time on its budget-measures bill, the Prosperous and Fair Ontario Act. The bill passed with the approval of the NDP as a condition of the deal that their leader, Andrea Horwath, had struck with the government on its spring budget. Progressive Conservative MPP Randy Hillier expressed disappointment that the NDP would support time allocation after fiercely opposing it for nearly two decades since leaving office.

> They've been a very, very vigorous defender against time allocations and closures. I find it disappointing that the NDP are now throwing away that history, throwing away that commitment when, really, in time of minority Parliament there is no greater time and more important time to uphold that scrutiny of public policy and that demand and expectation for full and wholesome discussion and debate of the government. (Hillier 2013)

The New Democrats justified the decision as a necessary evil to ensure that the premier appointed an independent financial accountability officer, as she had promised Horwath during the budget negotiations.

In the fall of 2013, the Liberals struck an agreement with the Progressive Conservatives to pass a massive time allocation motion that would allow the government to usher several of its bills through the legislature before winter recess. The motion restricted the time provided for debate and committee hearings on eight of the government's signature bills. In exchange, the government pledged its support for a private member's bill, sponsored by Progressive Conservative MPP Monte McNaughton, that proposed to repeal a fifty-five-year-old law requiring one of the province's largest construction companies, EllisDon, to hire unionized workers exclusively. When the NDP opposed the enormous motion, the government intervened after six and a half hours to invoke time allocation on the debate over the original time allocation motion. The NDP argued that it could not support the government's package of bills because of the "poison pill" inclusion of the EllisDon anti-union legislation (Di Novo 2013).

The Wynne government brought forward a time allocation motion just one more time during its minority mandate. This was on the School Boards Collective Bargaining Act, legislation designed to establish a two-tiered system for collective bargaining with the province's teachers. The NDP supported the government on the motion by abstaining from the vote and allowing it to pass, despite opposition from the Progressive Conservatives. When the massive time allocation package of eight bills is taken into consideration, the record shows that the Wynne government applied time allocation to ten bills and one motion, despite passing only fifteen bills throughout the entire second session. Ultimately, the minority 40th Parliament featured far fewer time allocation motions than the two Liberal majorities that had preceded it.

Once the Wynne government was elected to a majority mandate in 2014, it returned to using time allocation about as often as the McGuinty government had during its two mandates from 2003 to 2013. As displayed in table 9.1, during the 41st Parliament, from 2014 to 2018, the government brought forward thirty-nine time allocation motions relative to the ninety-three government bills passed by the legislature: more than 40 per cent.

The McGuinty and Wynne Liberals cannot be held solely accountable for the proliferation of the use of time allocation at Queen's Park. The practice had been in use for more than twenty years by the time they came to office, and it became commonplace under the Harris and Eves governments. However, it was arguably under their watch that the practice became institutionalized as a customary aspect of House scheduling. While it might be possible to suggest that the misuse of time allocation during the 1990s and 2000s was a consequence of the Tories' radicalism, the continuation of this practice by the

Liberals, with a frequency that mirrored that of their predecessors, embedded it in the institutional fabric of the legislature.

As the Doug Ford government has made clear since it was elected in 2018, it seems unlikely that the misuse of process to hasten the implementation of government initiatives will decline any time soon. In the two decades since the Harris revolutionaries took control of the parliamentary process with the single-minded aim of applying their agenda in the shortest possible time, the role of the opposition – to scrutinize the actions of the executive branch – has been marginalized by all governments; instead, they have prioritized their own political objectives over the legislature's pivotal role as a forum for public debate. The Liberals did not invent time allocation, but they normalized its expanded use as a pillar of the institutional culture at Queen's Park.

The Turbulent 40th Parliament of Ontario: New Procedural Tactics Emerge

The 40th Parliament under Dalton McGuinty was the first minority government in Ontario in nearly thirty years. Given the increased marginalization of Parliament under successive majority governments, many observers of Queen's Park watched with interest to see whether the legislative branch would take on a more active role in governing the province. The circumstances surrounding the 40th Parliament, however, were complicated by two important political variables, which would preclude the opposition from working in tandem to influence government policy. First, the New Democrats and Progressive Conservatives were far from natural political allies, holding opposite ideological positions. While NDP leader Andrea Horwath moved her party towards the centre to be better positioned to win disaffected Liberal votes, the Progressive Conservatives shifted to the far right under the stewardship of Tim Hudak, thereby eliminating any prospect that the parties could plausibly work together.

Second, both parties took the view that, as the result of a series of scandals, the Liberals had lost the moral authority to govern, and this situation ruled out the possibility that either party would forge a lasting alliance with them. The result was a Parliament that had become Balkanized; in an intensely partisan political environment, all three parties were primarily concerned with positioning themselves for the next election. The Liberals, meanwhile, were left to seek out temporary and transient alliances to pursue their legislative agenda. While the 40th Parliament did produce a handful of bills that were the product of inter-party negotiations, the inability of the parties to cooperate created a hostile environment in which the Liberals sought out new procedural tactics to circumvent the legislature and protect their political interests.

By the spring of 2012, the McGuinty government had recognized that while it could not reach common ground with the opposition to pass much of its signature legislation, it could potentially do so by passing its budget under the cover of a confidence motion. Polling data were showing that Ontarians had little appetite for another election mere months after the October 2011 campaign, and the Liberals calculated that if a political party were seen to be provoking an early election, it would cause at least one of the opposition parties to support their budget. On this gamble, the government moved forward with an aggressive austerity agenda based on a report by economist Don Drummond, which had provided advice on how the province could reduce its debt levels. The government took the position that the principal features of the budget would be non-negotiable.

The Hudak Tories, in an intensely political move designed to absolve itself of any blame for the Liberal government's record in the next campaign, rejected the Liberal budget almost immediately after it was introduced in the legislature. This tactic placed the New Democrats in the untenable position of having to either support the most severe austerity budget since the Harris era or defeat the government and force an election. After two weeks of negotiations, the NDP struck a deal with the Liberals on a series of demands that saw the government include in the budget a tax on individuals earning more than $500,000, $242 million for child care over three years, a 1 per cent increase in social assistance rates, and $20 million for hospitals in northern Ontario (Benzie and Ferguson 2012).

Ultimately, the Liberals were forced to concede little. Despite negotiating with a social democratic party, the government was able to use the bludgeon of confidence, and the prospect of an election that a defeat on the budget would have triggered, to pass its budget with its overall purpose and essential features intact. Additionally, it was able to include in the deal an agreement with the NDP to agree to pass its omnibus budget-implementation bill and the eventual time allocation motion associated with it. Leveraging the confidence threat to pass omnibus budget bills is a practice the Liberals would turn to again during the 40th Parliament as it continued under Kathleen Wynne.

Contempt of Parliament: The Use of Prorogation as an Escape Hatch

The most pervasive issue to arise during the 40th Parliament was the inquiry into the government's role in the cancellation of two gas power plants, which had been planned for Mississauga and Oakville, during the 2011 election campaign. As an election loomed in late 2010, both Tim Hudak and Andrea Horwath promised to cancel the plants if they were elected as the province's next government. They undoubtedly sensed the Liberals' vulnerability on this critical local issue and recognized the importance of making gains in the crucial

905 region, a belt of suburban ridings surrounding Toronto named after its area code. Observers anticipated that this area would likely determine the outcome of the 2011 general election.

The Liberals initially refused to cancel the construction of the gas plants, citing the costs associated with ending projects that were already well underway. However, during the middle of a tight election, with polls showing that Liberal seats in Mississauga and Etobicoke were in jeopardy, McGuinty shifted course and announced that his government intended to cancel the plants, effective immediately. While the Liberals surely understood that the cost of ending the projects, which some projections suggested could be in the hundreds of millions of dollars, would have long-term political consequences, they determined that their immediate interests were of primary importance during a close election campaign.

Predictably, after the election, questions abounded about whether the government had been involved in a conflict of interest by making expensive policy decisions for the purposes of political opportunism. Government members denied that the decision was made for partisan reasons, but the opposition continued to press for an admission of guilt from senior members of the McGuinty Cabinet. The closest that any member of the government came to such an admission occurred during Finance Minister Dwight Duncan's annual summer appearance before the Committee on Estimates. When pressed by NDP MPP Gilles Bisson on the nature of the decision, Duncan replied that it was "a campaign undertaking ... at a time when I think we were still behind in the polls, so it required a government decision, which occurred after the election" (Duncan 2012). Duncan stopped short of admitting that the Liberals had cancelled the plants for deliberately partisan reasons, but by revealing that the decision had been made by the campaign team and then implemented by the government after the election, he implied that politics had influenced the policy-making process.

In search of answers, the opposition used its majority in committee to force the government to release all the documents related to its decision to cancel the gas plants. In May 2012, the Standing Committee on Estimates passed a motion directing

> the Minister of Energy as well as the Ministry of Energy and Ontario Power Authority to produce, within a fortnight, all correspondence, in any form, electronic or otherwise, that occurred between September 1, 2010, and December 31, 2011, related to the cancellation of the Oakville power plant as well as all correspondence, in any form, electronic or otherwise, that occurred between August 1, 2011, and December 31, 2011, related to the cancellation of the Mississauga power plant. (Leone 2012a)

In July 2012, the government released five hundred pages of emails, letters, and PowerPoint files related to the cancellation of the gas plants. Numerous documents were missing, and those that had been filed appeared to have been edited by government staff (Green 2013). The opposition was incredulous that the government would fail to comply with an order of a standing committee of the legislature and demanded that it hand over the remaining documents. When the legislature returned on 27 August, Progressive Conservative MPP Rob Leone argued that his privilege as a member had been breached by the government's failure to produce all the information related to cancelling the gas plants. The government argued that the minister of energy had been placed in a difficult position by the committee's request, since the matter contained sensitive solicitor-client information that was presently before the courts. Leone, however, argued that this excuse could create a problematic precedent:

> If we accept the government's central arguments against the release of these documents, namely the sub judice argument, the commercially sensitive argument and the solicitor-client privilege argument, the government could use such arguments to restrict virtually all information from the legislature's committees. This would be a precedent that would run against the spirit of openness, accountability and transparency in our democratic institutions. (Leone 2012b)

On 13 September, Speaker Dave Levac ruled on Leone's point of privilege. He determined that the Estimates Committee was "unquestionably entitled" to request the documents related to the cancellation of the gas plants, and "in the end the minister had an obligation to comply with the committee's call for those documents." In light of the fact that "the committee did not accept the minister's reasons for withholding the document[s] and persisted in its demand during an extended period of time" (Levac 2012), the Speaker ruled that a *prima facie* case of privilege had indeed been established. Rather than find the government in contempt of Parliament, Levac gave the three House Leaders ten days to find a solution to the situation that would satisfy the Estimates Committee. If no such agreement could be arrived at, he ruled that Leone would be within his rights to file a motion of contempt against the minister of energy.

The opposition later alleged that in the days that followed his finding of a breach of privilege, members of the Premier's Office had attempted to intimidate Levac into changing his decision. In an email that became public in 2013, senior McGuinty insider Don Guy allegedly wrote, the "Speaker needs to follow up his prima facie finding and change his mind." He further warned that Liberal staffer Dave Gene was "putting the member from Brant on notice that we need better here" (Guy, quoted in Ferguson 2013). Levac downplayed the allegations, claiming, "I have never felt unable to make an informed, objective and procedurally sound decision, free of political interference. The fact that the ruling did stand should also speak for itself" (Dave Levac, quoted in ibid.).

On 24 September, the Liberals released 36,000 pages of documents that they claimed were a full disclosure of evidence related to the gas plants. Still unsatisfied that the government was providing everything at its disposal, and after the House Leaders were unable to reach an agreement to satisfy the Estimates Committee, Rob Leone brought forward a motion requesting the release of the remainder of the documents and finding the minister of energy, Chris Bentley, in contempt of Parliament. The debate on the contempt motion consumed House business for the balance of the next week, as sixty-six members rose to speak. On 2 October, the House voted 53–50 to adopt Leone's motion for contempt. The Estimates Committee would then convene over the next few weeks to determine the minister's fate. If it reported to the House that Bentley had indeed acted in contempt, and the report was adopted by the legislature, he faced the possibility of a number of penalties, including being disbarred from the Law Society of Upper Canada and/or prison time. In the event of such a scenario, it would be the first time in the history of any Canadian Assembly that a minister had been found in contempt (Ferguson 2012).

During Question Period, Premier McGuinty excoriated the opposition for the contempt motion:

> When you use the full force of the Ontario Legislature, a Legislature representing 13 million Ontarians, against one individual member in pursuit of a contempt motion as a matter of petty, partisan, shallow, self-interested, mean-spirited politics that is fundamentally wrong. That is not in keeping with our jobs. (McGuinty 2012)

After spending more than a week debating the contempt motion in the legislature, the opposition moved closure to bring about a vote on the matter. McGuinty, no doubt sensing that he had now been cornered, told Andrea Horwath that her party's support for closure was "a departure of 20 years of principled history." He continued,

> It is remarkable, it is noteworthy and, frankly, it is unprincipled for that member to have supported that closure motion, which cut off debate, which would have permitted more members of the government here to speak to a very important motion. I ask her to look at herself in the mirror and understand why she led that departure. (McGuinty 2012)

There was a good deal of irony in these comments from a premier who had used his majorities to pass more than one hundred time allocation motions.

As the committee began its investigation into the contempt charges against Bentley, the Ministry of Energy released an additional 20,000 pages that it claimed the bureaucracy had not accounted for in its initial release in September. In a press conference, Bentley told the media, "I deeply regret that this happened, very disappointed. I am the minister, I am responsible. I had thought when the 36,000 documents went over that they were all there" (Chris Bentley, quoted in Spears and Benzie 2012). However, any hope that the Liberals may have had that the opposition parties would be satisfied with the release of these new documents was short-lived. Almost immediately, it claimed that this was further evidence of the Liberals' contemptuous attitude towards Parliament (ibid.).

Confronted with the inevitability of one of his ministers being found in contempt, on 15 October, Dalton McGuinty made the surprising decision to resign as premier and advise Lieutenant-Governor David Onley to prorogue the legislature. Prorogation accomplished two central objectives. First, it ended the investigation into the issue of contempt against Bentley, since committees require the authorization of the Legislative Assembly to sit while the House is prorogued. While the committee could have resumed its investigation once the Assembly had been recalled, prorogation gave Bentley the time to gracefully exit politics on his own terms. With the minister responsible for the affair removed from his portfolio, McGuinty hoped that the opposition would drop its contempt motion against him.

Second, prorogation gave the Liberals time to hold a leadership convention and find another leader without having to endure opposition incriminations in a minority Parliament. Progressive Conservative MPP Jim Wilson argued that the premier had resigned "with his tail between his legs to save what was left of his party and his own reputation." He continued,

> There's nothing in the annals of the history of this place to indicate that that ever happened before. To do such a selfish act, to close this place down so the party could, as he said, lower the conversation, lower the tone, to run away, scared to face the accountability of this legislature, is shameful. (Wilson 2013)

While the premier justified his decision to prorogue on the grounds that political gamesmanship by the opposition parties had made it impossible for Parliament to function, his decision to evade the investigation of a parliamentary committee was an unheard-of circumvention of parliamentary authority in modern Ontario (*Toronto Star* 2012). When the legislature returned in February 2013, Rob Leone reintroduced his motion of contempt against the government for withholding documents from the Estimates Committee. While the issue had lost the object of its inquiry with Chris Bentley's predictable resignation from the Assembly, the opposition remained committed to expressing its lack of confidence in the government. On 29 April, Progressive Conservative MPP Jim Wilson introduced a motion of non-confidence in the government for a series of scandals, which, the motion stated, the Liberals had been responsible for dating back to the 39th Parliament.

Wilson argued that to expect the minority government to return after the government had acted in contempt and then prorogued the legislature, and to expect the opposition to "just blanketly say yes to everything you ask for and vote on everything you ask for," would constitute a further degradation of Parliament (Wilson 2013). Premier-elect Kathleen Wynne claimed that it would be superfluous to have a confidence vote on Wilson's motion when

> the members in this House will be confronting a budget in the next very short period of time, and they will have an opportunity to express confidence or not in the government. That is the confidence motion that I think we need to focus on. (Wynne 2013)

However, Wynne used the budget as an opportunity to leverage the New Democrats into a difficult position among their own political base if they were to oppose it. The 2013 budget provided millions of dollars for increases to social assistance, a youth jobs program, extra money for home care, and a promise to reduce automobile insurance rates by 15 per cent. For the NDP to oppose such a budget, despite its opposition to the government's ethics, would be to alienate elements of its own political constituency. The NDP ultimately did support the budget, averting the prospect of an election. However, Wynne's decision to avoid bringing forward Wilson's motion of non-confidence denied members the opportunity to express their collective will on an issue of contempt by the government against the Assembly itself.

While the minority 40th Parliament will not likely be remembered for its legislative achievements, the contempt saga was, without question, the most important expression of power from a parliamentary opposition since the 1985 Liberal-NDP Accord ended four decades of Tory rule. The opposition's use of its majority to demand compliance from the government and to ultimately bring down the premier was, despite its intensely partisan objectives, an important expression of the rights of the Assembly to act as a censor on the executive branch. The minority Parliament also established new precedents for evading the Assembly. The McGuinty government's prorogation of the legislature established a precedent for usurping an investigation into allegedly corrupt activities, and Wynne's failure to bring forward the a confidence vote on the contempt issue broke with the convention to allow the House the opportunity to express its will when its confidence in the government was in clear question.

Conclusion

In the epilogue to his 2015 memoirs, *Dalton McGuinty: Making a Difference*, the former premier claimed that true leaders govern with a healthy dose of idealism, which he called "a shining beacon that draws us forward and illuminates our way" (McGuinty 2015, 227). However, while he was elected to office on promises to repair the damage done by the CSR and to bring integrity back to the legislative chamber, his record is decidedly mixed on both counts. Instead, the Liberal era under both Dalton McGuinty and Kathleen Wynne can be described as a period of consolidation, one in which the government did little to overturn the radical institutional structures left in place by its reformist predecessors.

Like Mike Harris and Ernie Eves in their respective tenures in office, the Liberals demonstrated a general disregard for parliamentary institutions, continuing the use of precedents such as the brazen application of time allocation as a regular feature of parliamentary business, governance by regulation rather than through consultation with the Assembly, and a continued reliance on omnibus legislation. Later in their mandates, the Liberals introduced new tactics, including prorogation, to evade a parliamentary committee that was investigating whether the government should be found in contempt of Parliament. Far from replacing the revolutionary parliamentary apparatus that the Tories had forged at Queen's Park as they implemented the CSR, the Liberals continued most of these practices, anchoring them in the tradition of the legislature.

What differentiated the Liberals' tactics from the patterns established by previous governments was that they were the first to make such abuses of procedure a routine part of their approach to Parliament, without any consistent appeal to an economic or fiscal crisis as a justification. Although previous governments had been able to claim the need to circumvent the parliamentary process due to "extenuating circumstances," the Liberals came to office during a time of relative political and economic stability in Ontario. Additionally, because the Progressive Conservatives had undertaken comprehensive state restructuring during their eight years in power, there was less need for major neoliberal initiatives throughout much of the McGuinty/Wynne period.

It seems that the Liberals continued many of the legislative precedents of the Harris era because it was politically expedient for them to do so, rather than for any dignified cause. This distinction is crucial because it highlights a transition at Queen's Park from using these tactics as an emergency measure, reserved for crisis management, to making them an instrument of political opportunism. Stripped of any overarching ideological or communal purpose, those approaches became a customary part of House business at the Ontario Legislature.

As the logic of neoliberal parliamentarism becomes more engrained in the customs of the legislature, it is easier for new governments to make use of old rules, which they once criticized in opposition, for their own expedience. This is to say that once the executive branch breaks norms, it almost always normalizes them as new behavioural practices of the legislature. Some governments may choose to use the mechanisms left behind by other governments fleetingly or in less assertive ways, but rare is the government that rolls back the time restrictions imposed upon the legislature.

When the Liberal government's agenda turned back towards austerity in 2010, it suffered little public criticism for cutting debate short and packaging its measures into large omnibus bills, largely because it had been using these strategies since taking office in 2003. By 2010, Ontario had reached a stage where it was able to accommodate the introduction of a new retrenchment program without causing commotion among either the opposition parties or the public.

As Northrop Frye understood, although the flavour of a revolution is originally determined by a break from tradition, its true historical character is shaped by the ability of its ideas to carry on beyond the revolutionary moment. In the Ontario case, turning back the clock would have required the Liberal government to restore the Standing Orders to at least their pre-Harris standards and abandon its general disregard for parliamentary institutions. By neglecting to make changes to the way Parliament was practised during the Harris years, and continuing many of the approaches used during that era, the Liberals entrenched the architecture of neoliberal parliamentarism in the practice of legislative governance in Ontario.

10 "Common Sense" Austerity Returns to Ontario: The Ford Government, 2018–2021

Introduction

The year 2018 will be remembered as one of the most tumultuous in Ontario's political history. It began in the dead of night in early January, with the bizarre spectacle of the leader of Her Majesty's official opposition, Patrick Brown, being chased down the stairwells of the Legislative Building by hordes of journalists, seeking answers to the allegations of sexual misconduct that had surfaced in the media earlier that day. To get ahead of the story, Brown called a late-night news conference in his office, which did little to quell the controversy. Within days, the Progressive Conservatives had removed him, a moderate within his party, as leader, and announced a leadership convention. With less than six months remaining until the next provincial election, and with the Progressive Conservatives leading in the polls, the outcome of this leadership race had significant implications for the party.

By March, controversial former Toronto city councillor Doug Ford had become the leader of the Progressive Conservative Party. He promised a sharp departure from Liberal policies and a return to the politics of disruption witnessed under the Harris government in the 1990s. With this twist of fate, the province once again fell into the hands of a devoted neoliberal reformer, who would use a political approach that echoed the CSR.

Stefan Kipfer (2010, n.p.) remarked that right-wing populists "are more convincing if they have some claim, no matter how superficial, to being 'outsiders.'" Like Mike Harris, Premier Ford sought to portray himself as the representative of the interests of "the people," pitted against the mythical idea of a downtown Toronto elite represented by the Liberals and New Democrats. He achieved this by suggesting that the "real people" were to be found outside "the bubble" of downtown Toronto. When you "get out of the bubble, you get out of the downtown elites and the bunch of lefties downtown – all they want to do is tax and spend. You get to the real people." Ford claimed that his chief objective was "protecting the real people of this province, the hard-working people," while the opposition represented irrationality and profligacy (Ford 2019a).

Borrowing a theme from his late brother Rob's tumultuous term as mayor of the City of Toronto, Ford tried to shape his image as a commoner around the idea that he gave out his cell phone number to constituents and returned their calls. In response to a question about government accountability, Ford told the legislature that "if you want to talk to the government, call me on my cellphone" (Ford 2019b). In support of Ford's claims, Government House Leader Todd Smith insisted that there were "many millions who actually do have his cellphone number … The premier is very loyal to that smartphone and gets back to as many people as he possibly can" (T. Smith 2019b).

The idea that Ford was an "outsider" fighting for the "little guy" was used to great effect during the COVID-19 pandemic, when the premier used a variety of platforms to publicly shame individual businesses that were price-gouging on essential items. "I hear that they're selling hand wipes for $30 a tin," the premier said in response to a question from the press about a Toronto store inflating the prices of cleaning supplies and hand sanitizer. "That's disgusting. Absolutely disgusting a company like that would be selling hand wipes for that cost" (Doug Ford, quoted in Higgins 2020). By periodically attacking an individual business, while maintaining a general devotion to the overall objectives of the market, Ford portrayed himself as having an intrinsic connection to the concerns of the common person.

This rhetorical approach allowed the premier to claim that he had a direct line to the people and, therefore, the ability to address their concerns. Consequently, parliamentary institutions were instruments of vested interests, which the Liberals and the NDP had used to exploit the majority through taxes. The premier claimed that legislative institutions privileged these interests and undermined his ability to effectively regulate market relations. Like the ways in which neoliberal theory has undermined the idea of government as practice, contemporary, right-wing populism has increasingly employed rhetoric portraying legislative institutions as impediments to attaining its objectives.

Those individuals, and, critically, the government institutions that acted counter to this process, frustrating it and slowing it down, were invariably framed as oppositional to the interests not just of the government but also of "the people." Ford claimed that the resistance of the leader of Her Majesty's official opposition, Andrea Horwath, to government policy was primarily about "protecting her political, paid activists" and the salaries of NDP city councillors in the downtown core (Ford 2018d). The New Democrats, he maintained, were primarily motivated by a need "to protect a bunch of downtown politicians. They create their little fiefdom" (Ford 2018b). They were at once elitist and out-of-touch radicals, having only their own selfish interests in mind as opposed to the interests of society:

> Their method is attack, attack, attack, rather than create jobs, lower taxes, putting money back into people's pockets instead of lining their own pockets, taking care of all their downtown NDP councillors and taking care of their political activists. (Ford 2018e)

By establishing a narrative that the opposition represented the interests of bloated government and the politics of personal interest and decadence, Ford presented himself as the embodiment of a sensible economic rationality. Democracy was redefined in economic terms. Ford equated the idea of career success with the chief function of government:

> I've seen it over and over again in business: Someone might start at a lower level, work their way up to middle manager, manager, and then they could be running the show. That's what democracy is about, that's what free enterprise is about: giving everyone an opportunity to grow. (Ford 2018f)

Parliamentary processes were reframed as tools used by the obstructive opposition parties, standing in the way of development and economic rationalism. Parliament was, therefore, invariably a hurdle to be overcome rather than a necessary and useful part of the law-making process.

This chapter offers an assessment of the Ford government's first two and a half years in office and the ways in which its brand of right-wing populism has impacted legislative governance in Ontario. Although the political realities of the COVID-19 pandemic interrupted its austerity initiatives in 2020–1, it nevertheless remained committed to the principles of fiscal restraint. During those first years, there was conflict at the Ontario Legislature such as had not been witnessed since the Harris era. However, unlike the mid-1990s, when the opposition parties were able to delay the proceedings of the House, the Ford government did not have to make major reforms to the rules of the legislature to actualize its restraint agenda quickly and resolutely. Decades of reform by previous governments had left in place a parliamentary apparatus already designed to implement legislation rapidly and with a minimum of debate.

The Use of Regulatory Authority during the Ford Era

The "People's" Health Act

The Ford government continued the approach of using delegated legislation to shield controversial issues and decision-making processes from Parliament. The People's Health Care Act granted the government the authority to restructure the province's health care sector as a means of saving money. The bill dissolved the existing Local Health Integration Networks, established under the McGuinty government in an effort to bring a modicum of local decision-making to health care policy, and replaced them with what it termed a "Super Agency" (Bill 74, 2019).

Bill 74 empowered the new Super Agency, which was to be appointed by and accountable to the minister of health, with significant powers to oversee the operations of the province's health care system. It would have jurisdiction over the administration of health services, taking on responsibility for the planning, implementation, and assessment of all initiatives. Critically, this function involved the supervision of health care spending, including responsibility for labour relations.

Section 29 of the bill stipulated that the Super Agency was empowered to "designate a person or entity, or a group of persons or entities, as an integrated care delivery system" (Bill 74, 2019). The highly general nature of this provision, and the lack of an accountability mechanism requiring the provision of public health services, led some to believe that it allowed for the potential privatization of health care services in Ontario. The bill gave Minister of Health Christine Elliott the authority to issue directions regarding the actions of the committee, thus granting her sweeping discretionary authority to reform the health care sector, including amalgamating, closing, or repurposing any hospital in the province. Instead, accountability was primarily defined in fiscal terms because the Super Agency was required at least once every fiscal year to agree to an "accountability agreement" with the minister. The act set out performance goals, standards, and objectives and established fixed spending parameters (Bill 74, 2019).

When news of the government's plans for health care reforms leaked to the press before they were announced, Elliott reassured Ontarians that the government was "continuing to consult" with front-line workers in the health care sector about these changes (Christine Elliott, quoted in D'Mello 2019). However, groups representing doctors and nurses said that the government had made no effort to reach out to their organizations during the planning stages for the People's Health Care Act (ibid.); they had, in fact, had only a twenty-four-hour window to make oral submissions. In just one day, more than 1,500 people applied for one of the thirty spots the Tories made available to make their submissions on the controversial bill (Crawley 2019). When asked about this in the legislature, Government House Leader Todd Smith told the Assembly that it would simply take too long to review each request to speak before the Standing Committee on Social Policy. Smith asked the opposition, rhetorically, "Do you know how long it would take us to get through that process of hearing from them directly? It would take us 50 weeks. It would take us a full year of inaction on this front" (T. Smith 2019a).

The Ford government also moved to eliminate the independence of the officers of the legislature through the enactment of Bill 57, the Restoring Trust, Transparency and Accountability Act. In addition to eliminating three offices of the legislature – the Ontario Child Advocate, the Environmental Commissioner of Ontario, and the Office of the French Language Services Commissioner of Ontario – the bill contained a provision that compromised their independence. Bill 57 included amendments to the Freedom of Information and Privacy Act to expand the authority to suspend a commissioner. It also contained extraordinarily vague language surrounding the suspension or expulsion of a commissioner, saying that the corresponding minister would be empowered to carry this out where the "Assembly is of the opinion the suspension is warranted" (Bill 57, 2018). This broad language could be interpreted as meaning a simple plurality of votes. If this were the case, a majority government could, so long as it could maintain party discipline, suspend an officer of the legislature, at its will, with a simple majority of votes.

The bill was subsequently amended at committee, after the government had "put some water into its wine" and accepted a two-thirds-majority threshold of members' support for suspension or expulsion. Nonetheless, a government with a significant majority could still direct the suspension of an independent officer of the legislature.

The Restoring Ontario's Competitiveness Act

The Ford government also brought forward a significant omnibus bill, designed to eliminate or weaken laws and regulations that had been put in place to protect the environment. Schedule 10 of Bill 66, the Restoring Ontario's Competitiveness Act, granted sweeping powers to the minister of economic development, job creation and trade to make regulations regarding the removal of perceived obstructions to private-sector investment (Bill 66, 2018). The government argued that a reformed process would allow it to respond more quickly to development applications. Furthermore, municipalities would have the option to use these "streamlined processes" to "act quickly to attract major employers" rather than working through the existing process, already set out in other government legislation (Ontario. Ministry of Economic Development, Job Creation and Trade 2018).

With the approval of the minister, municipalities could enact "open-for-business planning by-laws," which would exempt them from laws such as the Clean Water Act, the Great Lakes Protection Act, and the Greenbelt Act (Bill 66, 2018). Municipalities would be required to provide details about the economic impact of each development proposal. The open-for-business by-laws would supersede any existing municipal plans or policies designed to ensure that development applications did not threaten public safety or the environment.

Additionally, a municipality would not be required to inform the public that it intended to pass an open-for-business by-law, thus raising the possibility that it could initiate this process without the public even being aware that it was doing so before it was too late (McGrath 2018a). After considerable popular backlash to the notion that the bill could allow municipalities to "punch factory-sized holes" in the environmentally precarious Greenbelt surrounding the Greater Toronto Area, the government again backtracked, removing Schedule 10 from the bill (ibid.).

The Better Local Government Act

In July 2018, as hundreds of candidates for Toronto City Council seats were in the middle of fighting an election to be held in October, the Ford government made the unprecedented decision to redistribute Toronto's ward boundaries, slashing the number of council seats nearly in half, without so much as a single formal public consultation. Much as the Harris government had done with its municipal restructuring agenda, the Ford government used its executive authority to shelter its decisions from widespread public resistance. Schedule 2, subsection (4) of Bill 5, the Better Local Government Act, stipulated that the minister might make regulations allowing the province oversight over every aspect of the implementation process and in matters involving the transitional period during which the ward boundaries were being changed. Bill 5 also included a provision expanding this regulatory capacity to include *any* other legislation that might conflict with it. Subsection (6) stipulated: "In the event of a conflict between a regulation made under subsection (4) and a provision of this Act or of any other Act or regulation, the regulation made under subsection (4) prevails" (Bill 5, 2018). This provision permitted regulations related to the redistribution of Toronto's ward boundaries specified in the bill to supersede other regulations.

NDP MPP Peter Tabuns argued that the inclusion of this power to govern through regulation "undermines your power – our power as legislators – to determine what goes out and what exists on the ground." He argued that while members could "go into committee, we can try to amend it, but the minister will be able to rewrite as much as he wants." The result, Tabuns contended, was that Bill 5 "rolls back democracy" in the affected communities and further undermined the capacity of the legislature to hold the executive to account. He warned that "a lot of games can be played when vague legislation gives a lot of power into the hands of one man" (Tabuns 2018).

The Ford government, however, justified its decision on the grounds that fewer politicians meant for less government and additional cost savings. Minister of Municipal Affairs and Housing Steve Clark claimed that the existing forty-seven-member council "hinders decision-making." The government was not simply concerned with reducing the size of council to cut costs. Rather, it viewed democratic debates *themselves* as being inherently wasteful. Justifying the decision to reduce the size of council, he contended:

> Debates are time-consuming, inefficient and costly. Forty-four independent councillors, each with their own agenda and outlook, hamstring the city's decision-making on so many, many issues the city is facing. Allowing Toronto city council to then grow to 47 councillors, I think, would make that even worse. (Clark 2018a)

Bill 5, Clark claimed, would result in "a streamlined council that will be ready to make quick decisions in the best interests of the people of Toronto" (Clark 2018a). In addition to preparing for the quick passage of reforms, a more streamlined democratic process would have the added benefit of saving taxpayers' money. He contended: "The current 44-member council has created a huge challenge for Toronto's bureaucracy, which has to respond to motion after motion, report after report, deferral after deferral" (Clark 2018d).

Clark argued that the government "need[ed] to have this bill go through the legislative process as fast as possible" to ensure that council would be realigned in time for the October election (Clark 2018c). Doing so, he claimed, would

> help the largest city in the province run like a well-oiled machine, one that puts the interests of taxpayers first. Right now, council debates, discusses and argues. They ask for reports and more reports. They drown themselves in a sea of paper and red tape. But a streamlined council would make decisions effectively and efficiently and get on with the important work that they have to end gridlock. It could take on the task of building more housing. It could undertake the need for repairs of infrastructure. By doing this, it would create jobs, which our government feels is extremely important in getting Ontario open for business. A streamlined council is not just good for Toronto taxpayers; it's good for taxpayers in Ontario. (Clark 2018b)

From this point of view, debates and motions are understood not as necessary elements of a legislative institution, but rather as tools that opposition forces can use to interfere with the government's plan to deliver on promises to taxpayers.

Premier Ford said that the government would be "protecting the environment" and "protecting trees" because "it's going to be 500,000 less sheets of paper" by eliminating the need for more process and deliberation (Ford 2018a). For the Progressive Conservatives, the logic that had long been applied to the administrative state – that regulations and processes were largely wasteful and in need of streamlining – could be applied to democratic institutions as well. They became instruments used by "the elite" to obstruct the ability of the government to deliver on their promises to "the people."

The Notwithstanding Clause

The City of Toronto took the province to court on the grounds that changing the ward boundaries in the middle of an election, which was without precedent in Canada's history, was a violation of the principles of the rule of law and the rights of the candidates under the Canadian Charter of Rights and Freedoms. In his decision, Justice Edward Belobaba of the Ontario Superior Court struck down Bill 5, arguing that by changing course in the middle of the election, the province had "clearly crossed the line" and contravened the candidates' right to freedom of expression (*City of Toronto et al. v. Attorney General of Ontario* 2018). The judge did not hide his disapproval of the hasty way in which the legislation had been drafted or the way in which it was being implemented without public consultation.

Justice Belobaba also criticized the government for violating "the unwritten constitutional principles of the rule of law and democracy" by applying these changes so brazenly in the middle of an election campaign. He noted that the government was justifying its actions by relying on notions of "improved efficiency" and a "more streamlined" council, but that it had hardly considered the issues of voter parity and rights in debate or public dialogue on the issue. Furthermore, there existed "no evidence that any other options or approaches were considered or that any consultation ever took place." Instead, the legislation was "hurriedly enacted," so that it would be in place in time for the October election, "without much thought at all, more out of pique than principle" (*City of Toronto et al. v. Attorney General of Ontario* 2018).

When the Better Local Government Act was struck down by the court, the Ford government moved to immediately introduce new legislation to enact the notwithstanding clause. This clause is a provision in the Charter that allows Parliament or any provincial legislature to override section 2 or sections 7–15. This was exactly the purpose of Bill 31, the Efficient Local Government Act: it was substantively the same as Bill 5, with the exception that it included a provision invoking the notwithstanding clause so that the provincial government could proceed with the redistribution of Toronto's ward boundaries (Bill 31, 2018). This marked the first time in the province's history that a government had taken such an action.

Recalling his statement from the campaign that he would govern through "the people" rather than through institutions, Premier Ford displayed contempt for judicial interference in the policy process, calling the judge's decision "unacceptable" and vowing that his government would be "taking a stand" against it (Doug Ford, quoted in Rieti 2018).

Ford did not merely take issue with the substance of the decision, however. He questioned one of the core building blocks of a constitutional democracy – that the courts function as an accountability mechanism to ensure that governments uphold the principles enshrined in the Constitution. "I was elected. The judge was appointed," Ford said about the ruling (Doug Ford, quoted in Crawley 2018). He suggested that the government would use "every tool at our disposal" to preserve the integrity of the democratic process in Ontario, and he threatened to use the notwithstanding clause again, if necessary (Doug Ford, quoted in *City News* 2018). As part of his prepared remarks, Ford said, "I also want to make it clear that we are prepared to use Section 33 again in the future" (Doug Ford, quoted in Lilley 2018).

Ford argued that "the people" would have another opportunity to elect their government "in four years," but, until then, he would control the province. He continued, telling the legislature, "I'll tell you who won't decide: a politically appointed judge by one person" (Ford 2018c). Tellingly, he said,

> We live in a democracy. This is going to be the will of the people. We were elected by 2.3 million people to move forward and make changes in this province. (Ford 2018d)

Democracy, on this view, exists to serve the 2.3 million Ontarians, less than 20 per cent of the province's total population, who had voted for the governing party. That an unelected judge should upend the decision of a democratically elected government was inconsistent with an approach to government that viewed politics through a "winner takes all" lens and whose objectives were about fundamentally reshaping the structure of government.

Ford was calling into question not only the judge's decision but also the foundational tenets of the rule of law. Leo Panitch argued that the threat to make brazen use of the notwithstanding clause reflected a new terrain for "authoritarian Fordism." It "sought to alter the overall political balance of forces this government would face over the next four years by shifting the terrain to one of the few counterforces on its authority, the judiciary" (Panitch 2018). Having gained control over other moderating forces, Ford's threat to weaponize the notwithstanding clause constituted a further encroachment upon Canada's constitutional democracy.

However, while remarking that legislative processes led to "gridlock," the government was, at the same time, acknowledging that it was using parliamentary sovereignty as a shield for the premier's heavily criticized rhetoric about the role of the judiciary. The government appealed directly to the integrity of legislative institutions and the importance of the separation of powers from an activist judiciary in its effort to rationalize its decision to act so hastily to reform Toronto's City Council. In debate on Bill 31, Government House

Leader Todd Smith claimed that by applying the notwithstanding provision of the Charter, the government was protecting itself from overreach by the judicial function of the state. The legislature, he argued, was the "nativity scene of democracy." He continued,

> It is a sometimes noisy Eden; there is no question about that … If the House's rights can be offended or limited, as was attempted in this case – and it would have succeeded without Bill 31 – then we do not have a democracy. (T. Smith 2018b)

In reference to Justice Belobaba's decision, Smith said, "Once someone beyond the 124 of us enjoys the ability to tell this House when it can meet and what it can discuss when it does, then we cease to be a democracy." He continued, arguing that "you cannot only partially abridge the rights and privileges of this place. And when there is an attempt to, the House must condemn it. It must defend its own rights. We must defend ourselves" (T. Smith 2018b).

Although this perspective may seem at odds with the government's view that process hindered the free hand of the executive to "get things done," it was in fact consistent with it. The legislative branch should continue as a site of authority and legitimacy, but it should be deprived of its content, streamlined, and made subject to the control of the executive branch. Appropriately configured, parliamentary supremacy became a shield that the government can use to legitimize its decisions and protect its policies from the reach of the judiciary.

The Ford Government's Use of Omnibus Legislation

The Ford government continued the tactic of using omnibus legislation as an important instrument in its approach to Parliament, but as of early 2021, nearly three years into its mandate, it had not done so nearly as prodigiously as the Harris government did during the first phase of its neoliberal restructuring program. Although the Ford government had not hesitated to group multiple, unrelated bills together, it had not yet reached the scale and size of the omnibus legislation enacted during the Harris years.

In its first few days in office, the government brought forward an omnibus bill, continuing this now well-established approach to legislative governance. Bill 2, the Urgent Priorities Act, cancelled the White Pines Wind Project, proposed new accountability measures for the board of directors of Hydro One, and legislated employees at York University back to work (Bill 2, 2018). It was subject to time allocation and received royal assent nine days after being brought forward. Although Bill 2 paled in comparison to some of the omnibus initiatives passed by the Harris government, it indicated a willingness to use this approach.

Bill 57, the Restoring Trust, Transparency and Accountability Act, also made amendments to several unrelated bills and included 45 separate schedules. This is the legislation that, among other things, eliminated the three Independent Officers of the Legislature. In addition, the bill amended everything from the Financial Accountability Act to the Electricity Act (Bill 57, 2018). Bill 66, the Restoring Ontario's Competitiveness Act, also made multiple amendments under the nebulous notion of economic policy, which has been broadly interpreted in the neoliberal era.

Radicalism Returns to Queen's Park: Parliamentary Procedure during the Ford Era

The Ford government assumed office in June 2018 with an aggressive agenda to implement. Given that the Liberals had left the procedural architecture implemented by the Harris government during the 1990s largely in place, the legislature remained organized to accommodate a radical, aggressive agenda. While the Harris government had been forced to endure the longest opposition-obstruction efforts in the legislature's modern history during its initiative to amalgamate the City of Toronto, the Ford government came to office with a legislature already prepared to rapidly implement its agenda.

One of the first issues for the Progressive Conservatives was how to deal with what remained of the Liberal caucus, reduced to just seven members in the legislature. The Liberals – whom Premier Ford ridiculed as "the minivan party" (Ford 2018c), inferring that their caucus was so small that it could travel together in one vehicle – fell one seat short of recognized party status. As a result, the entire Liberal caucus would be treated as independent members, having to notify the Speaker of their intention to ask a question in Question Period, make Members' Statements, or debate on a motion or bill, rather than having time set out for them.

Given that the Standing Orders are subject to the will of the House, the government had the option to either reduce the threshold for recognized party status to seven or make amendments to allow the Liberals certain privileges; they had, after all, received more than a million votes, representing just under 20 per cent of the total vote. When the legislature was recalled in early July, however, the government quietly announced that it would not extend recognized party status or any other concession to the Liberals. They would sit as independent members, who would have to appeal to the Speaker for opportunities to participate in regular House privileges and would do so without the benefit of considerable staffing and research funding.

But the Ford government was not content to stop at denying recognized party status. On the understanding that if just one disgruntled government member were to cross the floor, or if the Liberals were to win a single by-election seat, they would be entitled to recognized party status, the Progressive Conservatives raised the bar from eight members from twelve. The government justified its decision to change the Standing Orders to increase the threshold on the grounds that the number of seats in the legislature had grown to 124 from 107 after the 2018 election. Government House Leader Todd Smith said that the decision had been made to "take the politics out" of the recognized party status issue by resolving it once and for all (Smith, quoted in Ferguson 2018).

The Return of the Zebra Mussels Bill

The new Parliament was not even a month old when the government made the shock announcement to unilaterally reduce the size of Toronto's City Council. This decision immediately intensified the already highly fraught and partisan climate in the legislature. The government introduced Bill 5, the Better Local Government Act, on 30 July and passed it by 14 August, without granting opportunities for public hearings, despite overwhelming opposition to the decision among Toronto residents (Bill 5, 2018). In protest, the opposition sought to use whatever tools it had at its disposal to slow down the business of the legislature and to encourage the government to at least take time for a full public debate on such a significant issue.

With nearly every conceivable option to hold up the business of the House closed off, the time had come for the NDP to take a symbolic stance. It did so by resurrecting the Zebra Mussels Act, used by Mike Harris while still in opposition to obstruct the Rae government's 1991 budget. However, because the Standing Orders had been amended to place a five-minute time limit on the introduction of bills, House Leader Gilles Bisson and the New Democrats could only place speed bumps in the way of the government's effort to rush Bill 5 through the House.

In lieu of this restriction, Bisson brought forward fifteen separate zebra mussel–related bills over a series of days, thus enabling the New Democrats to hold up proceedings for a grand total of 75 minutes. When he rose to introduce each bill, Bisson would proceed to read the next list of lakes and rivers in the title of the bill until his five minutes had concluded. The point, however, was to reflect the opposition's displeasure with the government's efforts to trample on institutional processes.

The New Democrats also brought forward several reasoned amendments, and used motions for adjournment where possible, to hinder the government's efforts to pass its agenda. When the government announced its intention to table Bill 31 to enact the notwithstanding clause, for example, New Democrat members banged on their desks in the legislature repeatedly, shouting "No!" to delay its introduction. When they refused Speaker Ted Arnott's directions to abstain, he proceeded to remove them, one at a time, from the House. The tactics were successful in delaying the government's tabling of the bill by approximately 20 minutes (Janus 2018). NDP leader Andrea Horwath claimed that her party had undertaken such a noisy and disruptive approach to "represent all of those people who are frustrated, who are upset with the actions of this Ford government in the choice they have made to invoke the notwithstanding clause and trample on people's Charter rights" (Horwath, quoted in ibid.).

Time Allocation

Where time allocation is concerned, the early indications are that the Ford government will use it simply as a conventional means of parliamentary business. As of January 2021, the government had moved time allocation on thirty-five occasions, while fifty government bills had received royal assent. During the government's first two years in office, nearly every government bill that passed was subject to time allocation.

However, the COVID-19 crisis represented a turning point in the government's approach to the legislature. In early 2020, as the reality of the pandemic began to set in, a temporary spirit of collaboration emerged: the major parties agreed to allow the government to pass its emergency legislation rapidly, and without time allocation, so that it could respond to the crisis. In a testament to this unique display of unity, each party sent only a minimum number of members to vote so that it could observe social-distancing protocols. This occurred as Premier Ford softened his public image; he sought to be less divisive and partisan. In this collaborative environment, the Progressive Conservative and NDP House Leaders were able to agree to avoid time allocation on other bills that came before the House. Nonetheless, as table 10.1 indicates, the Ford government made unprecedented use of time allocation during its first two and a half years in office.

Standing Orders Reforms

Efforts by the New Democrats to place roadblocks in the way of the government's policy agenda compelled the government to make a series of changes to the Standing Orders. In November 2018, Government House Leader Todd Smith brought forward reforms, which he argued were part of the government's effort to bring "trust and accountability back to Queen's Park" (T. Smith 2018a).

The government made four notable changes to the Standing Orders. First, it restricted any members from moving the adjournment of the House unless they had acquired unanimous consent. This change was designed to put an end to the use of motions for adjournment to delay the proceedings of the legislature. Second, the government deleted Standing Order 98(e), which required the Speaker to suspend the House if debate on private members' business had

Table 10.1. Time allocation motions to government bills passed, 1981–2021

Parliament	Date	Number of government bills passed	Number of time allocation motions	Percentage of time allocation motions to government bills passed, %
32nd Parliament PC	1981–5	292	3	1.0
33rd Parliament LIB	1985–7	129	1	0.8
34th Parliament LIB	1987–90	183	3	1.7
35th Parliament LIB	1990–5	97	21	21.6
36th Parliament PC	1995–9	118	35	29.7
37th Parliament PC	1999–2003	111	67	60.4
38th Parliament LIB	2003–7	109	28	25.7
39th Parliament LIB	2007–11	94	41	43.6
40th Parliament LIB	2011–14	25	4	16.0
41st Parliament LIB	2014–18	93	39	41.9
42nd Parliament PC	**2018–21**	**50**	**35**	**70.0**

Note: The bolded row indicates the Ford government; updated to 11 January 2021.

expired. This procedure had worked well in a legislature with three recognized parties, but now, with only two, some debates had time left over that was not being used. Every Thursday, at the end of private members' business, the House sat suspended for thirty-one minutes because the parties had completed their rotations and no debates were scheduled to fill the time. The government eliminated the suspension requirement to allow the House to carry on with regular business and put an end to what Smith called "this strange, bizarre occurrence" of a gap created by the lack of a third recognized party (T. Smith 2018a). But it placed a sunset on this amendment, allowing for Standing Order 98(e) to be reinstated at the dissolution of the 42nd Parliament.

The third change to the Standing Orders allowed five minutes for independent members' business during Ministerial Statements and Opposition Days, whereas they had previously had no formally recognized role. Fourth, the reforms changed the number of days that the House might hold night sittings at the end of a sessional period from eight to twelve (T. Smith 2018a).

While the changes to the Standing Orders afforded the government additional capacity to implement its reforms by further restricting opposition privileges, it chose to frame the amendments as helping to democratize the legislature by providing more time for debate. Smith maintained that the Tories were offering "a greater opportunity for the opposition to voice their opposition to what the government is doing." The purpose of the amendments, then, was to encourage the "efficient use of the House" and to "ensure that as much debate takes place as possible in here, not as little" (T. Smith 2018a).

Official opposition House Leader Gilles Bisson took exception to the government's attempt to portray its Standing Orders reforms as being anything other than a cynical effort to further undermine the privileges exercised by the opposition in its effort to hold the executive to account. He argued that the government was "not doing it for the good of the House; they're doing it for the good of their own government." He noted that had the government been interested in collaboration, "they could have invited the opposition, the official opposition and others, to discuss these matters this summer, about what standing orders could be changed" (Bisson 2018). Although the government claimed to be expanding opposition privileges by providing the potential for an extra four night sittings at the end of a session, Bisson noted that the real impact was ensuring that "the government is going to have more time to pass its agenda." For him, the Tory rhetoric was little more than an effort to distract from the fact that it was taking steps to further formalize the curtailment of opposition privileges:

> It's not a great gift you're giving to the House: it's a gift you're giving to yourself. It's like going to the Christmas tree, wrapping up your own present, putting it underneath, pulling it out and saying to the whole family, "Surprise!" All you're really doing is giving yourself a little gift. (Bisson 2018)

Bisson, who had been at the legislature since 1990, offered context spanning multiple governments, including his own party's term in office. He argued that governments nearly always claimed that the changes were "good for democracy and will add more to debate," but that this distracted from the fact that they were undermining the accountability function of the legislature in the process. Without some form of external incentive, Bisson argued, "governments never change standing orders for the good of the House; they always change it for the good of themselves" (Bisson 2018).

Conclusion

The first two and a half years of the Ford government's tenure in office witnessed the continuation of both the policy and the parliamentary legacy of the Harris era. Not only did the government seek to carry out an austerity program on a scale not seen since the Harris years, but it also adopted a corresponding and similarly aggressive approach to legislative governance. It did not have to make the substantial changes to the Standing Orders that the Harris government had made because the Liberals had largely continued to use them during their tenure from 2003 to 2018.

From a procedural standpoint, the Ford government did not establish many new benchmarks, but it made more than 70 per cent of the government bills that it passed subject to time allocation. It was only the unique circumstances brought about by the COVID-19 crisis, which fostered an all-party consensus, that led to a temporary relaxation of time allocation. Instead, what set the Ford government apart during its first two and a half years was the tone of its political discourse. Its populist rhetoric actively sought to eliminate the space between the premier and "the people," portraying legislative institutions as instruments of those who would undermine their interests. It assumed the argument long espoused by advocates of neoliberalism – that a sovereign legislature is antagonistic to the public interest – and applied it to parliamentary institutions in Ontario. The concentration of political power in the executive secured the state against the excesses of parliamentary democracy, which existed to serve entrenched special interest groups who make continual claims on the state.

Legislative process was thus recast as an instrument of "the elite" and thereby opposed to that of "the people," whose interests Ford purported to channel by remaining in constant contact with "the little guy" (Ford 2018e). Rather than standing in the way of Ford's ability to govern, institutions should be streamlined and flattened to allow the government to provide optimal service to the 2.3 million voters who had supported the Progressive Conservative Party in the 2018 election. The final chapter claims that this populist discourse reflects the rise of an authoritarian variety of neoliberalism that has emerged around the world in recent years.

11 Parliament in the Age of Authoritarian Neoliberalism

Introduction

This book has sought to grapple with the impact of neoliberalization over the last several decades on the way the Ontario Legislature functions. It has made the case that the political contradictions confronting governments during their efforts to implement contentious neoliberal reforms have necessitated reconfiguring the parliamentary apparatus so that they can pass legislation quickly. Reforms to the legislature have expressed themselves in two ways: first, as a battle over control for the time that must be spent debating and scrutinizing government business; and second, as a struggle between the executive and legislative branches for the right to subject issues of public importance to additional scrutiny.

While the shift in the balance of forces towards a more powerful executive branch can be attributed in part to an interplay of dynamics within the Ontario Legislature's own unique political culture, the demand to implement neoliberal legislation has played a critical role. This is evident in three central ways. First, several major parliamentary precedents were established to enable the passage of neoliberal legislative initiatives that had been met with opposition resistance in the legislature. Second, just as many of the major precedent-setting parliamentary reforms were introduced as part of the neoliberal reorganization of the province, so too was every signature piece of neoliberal legislation subject to at least one, and often several, of the parliamentary practices surveyed in this book. Third, the evidence suggests that, during the most aggressive periods of neoliberal reform, approaches designed to restrain the legislature were indispensable to implementing and actualizing the restructuring process.

The fact that the decline of the role of parliament in Ontario emerged at the same time as neoliberalism can be explained, in part, by the province's unique pattern of historical development. It underwent its radical transformation much later than most other jurisdictions. While the politics of Thatcherism gripped much of the Western world during the 1980s, Ontario experienced a revival in social spending under the Peterson Liberals. Although the Davis Conservatives did implement some restraint measures in the 1970s and 1980s, they stopped well short of the wholesale structural changes being undertaken to the state's administrative apparatus elsewhere. Meaningful attempts at neoliberal restructuring would not be made again until the final two and a half years of the Rae government, when the deficit-weary New Democrats implemented a variety of retrenchment reforms. They were not able to see their agenda through before being reduced to third-party status in the 1995 election, but the initial steps taken during Bob Rae's mandate blazed a trail for the radical restructuring process that was to follow during Mike Harris's CSR. This pattern of development led to a significant rupture in approaches to public policy and, consequently, parliamentary governance, as the neoliberalization process occurred rapidly under the Harris government in the mid-1990s.

As was most clearly exemplified by the conflict between the government and opposition parties during the Harris era, the historical contradictions created by neoliberalism have become subsumed into a political crisis within parliamentary assemblies generally. The reconfiguration of parliamentary institutions, or what I have called neoliberal parliamentarism, can be understood as being part of a broader reorganization of the balance of forces in society, as governments have made changes to institutions to make it easier to pass radical reforms. By limiting the effectiveness of parliamentary institutions, or avoiding them altogether, governments have managed to sidestep the deliberation, scrutiny, and consensus-building that democratic institutions are designed to encourage.

Reforming the Ontario Legislature

The emergence of neoliberal parliamentarism at the Ontario Legislature implies neither that the legislature has become an appendage of the executive branch nor that it has become a mere decorative relic of some past society that no longer corresponds to our own – although, if current trends persist, it is in danger of becoming so. It continues to play an important role in bringing public exposure to issues, holding the government to account during Question Period, and allowing for the examination and amendment of legislation at chosen intervals, for the passage of some private members' legislation, and for issues to be given consideration through parliamentary debate. Despite its imperfections, it also serves as one of the few institutional channels through which it is possible to hold power to account today.

However, when we look back at the configuration of procedure at the Ontario Legislature in 1981, we find that the legislature operates in a fundamentally different way today, and within the framework of a much more partisan and disruptive political culture, than it did nearly four decades ago. The critical moment at which the polarization of external events began to reshape its political configuration can be traced back to the early 1980s. As extra-parliamentary social conflict over the inflation crisis began to articulate itself in the legislature in the political discord between the government and the third-party New Democrats, the issue of fiscal retrenchment was reduced to a dispute over the amount of time it would take to pass legislation to enable the Davis government to pass its restraint agenda.

The conflict surrounding the passage of the Inflation Restraint Act represents the moment, insofar as one can be recognized, in which the trend towards a new form of parliamentary governance can be said to have begun in the province of Ontario. This story played itself out repeatedly over the next several years. Successive governments began using time allocation as an instrument to pass their legislation. It was not until the Harris era, however, that this approach to legislative governance was formalized and a coherent logical structure began to coalesce around it.

Today, we find a legislature much differently configured. Time allocation now serves as a conventional part of House business since the Standing Orders have been amended several times to guarantee that the government has the capacity to have its legislation passed by the House in a matter of days. The use of large omnibus bills and delegated legislation to circumvent the legislature has become commonplace. Although governments sometimes engage in public consultation and allow some legislative debate, nearly every controversial neoliberal reform since the Davis era has been rushed through the House using time allocation or one of these procedural approaches. Time allocation was initially used as a temporary mechanism to overcome legislative stasis, but it has become a customary element of House procedure at Queen's Park. The evolution of this process over four decades has left in place procedural rules that are able to rapidly institute a radical reform agenda.

The Periodization of Legislative Governance in Ontario

Bob Jessop (2019, 346) has argued that the history of neoliberalism can be understood as unfolding through "periodization," or the division of its development into a series of chronological periods. Jessop claimed that the establishment of "control over the legislature and executive branch in the face of opposition inside the government or from other forces" can be dated to the beginning of the neoliberal project in the 1970s and 1980s. This approach serves as one of the early and important variables entrenching neoliberalism's hegemony (347).

Parliamentary reform in Ontario may be divided into five eras, which cut across several different government mandates. The first period, from 1981 until 1985, can be defined as a period of *crisis management* in Ontario politics. Under the cloud of an economic crisis, the Davis government made unprecedented use of procedure to break legislative deadlock and secure the implementation of its restraint program. It is notable that Jessop's categorization of legislative and executive reform as the second moment in the emergence of neoliberalism is consistent with the argument presented in this book: that the beginnings of parliamentary reform can be traced back to the early stages of the neoliberal period; they were a necessary condition for its implementation (Jessop 2019).

The second era, which this book has referred to as an *interregnum* period, lasted from 1985 to the end of 1991 and encompassed both Peterson governments as well as the first years of the Rae government. During this time, the opposition parties pushed back against the government, beginning with the accord between the opposition Liberals and the NDP to end the forty-three-year rule of the governing Tories and culminating in a series of lengthy obstructions to House proceedings, which caused the government to amend the legislature's Standing Orders. This period was also characterized by a return to the principles of Keynesianism, as a temporary economic upswing, along with a series of tax increases, gave the government a considerable revenue base from which to draw. The practice of time allocation was continued, but it was used largely as a means of overcoming the stalemate that resulted from an increasingly partisan and divided House.

The third period, lasting from 1992 to the end of 2001, was the period of *neoliberal restructuring*. It began with major public-sector restructuring under the Rae government, through the CSR, until the retirement of Premier Mike Harris at the end of 2001. It is characterized by aggressive restructuring of the state apparatus, which was accompanied by extreme measures to circumvent Parliament and local democratic institutions.

The fourth period, from 2002 to 2018, was the period of *consolidation*. It witnessed the continuation of both the neoliberal state structure put in place during the CSR and its approach to parliamentary relations. The result was to make permanent the restrictive Standing Orders put in place by the Harris government and to ensure that the legislature's parliamentary apparatus was appropriately configured to accommodate future rounds of reforms.

The final period, which began with the election of the Ford government in 2018 and continues to the present, marks a return to the *right-wing populism* of the Harris era, with similar objectives for enacting an aggressive retrenchment agenda.

Neoliberal Parliamentarism and the Erosion of Forbearance

Levitsky and Ziblatt (2018, 106) claim that one of the elements most critical to the preservation of democracy is "institutional forbearance," which can be described as the exercise of restraint on the customary or unwritten rules that govern political systems. It is the glue that binds institutions together through a series of centuries-old, often tacit covenants, which hold that the preservation of political institutions and their processes is a shared objective, superseding partisan or individual motivations, and fusing the past, present, and future in a common objective.

Since parliamentary governance is determined by both formalized Standing Orders and centuries of unwritten tradition, the rules that are in place are, to a significant degree, determined by the restraint exercised by governments so that they act in accordance with the spirit of responsible government and democratic accountability.

The erosion of the standards of institutional forbearance has played a critical role in the decline of the Ontario Legislature. One of the characteristic trends of the last four decades has been the willingness of governments to test the limits of these unwritten norms by using them outside their historical context. For instance, time allocation had never been used at Queen's Park before the Davis government applied it to break a parliamentary deadlock. In the years since, its use has become customary. Similarly, before the Rae era, omnibus legislation was commonly used, but in a manner that was almost always benign. Governments from all three parties have failed to observe norms that have helped to maintain the integrity of the institution of Parliament. This failure has played a crucial role in the decline of the capacity of the legislature to effectively scrutinize the executive branch.

Neoliberal parliamentarism has emerged through a gradual erosion of norms, as boundaries have been pushed to minimize the spaces where accountability within the system may be realized. In the Ontario case, the clear trend has been that as one government has moved the goalposts, other governments, emboldened by these actions, have moved the goalposts farther and more aggressively. Such examples become enshrined as new precedents, which further incentivize governments to use them again, even when the original justification was to address an emergency or crisis by circumventing the traditional rules of Parliament. These precedents, like time allocation, often become so customary to the operation of Parliament, or expeditious to a government's agenda, that they are formalized in the Standing Orders. This allows the government to "lock in" its leverage over the opposition, ensuring that it is able to pursue its agenda unobstructed.

The opposition parties, too, have played a role in the decline of forbearance in Ontario. All three parties have engaged in tactics designed to deliberately forestall the process of law-making for primarily partisan ends. Although this process has, no doubt, played a role in the erosion of forbearance more broadly, the considerable power afforded to majority governments to determine the activities of Parliament has allowed them to use these instances as justifications for further crackdowns on House procedure. Opposition efforts to delay proceedings have served as a trigger for implementing neoliberal parliamentarism by providing the executive with the political cover to change the rules to its benefit, but it is ultimately the parties in power that have made structural reforms to procedure.

This is why it is necessary to study the trajectory of governance in a parliamentary Assembly over a series of decades, rather than a few months or years. Many of the most important changes occurred incrementally and became fully implemented as institutional practice only after many examples of precedent-breaking behaviour had occurred over several years.

The demand to overcome political resistance in Parliament during the neoliberal turn in the 1980s and 1990s served as a catalyst for curtailing the legislature's capacity to hold the executive to account, leaving in place a parliamentary apparatus at Queen's Park ideally configured to implement controversial policies rapidly.

Although the ascendency of the neoliberal orthodoxy was not the only reason for the decline of forbearance at Queen's Park over the last several decades, the embrace of an economic rationalism that viewed the dethronement of politics from the process of governance as essential to implementing neoliberal policy was a central force driving procedural change. Governments that were of both left and right political persuasions appealed to the idea of market competitiveness and fiscal efficiency as the primary public rationalizations for curtailing the capacity of the legislature to hold the government accountable.

Parliament in the Age of Authoritarian Neoliberalism

One of the objectives of this book has been to make the case that the rise of neoliberal parliamentarism at Queen's Park did not occur in a vacuum. Rather, it emerged in the context of a broader transformation in class forces under neoliberalism around the world that have required a weakened legislative apparatus to secure the legitimate actualization of policies that are inherently countermajoritarian. The declining popularity of neoliberal policies in the wake of the 2008 economic crisis, and the austerity measures that followed, have witnessed the fragmenting of neoliberalism's legitimacy and the rise of authoritarian forms of governance that can maintain the hegemony of the dominant class, while its popular legitimacy continues to erode (Peck and Theodore 2019).

The result of this "hegemonic unravelling" (Fraser 2019, 39) after the 2008–9 Great Recession was a realignment of political forces; it created an "unstable interregnum" that is likely to be characterized by political conflict and crisis as a new, sustainable governing coalition emerges (29).

The political morbidity of the present moment has resulted in a situation in which "actually existing neoliberalism continues to run on autopilot, as a default option with no positive legitimacy that persists simply because there appears to be no viable alternative" (Kotsko 2020, 461). Despite widespread popular sentiment that the financial crisis would bring an end to neoliberalism, the years that followed were characterized by deepening austerity and widening income inequality in most countries. Peck has argued that neoliberalism may have entered a "zombie phase," in which the essential features of its approach to governance remain, even while its intellectual and ideological foundations increasingly lose legitimacy among ever-larger segments of the population (Peck 2010, 109).

William Callison and Zachary Manfredi have recently claimed that neoliberalism's remarkable durability may be better understood by what they term "mutant neoliberalism." True to its chameleon nature, rather than fade from existence, neoliberalism has sought to consolidate its hegemony through "mutations," or changes to its "genetic code," and to adopt different, sometimes nationalist or xenophobic, forms to retain its legitimacy (Callison and Manfredi 2020, 3). Mutant neoliberalism subscribes to the view that, unlike zombies, mutants are "new life forms," which have the capacity to adapt and survive within challenging and rapidly evolving environments (4). Neoliberalism is "not on its deathbed but is instead splintering and mutating to survive in changing circumstances" (26).

In an effort to transcend this legitimization crisis, neoliberalism has transitioned to increasingly authoritarian approaches, which do not rely upon appeals to popular sovereignty to justify its hegemony. Ian Bruff contended that this period has witnessed the rise of "authoritarian neoliberalism," which involves "the reconfiguring of the state into a less democratic entity through constitutional and legal changes that seek to insulate it from social and political conflict" (Bruff 2014, 113). As neoliberalism has proved "increasingly unable to garner the consent, or even the reluctant acquiescence, necessary for more 'normal' modes of governance," it has turned to non-democratic solutions to carry out its objectives (114). Consequently, the authority of the state has been strengthened through the growth of a repressive state apparatus and the concentration of power in the executive branch, while, at the same time, it has become increasingly fragile, having been hollowed out and left to address "a range of popular struggles, demands, and discontent" (114).

In their recent article, "Still Neoliberalism?," Jamie Peck and Nik Theodore (2019, 263) reflect upon whether "neoliberalism's authoritarian (re)turn" marks its end, arguing that it seems to have "given up on its own future, as the horizons of even nominally free-market actions and imagination seem to be collapsing." Jessop, who had previously suggested that liberal democracy provided the best possible political shell for neoliberalism (Jessop 1993), recently reconsidered that theory in the context of the emergence of authoritarian state forms in recent years. He now argues that "the consolidation of authoritarian neoliberalism" has indeed functioned as "the best possible political shell" for the "still-evolving, and inevitably crisis-prone, predatory, finance-dominated accumulation regime," which cuts against the interests of the general population and requires a parliamentary form that can actualize these reforms against the headwinds of widespread public resistance (Jessop 2019, 359).

Erik Swyngedouw (2019) argues that the "alarming rise of autocratic liberalism" has been a characteristic feature of the latest phase of neoliberalization (269). He maintains that the rise of authoritarian approaches to governance are "a symptom of the deadlock produced by the contradictions and antagonisms that constitute present-day instituted post-democracy in its articulation with a deepening process of neoliberalization" (269). Contemporary authoritarian politics, in this respect, is "not the privilege of blinkered nativist and xenophobic populist right-wingers but is first and foremost the disavowed truth of the political and economic neoliberal project itself" (270). The present moment of right-wing-populist authoritarianism, then, is "an integral part – the other face – of liberal democracy itself" (271). As the contradictions of neoliberalism have intensified, particularly in the wake of the 2008 financial crisis, the state has been forced to further harden its political institutions, taking even more extreme measures to secure the implementation of neoliberal policy.

Matthew Ryan (2019), in reply to Bruff, contends that the concept of authoritarian neoliberalism, while useful as a means of understanding and categorizing the recent shift towards increasingly undemocratic approaches to the application of neoliberalism, can be misleading. He claims that separating the present era of neoliberalism from the past risks a conceptual separation that obscures the durability of authoritarian state forms under neoliberalism. Similar to Ryan's perspective, this book acknowledges that right-wing populism represents an intensification of existing trends, but holds that the gradual concentration of authority in the executive branch is a pattern that can be traced back to the beginning of the neoliberal era in Ontario and that was critical to the process of neoliberalization in the province.

This book has claimed that the institutional ground has been prepared for the rise of an authoritarian form of neoliberalism through decades of reforms to Parliament that have had the effect of minimizing the capacity of the legislature to hold the executive accountable. Not only has actually existing neoliberalism been actualized through the use of the strong state to overcome parliamentary and extra-parliamentary resistance, but it is also grounded in a logic that considers parliamentary sovereignty to be the primary cause of what its foundational thinkers believed was the crisis of modern liberalism.

As chapter 3 discusses, the foundational logic of the neoliberal intellectual tradition, espoused most clearly by Friedrich Hayek, but consistent with much of twentieth-century neoliberal thought, is steeped in a rejection of the idea of a sovereign parliament, which it understands as being institutionally incentivized to privilege rent-seeking special-interest groups, whose claims on public revenues interfere with the price mechanism and tend towards the tyranny of minority interests (Hayek 1982).

For Hayek, the liberal tradition became fatally corrupted around the beginning of the nineteenth century, when the scientism and rationalism of the seventeenth and eighteenth centuries merged with the constitutional radicalism of the Benthamites. The neoliberal perspective held that this new constitutional radicalism, which inspired the democratic reform of political institutions across the world throughout the nineteenth and twentieth centuries, led to the development of a political system predisposed to the constant expansion of the state.

Hayek believed that the granting of sovereignty to the legislature provided an essential explanation for the rise of welfare-state capitalism in the mid-twentieth century, which he claimed had defaced the classical liberal school to which the neoliberals subscribed. This position can be most closely associated with Scottish moralists such as Adam Smith and David Hume, who believed that knowledge about how to organize our social lives was best arrived at through spontaneous sources, in which no individual was responsible for designing the law; knowledge took its cues from the abstract, disparate, and unplanned outcomes transmitted through channels such as the market and tradition.

The expansion of the welfare state during the twentieth century, then, was primarily a *political* rather than an economic problem. Hayek believed that the conferral of sovereignty upon the legislature, granting it unrestrained authority, compelled legislators to behave in ways that were contrary to the community interest. He contended that in a parliamentary democracy, politicians were "mainly concerned to secure and retain the votes of particular groups by procuring special benefits for them" (Hayek 1982, 3:9). The problem was not the existence of a representative legislature, or even basing government upon popular rule, but granting legislators sovereignty to "command whatever they pleased simply by calling their commands 'laws'" (1:130). In the absence of a superior authority to "prevent the legislature from granting special privileges," there was "no limit to the blackmail to which government will be subject" (3:11).

Consequently, Hayek believed that the modern legislature should be deprived of its sovereignty and reduced to a largely technocratic role, regulating market relations and fine-tuning the agreed-upon general principles. This approach followed in the classical liberal, Lockean tradition, which held that individuals had already known how to live in a state of nature before government intervened in their lives. Accordingly, the role of the legislative branch should simply be to provide for "the laying down of rules of just conduct for the private citizen" within the framework of the general rules passed down through the common law (Hayek 1982, 3:22). A representative legislature should have limited power to make laws, and then only in accordance with the general rules common to individuals before political society was established, subject to revocation by way of revolution if these principles were violated.

This book has made the case that, at the Ontario Legislature, the concentration of political authority in the executive over the neoliberal period insulated critical decisions from the jurisdiction of Parliament and served as a counterforce to Parliament, thereby constraining its will. This strong executive has both enabled governments to pass controversial initiatives and kept the Legislative Assembly disciplined towards the pursuit of economic rationalism.

In this way, the concentration of power in the executive has served as a counterbalance to the powers of an unrestrained legislature to ensure that it did not legislate in ways that were inconsistent with economic reason or the need to cultivate a society based upon the rule of marketplace competition. Although neoliberal parliamentarism occurred in the context of a constitutional system with a sovereign parliament, the concentration of power in the executive functioned as a "check" against the powers of an unrestrained legislature, ensuring that the state was governed in ways that were consistent with neoliberal logic and the need to create the conditions for marketplace competition. The use by governments from all three major parties of fiscal and economic crises to justify reforms to parliamentary procedure in Ontario underscores the influence of neoliberal political rationality on legislative governance as neoliberalism has become hegemonic.

The essential features of this Hayekian anti-parliamentarism can be found in the rhetoric of modern, right-wing, populist politicians. The Ford government, for instance, commonly portrayed the legislative process as inefficient and superfluous, interfering with the timely and effective delivery of policy because it had become beholden to an obstructionist opposition. Taken to its logical extension, this approach eliminates the need for any accountability mechanisms, which largely function to insert themselves between the premier and his ability to deliver results for "the people." His government ought to have free reign to act without restrictions since curtailing such power amounts to undermining its capacity to cultivate economic advantage.

Both the Ford and the Harris governments openly embraced an anti-parliamentary attitude, attempting to portray the parliamentary opposition as out-of-touch elites who served special interests and the parliamentary process as a wasteful exercise of politics. This perspective holds that a government, captured by these competing interests that are pursuing "special advantages," leans invariably towards a system that is unworkable, inefficient, and ineffective, one in which everyone is in competition for scarce resources. Procedure is understood not as a necessary element of parliamentary systems, but rather as an instrument that these opposition forces and special interests can manipulate to interfere with the government's plan to deliver on promises to taxpayers and deliver efficient government. Parliamentary process is reduced to another systemic inefficiency that must be removed or streamlined to facilitate the government's reform agenda. When the government violates traditional institutional norms, it is doing what is necessary to "get things done" and to deliver on promises to taxpayers. This perspective conflates neutral institutions with partisan actors, creating the impression that governments are unable to function because the institutions *themselves* have been corrupted by these forces and are therefore antagonistic to the interests of "the people."

As we contend with the rise of increasingly authoritarian forms of right-wing populism, it is important to recall that the objective of neoliberalism's early thinkers was not to throw out liberalism entirely, but to "renovate" it by embedding the market mechanism as the primary end of government activity (Friedrich Hayek, quoted in Caldwell and Montes 2015, 303).

It was for this reason that Hayek believed that a liberal society, governed according to the principles of social justice and equality, was worse than a limited dictatorship. Of primary importance was not the extension of democratic rights, but rather the capacity to participate in market interactions, where the wisdom of discrete, individual exchanges could offer guidance as to how society should be organized. It was on these grounds that Hayek was able to justify the abuses of the Pinochet regime in Chile as necessary, during a time of crisis, to impose a market system (Caldwell and Montes 2015). A strong executive could protect the community from an omnipotent Parliament predisposed to state expansionism and market interventionism and could safeguard the general principles.

Parliament in the age of authoritarian neoliberalism is not a "dead letter"; instead, it has been repurposed to facilitate the implementation of contentious neoliberal legislation. This is a legislative form that has emerged to meet the specific political contradictions of the neoliberal era, actualizing a formal shift in the balance of class forces by extinguishing efforts at resistance within the legislative apparatus. The rejection of parliamentary sovereignty at the root of neoliberal thought has provided a theoretical foundation for this emergent anti-parliamentarism.

As the tides of authoritarianism wash across the shores of Europe and North America, there is a need today to better understand how institutional processes have held up against the anti-democratic forces that swirl around us. While the study of parliament has been neglected for decades as an object of serious academic analysis, changing realities should cause us to once again fix our gaze on our legislative institutions.

What is needed is a comparative analysis of the evolution of neoliberal parliamentarism so that we can establish the extent to which the process of neoliberalization has necessitated making changes to the practice of legislative governance to actualize its efforts at state restructuring. Doing so is essential – not merely to understand how parliamentary procedure has changed in recent years but also to recognize the way in which this shift has led to the present moment, one in which legislative institutions around the world appear more unstable than they have in decades.

References

Books, Articles, and Other Sources

Albertazzi, D., and D. McDonnell, eds. 2008. *Twenty-First Century Populism: The Spectre of Western European Democracy.* New York: Palgrave Macmillan.

Aucoin, P. 1986. "Organizational Change in the Machinery of Canadian Government: From Rational Management to Brokerage Politics." *Canadian Journal of Political Science* 19 (1): 3–27. DOI:10.1017/S0008423900057954.

Aucoin, P., and R. Heintzman. 2000. "The Dialectics of Accountability for Performance in Public Management Reform." *International Review of Administrative Sciences* 66 (1): 45–55. DOI:10.1177/0020852300661005.

Aucoin, P., L. Turnbull, and M.D. Jarvis. 2011. *Democratizing the Constitution: Reforming Responsible Government.* Toronto: Emond Montgomery Publications.

Bagehot, W. 1873. *The English Constitution.* 2nd ed. London: Chapman & Hall. First published 1867.

Bakvis, H. 2001. "Prime Minister and Cabinet in Canada: An Autocracy in Need of Reform?" *Journal of Canadian Studies* 35 (4): 60–79. DOI:10.3138/jcs.35.4.60.

Bates, T.S.N. 1986. "Parliament, Policy and Delegated Power." *Statute Law Review* 79 (2): 114–23. DOI:10.1093/slr/7.2.114.

Beith, A. 1981. "Prayers Unanswered: A Jaundiced View of the Parliamentary Scrutiny of Statutory Instruments." *Parliamentary Affairs* 34 (2): 165–73. DOI:10.1093/oxfordjournals.pa.a054195.

Bellefontaine, M. 2018. "UCP Leader Finally Dropping the Mask on His True Beliefs, NDP Minister Says." *CBC News*, October 15.

Bentham, J. 1830. *Constitutional Code: For the Use of All Nations and All Governments Professing Liberal Opinions,* vol. 1. Heward.

Benzie, R., and R. Ferguson. 2012. "Ontario Budget: McGuinty Agrees to Horwath's Tax-the-Rich Scheme." *Toronto Star*, 23 April.

Biebricher, T. 2019. *The Political Theory of Neoliberalism.* Stanford, CA: Stanford University Press.

Brodie, I. 2018. *At the Centre of Government: The Prime Minister and the Limits on Political Power.* Montreal and Kingston: McGill-Queen's University Press.

Brown, W. 2006. "American Nightmare: Neoliberalism, Neoconservatism, and De-democratization." *Political Theory* 34 (6): 690–714. DOI:10.1177/0090591706293016.

– 2015. *Undoing the Demos: Neoliberalism's Stealth Revolution.* Cambridge, MA: MIT Press.

– 2019. *In the Ruins of Neoliberalism: The Rise of Antidemocratic Politics in the West.* New York: Columbia University Press.

Bruff, I. 2014. "The Rise of Authoritarian Neoliberalism." *Rethinking Marxism* 26 (1): 113–29. DOI:10.1080/08935696.2013.843250.

Bryden, K. 1975. "Executive and Legislature in Ontario: A Case Study on Governmental Reform." *Canadian Public Administration* 18 (2): 235–52. DOI:10.1111/j.1754-7121.1975.tb01939.x.

Buchanan, J.M. 1988. "Contractarian Political Economy and Constitutional Interpretation." *American Economic Review* 78 (2): 135–9. https://www.jstor.org/stable/1818111.

Bücker, J. 1989. "Report on the Obstruction of Parliamentary Proceedings." *Constitutional and Parliamentary Information* 158: 243–64.

Caldwell, B., and Montes, L. 2015. "Friedrich Hayek and His Visits to Chile." *Review of Austrian Economics* 28 (3): 261–309. DOI:10.1007/s11138-014-0290-8.

Callison, W., and Z. Manfredi. 2020. "Introduction: Theorizing Mutant Neoliberalism." In *Mutant Neoliberalism: Market Rule and Political Rupture*, edited by W. Callison and Z. Manfredi, 1–38. New York: Fordham University Press.

Cameron, D., C. Mulhern, and G. White. 2003. "Democracy in Ontario." Research paper no. 35. Prepared for the Panel on the Role of Government.

Campion-Smith, B., and T. MacCharles. 2013. "Alberta MP Brent Rathgeber Blasts Conservatives as He Quits Party." *Toronto Star*, 6 June.

Cerny, P.G. 1997. "Paradoxes of the Competition State: The Dynamics of Political Globalization." *Government and Opposition* 32 (2): 251–74. DOI:10.1111/j.1477-7053.1997.tb00161.x.

– 1999. "Globalization and the Erosion of Democracy." *European Journal of Political Research* 36 (1): 1–26. DOI:10.1111/1475-6765.00461.

Charlton, C. 1997. "Obstruction in Ontario and the House of Commons." *Canadian Parliamentary Review* 20 (3): 21–8. http://www.revparl.ca/english/issue.asp?param=64&art=71.

Christie, A. 1985. "We'll Back Liberals, NDP Says." *Toronto Star*, 25 May, A1.

City News. 2018. "Doug Ford Invoking Notwithstanding Clause in Order to Cut Toronto City Council Size." 10 September. https://toronto.citynews.ca/2018/09/10/doug-ford-invoking-notwithstanding-clause-order-cut-toronto-city-council-size/.

City of Toronto et al. v. Attorney General of Ontario. 2018. ONSC 5151.

Coulter, K. 2009. "Deep Neoliberal Integration: The Production of Third Way Politics in Ontario." *Studies in Political Economy* 83 (1): 191–208. DOI:10.1080/19187033.2009.11675061.

Courchene, T., and C. Tellmer. 1998. *From Heartland to North American Regional State: The Social, Fiscal and Federal Evolution of Ontario.* Toronto: University of Toronto Press.

Crawley, M. 2018. "Doug Ford 'Won't Be Shy' to Use Notwithstanding Clause Again, and He's Getting Support for That." *CBC News*, 12 September. https://www.cbc.ca/news/canada/toronto/doug-ford-notwithstanding-charter-1.4818730.

– 2019. "Doug Ford's Health-Care Bill Provokes Avalanche of Public Response." *CBC News*, 30 March. https://www.cbc.ca/news/canada/toronto/doug-ford-ontario-health-care-bill-74-public-hearing-1.5076811.

Crone, G. 1997. "No Relief in Sight as Filibuster Takes Its Toll on MPPs: Party House Leaders Try to Find Ways for Vote to Proceed in Ontario." *Hamilton Spectator*, B3, 10 April.

Crouch, C. 2004. *Post-democracy.* Malden, MA: Polity Press.

Cruickshank, J. 1985. "Ontario Liberals Set to Take Power: It's Over; Tory Dynasty Toppled." *Globe and Mail*, A1, 19 June.

Decker, T. 1997. "Ontario Legislative Reports." *Canadian Parliamentary Review* 20 (4): 35–44. http://www.revparl.ca/english/issue.asp?param=65&art=83.

Dewey, J. (1935) 1963. *Liberalism and Social Action.* Vol. 74 of the Page-Barbour Lectures. Reprint, New York: Capricorn Books.

Dixon, J., A. Kouzmin, and N. Korac-Kakabadse. 1998. "Managerialism: Something Old, Something Borrowed, Little New." *International Journal of Public Sector Management* 11 (2/3): 164–87. DOI:10.1108/09513559810216483.

Djelic, M.L., and S. Quack. 2007. "Overcoming Path Dependency: Path Generation in Open Systems." *Theory and Society* 36 (2): 161–86. DOI:10.1007/s11186-007-9026-0.

D'Mello, C. 2019. "Doctors, Nurses Say They Were Never Consulted on Proposed Ontario Health Care Reforms." *CTV News*, 5 February.

Dodek, A.M. 2016. "Omnibus Bills: Constitutional Constraints and Legislative Liberations." *Ottawa Law Review* 48, 1–42.

Döring, H. 1995. "Time as a Scarce Resource: Government Control of the Agenda." In *Parliaments and Majority Rule in Western Europe*, edited by H. Döring, 223–46. Mannheim, Germany: Mannheim Centre for European Social Research.

Duffy, R. 1983. "Parliament Session Shows Urgent Need for Parliamentary Reform." *Toronto Star*, 20 February.

Duménil, G., and D. Lévy. 2011. *The Crisis of Neoliberalism*. Cambridge, MA: Harvard University Press.

Elgie, R., and J. Stapleton. 2006. "Testing the Decline of Parliament Thesis: Ireland, 1923–2002." *Political Studies* 54 (3): 465–85. DOI:10.1111/j.1467-9248.2006.00611.x.

Eucken, W. 2012. *The Foundations of Economics: History and Theory in the Analysis of Economic Reality*. Translated by T.W. Hutchinson. New York: Springer-Verlag. First published 1950.

Evans, B. 2005. "How the State Changes Its Mind: A Gramscian Account of Ontario's Managerial Culture Change." *Philosophy of Management* 5 (2): 25–46. DOI:10.5840/pom20055220.

– 2007. "Treading Water: Four Years of Ontario's Liberals." *The Bullet* (blog), *Socialist Project*. 23 September.

– 2008. "From Pragmatism to Neoliberalism: The Politics of the Remaking of the Ontario Administrative State, 1970–2002." PhD diss., York University, Toronto.

Evans, B., and G. Albo. 2011. "Permanent Austerity: The Politics of the Canadian Exit Strategy from Fiscal Stimulus." *Alternate Routes* 22: 7–28. http://www.alternateroutes.ca/index.php/ar/article/view/14414.

Evans, B., and C. Fanelli. 2018. "Ontario in an Age of Austerity: Common Sense Reloaded." In *The Public Sector in an Age of Austerity: Perspectives from Canada's Provinces and Territories*, edited by B. Evans and C. Fanelli, 128–60.

Fanelli, C. 2018. "It's Time We Dispel the Myth of 'Progressive' Liberalism in Ontario." *Huffington Post*, 10 October.

Fanelli, C., and M.P. Thomas. 2011. "Austerity, Competitiveness and Neoliberalism Redux: Ontario Responds to the Great Recession." *Socialist Studies* 7 (1/2): 141–70. DOI:10.18740/S4BS31.

Ferguson, R. 1997. "Filibustering Finished: Final Vote on Bill 103 Will Kill Metro Toronto." *Hamilton Spectator*, B7, 12 April.

– 2012. "Chris Bentley Could Face Jail Time If Found in Contempt of Parliament." *Toronto Star*, 2 October.

– 2013. "Ontario Gas Plants Scandal: Speaker Shrugs Off Liberal 'Intimidation.'" *Toronto Star*, 30 July.

– 2018. "Liberals Fall Further from Official Party Status after Ford Government Raises the Bar." *Hamilton Spectator*, 13 November.

Flinders, M. 2004. "MPs and Icebergs: Parliament and Delegated Governance." *Parliamentary Affairs* 57 (4): 767–84. DOI:10.1093/pa/gsh060.

Foucault, M. 2008. *The Birth of Biopolitics: Lectures at the Collège de France, 1978–79*. Translated by G. Burchell and A. Davidson. New York: Palgrave Macmillan.

Franks, C.E.S. 1995. "Representation and Policy Making in Canada." In *Canada's Century: Governance in a Maturing Society*, edited by C.E.S. Franks, 68–86. Montreal and Kingston: McGill-Queen's University Press.

– 1999. *Parliament, Intergovernmental Relations, and National Unity*. Kingston, ON: Queen's University, Institute of Intergovernmental Relations.

– 2010. "Omnibus Bills Subvert Our Legislative Process." *Globe and Mail*, 14 July.

Fraser, N. 2019. *The Old Is Dying and New Cannot Be Born: From Progressive Neoliberalism to Trump and Beyond*. New York: Verso.

Friedman, M., and R. Friedman. 1980. *Free to Choose: A Personal Statement*. New York: Harcourt Brace Jovanovich.

Frye, N. 1991. *The Double Vision: Language and Meaning in Religion*. Toronto: University of Toronto Press.

Gamble, A. 1988. *The Free Economy and the Strong State: The Politics of Thatcherism*. Durham, NC: Duke University Press.

– 2006. "Hayek on Knowledge, Economics, and Society." In *Hayek: The Cambridge Companion*, edited by E. Feser, 111–31. London: Cambridge.

Gill, S. 1995. "The Global Panopticon? The Neoliberal State, Economic Life, and Democratic Surveillance." *Alternatives: Global, Local, Political* 20 (1): 1–49. https://www.jstor.org/stable/40644823.

– 2008. *Power and Resistance in the New World Order*. New York: Palgrave-Macmillan.

Globe and Mail. 1982. "Ontario Tories Use Tactics of Ottawa for Wage Restraint." 9 December. Proquest Historical Newspapers, 5.

Goet, N.D., T.G. Fleming, and R. Zubek. 2020. "Procedural Change in the UK House of Commons, 1811–2015." *Legislative Studies Quarterly* 45 (1): 35–67. DOI:10.1111/lsq.12249.

Gramsci, A. 1971. *Selections from the Prison Notebooks*. London: Lawrence and Wishart.

Green, J. 2013. "Gas Plant: Timeline on the Life and Death of Two Gas Plants." *Toronto Star*, 30 April. http://www.thestar.com/news/queenspark/2013/04/30/gas_plant_timeline_on_the_life_and_death_of_two_gas_plants.html.

Harrington, D., and B. Walker. 1985. "Peterson, Rae Repeat Vow to Oust Miller's Tories." *Toronto Star*, A16, 5 June.

Harris, M. 2014. *Party of One: Stephen Harper and Canada's Radical Makeover*. Toronto: Penguin Canada.

Hart, G. 2013. "Gramsci, Geography and the Languages of Populism." In *Gramsci: Space, Nature, Politics*, edited by M. Ekers, G. Hart, S. Kipfer, and A. Loftus, 301–20. London: Routledge.

Hayek, F.A. 1973. *Economic Freedom and Representative Government*. London: Wincott Foundation.

– 1982. *Law, Legislation and Liberty*. 3 vols. London: Routledge.

– 1988. *The Fatal Conceit: The Errors of Socialism*. Vol. 1 of *The Collected Works of F.A. Hayek*, edited by W.W. Bartley. London: Routledge.

Helms, L. 2004. "Five Ways of Institutionalizing Political Opposition: Lessons from the Advanced Democracies." *Government and Opposition* 39 (1): 22–54. DOI:10.1111/j.0017-257x.2004.00030.x.

– 2008. "Studying Parliamentary Opposition in Old and New Democracies: Issues and Perspectives." *Journal of Legislative Studies* 14 (1–2): 6–19. DOI:10.1080/13572330801920788.

Higgins, M. 2020. "Doug Ford Declares War on Price Gougers Taking Advantage of COVID-19 Outbreak." *National Post*, 28 March.

Howlett, K. 2012. "McGuinty Calls On Ontario Public Service Workers to Accept Wage Freezes." *Globe and Mail*, 12 September.

Ibbitson, J. 1997. *Promised Land: Inside the Mike Harris Revolution*. Scarborough, ON: Prentice Hall.

– 2013. "Ignatieff: Too Much Executive Power Is Harming Democracy." *Globe and Mail*, 2 February.

Jackson, D. 1991. "Halevy Reconsidered: The Importance of Bentham's Psychological Epistemology in His 'Conversion' to Democracy." Paper presented to the Bentham Project Conference, University College London, March.

Janus, A. 2018. "NDP Kicked Out of Ontario Legislature as Bill to Cut Toronto Council Reintroduced." *CBC News*, 12 September.

Jessop, B. 1990. *State Theory: Putting Capitalist States in Their Place*. University Park: Pennsylvania University State Press.

– 1993. "Schumpeterian Welfare State? Remarks on Post-Fordist Political Economy." *Studies in Political Economy* 40: 7–39. DOI: https://doi.org/10.1080/19187033.1993.11675409.

– 2019. "Authoritarian Neoliberalism: Periodization and Critique." *South Atlantic Quarterly* 118 (2): 343–61. DOI:10.1215/00382876-7381182.

Karsten, S.G. 1985. "Eucken's 'Social Market Economy' and Its Test in Post-War West Germany: The Economist as Social Philosopher Developed Ideas That Paralleled Progressive Thought in America." *American Journal of Economics and Sociology* 44 (2): 169–83. https://www.jstor.org/stable/3486836.

Kipfer, S. 2010. "The Hordes at the Gate? Hard-Right Populism Defines Toronto Mayoral Election." *The Bullet* (blog), *Socialist Project*. 13 October. https://socialistproject.ca/2010/10/b419/.

Kipfer, S., and P. Saberi. 2014. "From 'Revolution' to Farce? Hard-Right Populism in the Making of Toronto." *Studies in Political Economy* 93 (1): 127–52. DOI:10.1080/19187033.2014.11674967.

Kirchhoff, D., and L.J. Tsuji. 2014. "Reading between the Lines of the 'Responsible Resource Development' Rhetoric: The Use of Omnibus Bills to 'Streamline' Canadian Environmental Legislation." *Impact Assessment and Project Appraisal* 32 (2): 108–20. DOI:10.1080/14615517.2014.894673.

Kotsko, A. 2020. "American Politics in the Era of Zombie Neoliberalism." *Public Culture* 32 (3): 453–63.

Lajoie, D. 2012. "Province Appoints Supervisor for Windsor-Essex RC School Board." *Windsor Star*, 28 August.

Leduc, L., and W.L. White. 1974. "The Role of Opposition in a One-Party Dominant System: The Case of Ontario." *Canadian Journal of Political Science* 7 (1): 86–100. DOI:10.1017/S0008423900037987.

Leslie, K. 2012. "Unions Go to Court to Challenge Ontario Bill Freezing Teachers' Salaries for Two Years." *Canadian Press*, 11 October.

Levitsky, S., and D. Ziblatt. 2018. *How Democracies Die*. New York: Crown Publishing.

Lilley, B. 2018. "Ford Makes Right Call to Trigger Notwithstanding Clause." *Toronto Sun*, 11 September.

Locke, J. (1689) 2014. *Second Treatise of Government: An Essay Concerning the True Original Extent and End of Civil Government*. Edited by R.H. Cox. Hoboken, NJ: John Wiley & Sons.

Loreto, R. 1997. "Making and Implementing the Decisions: Issues of Public Administration in Ontario." In *The Government and Politics of Ontario*, 5th ed., edited by G. White, 93–125. Toronto: University of Toronto Press.

Lyon, V. 1984. "Minority Government in Ontario, 1975–1981: An Assessment." *Canadian Journal of Political Science* 17 (4): 685–706. DOI:10.1017/S0008423900052549.

MacDonald, D. 1998. *The Happy Warrior: Political Memoirs*. Hamilton, ON: Dundurn Press.

Mackie, R. 2003. "Ontario MP Changes Name in Protest." *Globe and Mail*, 8 November.

MacLellan, D. 2009. "Educational Restructuring and the Policy Process: The Toronto District School Board 1997–2003." Article 11. *Academic Leadership: The Online Journal* 7 (4): 1–16. https://scholars.fhsu.edu/alj/vol7/iss4/11.

Macpherson, C.B. 1965. *The Real World of Democracy*. Toronto: CBC Publications.

– 1980. "Editor's Introduction" to *Second Treatise of Government*, by J. Locke, xvii–xxiv. Indianapolis, IN: Hackett.

Mair, P. 2006. "Ruling the Void: The Hollowing of Western Democracy." *New Left Review* 42: 25–51. http://hdl.handle.net/1814/6418.

– 2013. *Ruling the Void: The Hollowing of Western Democracy*. London: Verso.

Mallan, C. 2003. "Tory Backers to Provide Setting for Budget Day: Magna's Facility in Brampton Picked; Liberals Call Plan a Partisan Event." *Toronto Star*, A6, 22 March.

Mallory, J.R. 1953. "Delegated Legislation in Canada: Recent Changes in Machinery." *Canadian Journal of Political Science* 19 (4): 462–71. DOI:10.2307/138294.

– 1979. "Parliament: Every Reform Creates a New Problem." *Journal of Canadian Studies* 14 (2): 26–34. DOI:10.3138/jcs.14.2.26.

Malloy, J. 2004. "The Executive and Parliament in Canada." *Journal of Legislative Studies* 10 (2/3): 206–17. DOI:10.1080/1357233042000322319.

Manikel, T. 1992. "Ontario: Legislative Reports." *Canadian Parliamentary Review* 15 (3). http://www.revparl.ca/english/issue.asp?param=142&art=944.

Marcetic, B. 2017. "New Zealand's Neoliberal Drift." *Jacobin*, March.

Marleau, R., and C. Montpetit. 2000. *House of Commons Procedure and Practice*. Toronto: McGraw-Hill.

Massicotte, L. 2013. “Omnibus Bills in Theory and Practice.” *Canadian Parliamentary Review* 36 (1): 13–17.

McDonald, A. 2005. “Evolution of the Ontario Standing Orders since 1985.” *Canadian Parliamentary Review* 28 (3): 33–9.

McDowell, T. 2020. “The Origins of Authoritarian Neoliberalism: The Role of the Legislature in Implementing Fiscal Retrenchment in British Columbia, 1983.” *Critique: A Journal of Socialist Theory*, 387–403.

– “The People vs. Parliament: Hayek and the Role of Parliamentary Sovereignty in the Brexit Crisis.” *Alternate Routes: A Journal of Critical Social Theory* (forthcoming).

McGrath, J.M. 2018a. “Tories’ Bill Could Punch Factory-Sized Holes in the Greenbelt.” *TVO*, 7 December. https://www.tvo.org/article/tories-bill-could-punch-factory-sized-holes-in-the-greenbelt.

– 2018b. “What Losing ‘Recognized Party’ Status Could Mean for the Liberals.” *TVO*, 7 June.

McGuinty, D. 1997. “‘Megaweek’ Goal Is Hiding Taxes, User Fees.” *Toronto Star*, A17, 4 February.

– 2015. *Dalton McGuinty: Making a Difference*. Toronto: Dundurn Press.

Mellor, L. 1988. “Legislative Reports: Ontario.” *Canadian Parliamentary Review* 11 (2): 35–46. http://www.revparl.ca/english/issue.asp?param=125&art=773.

– 1989. “Legislative Reports: Ontario.” *Canadian Parliamentary Review* 12 (3): 32–40. http://www.revparl.ca/english/issue.asp?param=130&art=827.

Miliband, R. 2009. *The State in Capitalist Society*. Talgarth, UK: Merlin Press. First published 1969.

Mouffe, C. 2005. “Populism and the Mirror of Democracy.” In *Populism and the Mirror of Democracy*, edited by F. Panizza, 50–71. New York: Verso.

Munroe, H.D. 2011. “Style within the Centre: Pierre Trudeau, the War Measures Act, and the Nature of Prime Ministerial Power.” *Canadian Public Administration* 54 (4): 531–49. DOI:10.1111/j.1754-7121.2011.00191.x.

Nesbitt, D. 2012. “Kill Bill 115: Where Is the Ontario Labour Movement Going?” *The Bullet* (blog), *Socialist Project*. 10 December. https://socialistproject.ca/2012/12/b742/.

O’Brien, A., and M. Bosc., eds. 2009. *House of Commons Procedure and Practice*. 2nd ed. Ottawa: House of Commons; Montréal: Éditions Yvon Blais. https://www.ourcommons.ca/procedure-book-livre/document.aspx?sbdid=7c730f1d-e10b-4dfc-863a-83e7e1a6940e&sbpidx=2.

O’Connor, J. 2003. *The Fiscal Crisis of the State*. Reprint, New York: Transaction Publishers. First published 1973.

Ontario. Administration Institute Hospital Restructuring Committee. 1994. “Report.” 8 March. File B421107. Toronto: Archives of Ontario.

– Council on University Affairs. 1982. “Restrictions on University Deficits: In Ministry of Training, Colleges and Universities Amendment Act.” Policy Compendium.

32nd Parliament, 2nd session. Sessional Paper No. 334, 21 December. Toronto: Government of Ontario.
– Legislative Assembly. 2020. Standing Committee on Regulations and Private Bills: Mandate. https://www.ola.org/en/legislative-business/committees/regulations-private-bills/parliament-42/mandate.
– Ministry of Economic Development, Job Creation and Trade. 2018. "Proposed Changes to Create Jobs and Reduce Regulatory Burden in Specific Sectors." News release. 6 December.
– Red Tape Review Commission. 1997. "Cutting the Red Tape: Barriers to Jobs and Better Government." Final Report. Archives of Ontario. File: B803357.
Ontario Public School Boards' Association v. Ontario (Attorney General). 1997. Ontario Supreme Court, 4 August 1998. https://www.canlii.org/en/on/onsc/doc/1997/1997canlii12352/1997canlii12352.html.
OPSEU et al. v. Ontario. 2016. ONSC 2197.
Ottawa Citizen. 1997. "Opposition Filibuster Ends." A3, 12 April.
Panitch, L. 2018. "Authoritarian Fordism in Ontario Trumps the Far Right Elsewhere." *Toronto Star*, 17 September.
Peck, J. 2010. *Constructions of Neoliberal Reason*. New York: Oxford University Press.
Peck, J., and N. Theodore. 2019. "Still Neoliberalism?" *South Atlantic Quarterly* 118 (2): 245–65. DOI:10.1215/00382876-7381122.
Pierson, P. 1994. *Dismantling the Welfare State? Reagan, Thatcher, and the Politics of Retrenchment.* New York: Cambridge University Press.
Pilon, D. 2017. "The Contested Origins of Canadian Democracy." *Studies in* Political Economy 98 (2): 105–23. DOI:10.1080/07078552.2017.1342990.
Pond, D. 2005. "Imposing a Neo-liberal Theory of Representation on the Westminster Model: A Canadian Case." *Journal of Legislative Studies* 11 (2): 170–93. DOI:10.1080/13572330500158599.
– 2008. "Legislative Control of Cabinet Appointments to the Public Service: A Canadian Case-Study in the Political Limits to Parliamentary Reform." *Parliamentary Affairs* 61 (1): 52–72. DOI:10.1093/pa/gsm052.
Poulantzas, N. 1978. *Political Power and Social Classes*. London: Verso.
– 2008. *The Poulantzas Reader: Marxism, Law and the State.* Edited by J. Martin. New York: Verso.
Pusey, M. 1991. *Economic Rationalism in Canberra: A Nation-Building State Changes Its Mind.* Cambridge: Cambridge University Press.
Rae, B. 1997. *From Protest to Power*. Toronto: Penguin.Raney, T., S. Tregebov, and G. Inwood. 2013. "Democratizing the Ontario Parliament: Change, but Change Enough?" Studies of Provincial and Territorial Legislatures, 7 March. Ottawa: Canadian Study of Parliament Group.
Rieti, J. 2018. "Premier Doug Ford to Use Notwithstanding Clause to Cut Size of Toronto City Council." *CBC News*, 9 September.

Röpke, W. 1950. *The Social Crisis of Our Time*. Chicago: University of Chicago Press.

Russell, P.H. 2009. "The Need for Agreement on Fundamental Conventions of Parliamentary Democracy." *National Journal of Constitutional Law* 27 (1): 205–15.

Russell, P.H., and L. Sossin, eds. 2009. *Parliamentary Democracy in Crisis*. Toronto: University of Toronto Press.

Rutherford, G.W. 1914. "Some Aspects of Parliamentary Obstruction." *Sewanee Review* 22 (2): 166–80.

Ryan, M.D. 2019. "Interrogating 'Authoritarian Neoliberalism': The Problem of Periodization." *Competition & Change* 23 (2): 116–37. DOI:10.1177/1024529418797867.

Savoie, D. 1999. *Governing from the Centre: The Concentration of Power in Canadian Politics*. Toronto: University of Toronto Press.

– 2010. *Power: Where Is It?* Montreal and Kingston: McGill-Queen's University Press.

Schindeler, F.F. 1969. *Responsible Government in Ontario*. Toronto: University of Toronto Press.

Sibenik, P. 1989. "Legislative Reports: Ontario." *Canadian Parliamentary Review* 12 (4): 32–41. http://www.revparl.ca/english/issue.asp?param=131&art=466.

Smith, D. 1979. "President and Parliament: The Transformation of Parliamentary Government in Canada." In *The Canadian Political Process*, 3rd ed., edited by R. Schultz, O.M. Kruhlak, and J.C. Terry, 305–25. Toronto: Holt, Rinehart and Winston of Canada.

– 2013. *The Invisible Crown: The First Principle of Canadian Government*. Toronto: University of Toronto Press; Halifax: Science Association.

Spears, J., and R. Benzie. 2012. "Liberals Release an Additional 20,000 Pages on Power-Plant Closures amid 'Cover-Up' Charges." *Toronto Star*, 13 October.

Speirs, R. 1985. "PCs to Be Defeated Gracefully." *Toronto Star*, A8, 25 May.

Statistics Canada. 2011. "Direct Taxes from Persons and Contributions to Social Insurance Plans and Other Transfers to Government, Provincial Economic Accounts, Annual, 1981–2009." CANSIM (Table 384-0006).

– 2015a. "Estimates of Population, by Age Group and Sex for July 1: Canada, Provinces and Territories, Annual." CANSIM (Table 051-0001).

– 2015b. "Gross Domestic Product, Expenditure-Based, Provincial and Territorial, Annual." CANSIM (Table 384-0038).

– 2016. "Labour Force Survey Estimates by Sex and Age Group, Seasonally Adjusted and Unadjusted, Annual." CANSIM (Table 282-0087).

Streeck, W. 2011. "The Crises of Democratic Capitalism." *New Left Review* 71 (Sept/Oct): 5–29.

– 2014. *Buying Time: The Delayed Crisis of Democratic Capitalism*. London: Verso Books.

Strom, K. 2000. "Delegation and Accountability in Parliamentary Democracies." *European Journal of Political Research* 37 (3): 261–90. DOI:10.1023/A:1007064803327.

Sutherland, S. 2009. "The Current State of Research Activities on the Parliament of Canada: Summary of Published Scholarship on Canadian Institutions and Scholars' Activities Other Than Publication, June 2009." Ottawa: Library of Parliament.

Swyngedouw, E. 1996. "Reconstructing Citizenship, the Re-scaling of the State and the New Authoritarianism: Closing the Belgian Mines." *Urban Studies* 33 (8): 1499–521. DOI:10.1080/0042098966772.

– 2019. "The Perverse Lure of Autocratic Postdemocracy." *South Atlantic Quarterly* 118 (2): 267–86. DOI:10.1215/00382876-7381134.

Taggart, M. 2005. "From 'Parliamentary Powers' to Privatization: The Chequered History of Delegated Legislation in the Twentieth Century." *University of Toronto Law Journal* 55 (3): 575–627. DOI:10.1353/tlj.2005.0030.

Thomas, P.G. 2004. "Governing from the Centre: Reconceptualizing the Role of the PM and Cabinet." *Policy Options* (December 2003–January 2004): 79–85.

– 2010. "Parliament and Legislatures: Central to Canadian Democracy?" In *The Oxford Handbook of Canadian Politics*, edited by J.C. Courtney and D.E. Smith, 153–71. Toronto: Oxford University Press.

Toronto Star. 2012. "Ontario Premier Dalton McGuinty Has No Good Reason to Prorogue Legislature." 16 October.

Walker, B. 1985a. "Aird, Rae Sip Coffee at Meeting to Describe Deal." *Toronto Star*, A19, 30 May.

– 1985b. "Rae Says He Rejected Tories Because They Were Inflexible." *Toronto Star*, A1, 25 May.

Walker, W. 1997. "Tories Begin Battle to Dispel Megaweek Confusion." *Toronto Star*, 18 January.

Weller, P. 2003. "Cabinet Government: An Elusive Deal?" *Public Administration* 81 (4): 701–22. DOI:10.1111/j.0033-3298.2003.00368.x.

White, G. 1979. "Teaching the Mongrel Dog New Tricks: Sources and Directions of Reform in the Ontario Legislature." *Journal of Canadian Studies* 14 (2): 117–32. DOI:10.3138/jcs.14.2.117.

– 1980. "The Life and Times of the Camp Commission." *Canadian Journal of Political Science* 13 (2): 357–75. DOI:10.1017/S0008423900033060.

Žižek, S. 2000. *The Ticklish Subject*. London: Verso.

– 2008. *Violence: Six Sideways Reflections*. New York: Picador.

Debates of the Legislative Assembly

Aird, J.B. 1985, 4 June. "Speech from the Throne." 33rd Parliament, 1st Session. http://www.ontla.on.ca/web/house-proceedings/house_detail.do?Date=1985-06-04&Parl=33&Sess=1&locale=en.

Alexander, L. 1990, 20 November. Speech from the Throne. 35th Parliament, 1st Session. http://www.ontla.on.ca/web/house-proceedings/house_detail.do?Date=1990-11-20&Parl=35&Sess=1&locale=en.

Baird, J. 2003, 14 May. Contempt of Parliament. 37th Parliament, 4th Session. http://hansardindex.ontla.on.ca/hansardeissue/37-4/l009.htm.

Barrett, T. 2006, 1 March. Time allocation. 38th Parliament, 2nd Session. http://hansardindex.ontla.on.ca/hansardeissue/38-2/l046b.htm.

Bartleman, J. 2003, 20 November. Speech from the Throne. 38th Parliament, 1st Session. http://www.ontla.on.ca/web/house-proceedings/house_detail.do?Date=2003-11-20&Parl=38&Sess=1&locale=en#P80_4617.

Bisson, G. 1992, 6 May. Gasoline Tax Amendment Act. 35th Parliament, 2nd Session. http://www.ontla.on.ca/web/house-proceedings/house_detail.do?Date=1992-05-06&Parl=35&Sess=2&locale=en.

– 1997, 16 December. Time Allocation. 36th Parliament, 1st Session. http://www.olip.ontla.on.ca/hansardeissue/36-1/l262b.htm.

– 2018, 13 September. Standing Orders. 42nd Parliament, 1st Session. https://www.ola.org/en/legislative-business/house-documents/parliament-42/session-1/2018-09-13/hansard.

Bradley, J. 1983, 23 February. Municipality of Metropolitan Toronto Amendment Act. 32nd Parliament, 2nd Session. http://hansardindex.ontla.on.ca/hansardeissue/32-2/l222.htm.

– 1993, 23 June. Social Contract. 35th Parliament, 3rd Session. http://hansardindex.ontla.on.ca/hansardeissue/35-3/l037a.htm.

– 1994a, 2 November. Time Allocation. 35th Parliament, 3rd Session. http://hansardindex.ontla.on.ca/hansardecat/35-3/l152-7.htm.

– 1994b, 28 November. Legislative Debate. 35th Parliament, 3rd Session. http://www.ontla.on.ca/web/house-proceedings/house_detail.do?Date=1994-11-28&Parl=35&Sess=3&locale=en.

– 1997a, 16 June. Standing Orders Reform. 36th Parliament, 1st Session. http://www.ontla.on.ca/web/house-proceedings/house_detail.do?Date=1997-06-16&Parl=36&Sess=1&locale=en#P347_94941.

– 1997b, 16 December. Time Allocation. 36th Parliament, 1st Session. http://www.ontla.on.ca/web/house-proceedings/house_detail.do?locale=en&Date=1997-12-16&Parl=36&Sess=1&detailPage=/house-proceedings/transcripts/files_html/1997-12-16_L262b.htm#tidyout.

– 1999, 20 December. Fewer Politicians Act. 37th Parliament, 1st Session. http://hansardindex.ontla.on.ca/hansardeissue/37-1/l031b.htm.

Breaugh, M. 1984, 25 June. Time Allocation. 32nd Parliament, 4th Session. http://hansardindex.ontla.on.ca/hansardeissue/32-4/l081.htm.

– 1989, 25 July. Standing Orders. 34th Parliament, 2nd Session. http://hansardindex.ontla.on.ca/hansardetitle/34-2/l047-54.html.

Broten, L. 2012, 28 August. Putting Students First Act. 40th Parliament, 1st Session. http://www.ontla.on.ca/web/house-proceedings/house_detail.do?Date=2012-08-28&Parl=40&Sess=1&locale=en#P817_203662.

Bryant, M. 2003, 9 December. Democratic Renewal. 38th Parliament, 1st Session. http://hansardindex.ontla.on.ca/hansardeissue/38-1/l012a.htm.

Caplan, D. 2004, 7 December. Time Allocation. 38th Parliament, 1st Session. http://www.ontla.on.ca/web/house-proceedings/house_detail.do?Date=2004-12-07&Parl=38&Sess=1&locale=en#P425_96892.

– 2006, 1 March. Time Allocation. 38th Parliament, 2nd Session. http://hansardindex.ontla.on.ca/hansardeissue/38-2/l046b.htm.

Caplan, E. 1994, 23 June. Budget Measures Act. 35th Parliament, 3rd Session. http://hansardindex.ontla.on.ca/hansardecat/35-3/l149b-1.htm.

Carr, G. 2003, 8 May. Contempt of Parliament. 37th Parliament, 4th Session. https://www.ola.org/en/legislative-business/house-documents/parliament-37/session-4/2003-05-08/hansard.

Charlton, B. 1993, 5 July. Time Allocation. 35th Parliament, 3rd Session. http://www.ontla.on.ca/web/house-proceedings/house_detail.do?Date=1993-06-08&Parl=35&Sess=3&locale=en#P469_113943.

Christopherson, D. 1999, 13 December. Fewer Politicians Act. 37th Parliament, 1st Session. http://hansardindex.ontla.on.ca/hansardeissue/37-1/l027a.htm.

– 2000, 27 April. Direct Democracy through Municipal Referendums Act. 37th Parliament, 1st Session. http://hansardindex.ontla.on.ca/hansardeissue/37-1/l049.htm.

Churley, M. 1997, 2 April. City of Toronto Act. 36th Parliament, 1st Session. https://www.ola.org/en/legislative-business/house-documents/parliament-36/session-1/1997-04-02/hansard-1.

Clark, S. 2018a, 2 August. Better Local Government Act. 42nd Parliament, 1st Session. https://www.ola.org/en/legislative-business/house-documents/parliament-42/session-1/2018-08-02/hansard#para1407.

– 2018b, 14 August. Better Local Government Act. 42nd Parliament, 1st Session. https://www.ola.org/en/legislative-business/house-documents/parliament-42/session-1/2018-08-14/hansard.

– 2018c, 13 September. Curriculum. 42nd Parliament, 1st Session. https://www.ola.org/en/legislative-business/house-documents/parliament-42/session-1/2018-09-13/hansard.

– 2018d, 17 September. "Efficient Local Government Act." 42nd Parliament, 1st Session. https://www.ola.org/en/legislative-business/house-documents/parliament-42/session-1/2018-09-17/hansard.

Clement, T. 1997, 3 April. City of Toronto Act. 36th Parliament, 1st Session. http://hansardindex.ontla.on.ca/hansardeissue/36-1/l176e.htm.

– 1999, 6 December. Municipal Restructuring. 37th Parliament, 1st Session. http://hansardindex.ontla.on.ca/hansardeissue/37-1/l023a.htm.

– 2000, 25 April. Direct Democracy through Municipal Referendums Act. 37th Parliament, 1st Session. http://hansardindex.ontla.on.ca/hansardespeaker/37-1/l047b-119.html.

Colle, M. 1997a, 15 January. City of Toronto Act, 1996. 36th Parliament, 1st Session. https://www.ola.org/en/legislative-business/house-documents/parliament-36/session-1/1997-01-15/hansard.

– 1997b, 11 December. Red Tape Reduction Act. 36th Parliament, 1st Session. http://www.olip.ontla.on.ca/hansardeissue/36-1/l260b.htm.

Conway, S. 1986, 28 April. Standing Orders Reform. 33rd Parliament, 2nd Session. http://hansardindex.ontla.on.ca/hansardeissue/33-2/l004.htm.

– 1989a, 19 January. Time Allocation. 34th Parliament, 1st Session. https://www.ola.org/en/legislative-business/house-documents/parliament-34/session-1/1989-01-19/hansard.

– 1989b, 18 July. Time Allocation. 34th Parliament, 2nd Session. http://www.ontla.on.ca/web/house-proceedings/house_detail.do?Date=1989-07-18&Parl=34&Sess=2&locale=en#P303_75522.

– 1989c, 25 July. Orders of the Day. 34th Parliament, 2nd Session. http://hansardindex.ontla.on.ca/hansardespeaker/34-2/l047-558.html.

– 1992, 14 July. Time Allocation. 35th Parliament, 2nd Session. http://www.ontla.on.ca:web:house-proceedings:house_detail.do%3FDate=1992-07-14&Parl=35&Sess=2&locale=en.

– 1995, 30 November. Parliamentary Procedure. 36th Parliament, 1st Session. http://www.ontla.on.ca/web/house-proceedings/house_detail.do?Date=1995-11-30&Parl=36&Sess=1&locale=en.

– 2003, 1 May. Contempt of Parliament. 37th Parliament, 4th Session. http://www.ontla.on.ca/web/house-proceedings/house_detail.do?Date=2003-05-01&Parl=37&Sess=4&locale=en#P375_114252.

Cooke, D. 1989a, 29 May. Executive Council Amendment Act. 34th Parliament, 2nd Session. https://www.ola.org/en/legislative-business/house-documents/parliament-34/session-2/1989-05-29/hansard.

– 1989b, 25 July. Standing Orders. 34th Parliament, 2nd Session. http://hansardindex.ontla.on.ca/hansardespeaker/34-2/l047-5101.html.

– 1989c, 20 December. Committee Business. 34th Parliament, 2nd Session. http://www.ontla.on.ca/web/house-proceedings/house_detail.do?Date=1989-12-20&Parl=34&Sess=2&locale=en.

– 1990, 3 April. Time Allocation. 34th Parliament, 2nd Session. http://www.ontla.on.ca/web/house proceedings/house_current.do?locale=en&Month=4&Year=1990.

– 1991, 10 April. Time Allocation. 35th Parliament, 1st Session. https://www.ola.org/en/legislative-business/house-documents/parliament-35/session-1/1991-04-10/hansard.

– 1992, 25 June. Parliamentary Procedure. 35th Parliament, 2nd Session. http://www.ontla.on.ca/web/house-proceedings/house_detail.do?Date=1992-06-25&Parl=35&Sess=2&locale=en.

Cordiano, J. 1997, 19 January. Time Allocation. 36th Parliament, 1st Session. http://www.ontla.on.ca/web/house-proceedings/house_detail.do?Date=1997-01-29&Parl=36&Sess=1&locale=en#P433_117556.

Cousens, D. 1991, 13 May. Parliamentary Process. 35th Parliament, 1st Session. http://hansardindex.ontla.on.ca/hansardespeaker/35-1/l032-311.html.

Damerla, D. 2012, 29 August. Putting Students First Act. 40th Parliament, 1st Session. http://www.ontla.on.ca/web/house-proceedings/house_detail.do?locale=en&Date=2012-08-29&detailPage=%2Fhouse-proceedings%2Ftranscripts%2Ffiles_html%2F29-AUG-2012_L071B.htm&Parl=40&Sess=1#PARA25.

Davis, B. 1981, 23 April. Severance Pay. 32nd Parliament, 1st Session. http://hansardindex.ontla.on.ca/hansardeissue/32-1/l002.htm.

– 1983, 15 February. Metro Toronto Bill. 32nd Parliament, 2nd Session. http://www.olip.ontla.on.ca/hansardespeaker/32-2/l212-380.html.

Di Novo, C. 2013, 2 October. Time Allocation. 40th Parliament, 2nd Session. http://hansardindex.ontla.on.ca/hansardeissue/40-2/l067.htm.

Di Santo, O. 1982, 5 October. Inflation Restraint Act. 32nd Parliament, 2nd Session. http://hansardindex.ontla.on.ca/hansardeissue/32-2/l112.htm.

Drainville, D. 1993, 5 July. Time Allocation. 35th Parliament, 3rd Session. http://www.ontla.on.ca/web/house-proceedings/house_detail.do?Date=1993-06-08&Parl=35&Sess=3&locale=en#P469_113943.

Duncan, D. 2003, 2 December. Business of the House. 38th Parliament, 1st Session. http://www.ontla.on.ca/web/house-proceedings/house_detail.do?locale=en&Date=2003-12-02&Parl=38&Sess=1&detailPage=/house-proceedings/transcripts/files_html/2003-12-02_L008B.htm#tidyout.

– 2004, 10 June. Time Allocation. 38th Parliament, 1st Session. http://www.ontla.on.ca/web/house-proceedings/house_detail.do?Date=2004-06-10&Parl=38&Sess=1&locale=en.

– 2012, 19 July. Ministry of Finance. Official Transcripts of the Standing Committee on Estimates. 40th Parliament, 1st Session. http://www.ontla.on.ca/web/committee-proceedings/committee_transcripts_details.do?locale=en&Date=2012-07-19&ParlCommID=8956&BillID=&Business=Ministry+of+Finance&DocumentID=26502.

Edighoffer, H. 1988, 14 April. Petitions. 34th Parliament, 1st Session. http://www.ontla.on.ca/web/house-proceedings/house_detail.do?Date=1988-04-14&Parl=34&Sess=1&locale=en.

– 1989a, 23 January. Time Allocation. 34th Parliament, 1st Session. http://www.olip.ontla.on.ca/hansardeissue/34-1/l133.htm.

– 1989b, 29 May. Premier's Comments. 34th Parliament, 2nd Session. http://www.olip.ontla.on.ca/hansardeissue/34-2/l019.htm.

Elston, M. 1994, 13 June. Budget Measures Act. 35th Parliament, 3rd Session. http://hansardindex.ontla.on.ca/hansardecat/35-3/l142a-6.htm.

Eves, E. 1991, 10 April. Time Allocation. 35th Parliament, 1st Session. http://www.ontla.on.ca/web/house-proceedings/house_detail.do?Date=1991-04-10&Parl=35&Sess=1&locale=en.

– 1992, July 14. Time Allocation. 35th Parliament, 2nd Session. http://www.ontla.on.ca/web/house-proceedings/house_detail.do?Date=1992-07-14&Parl=35&Sess=2&locale=en.

Faubert, F. 1988, 14 April. Petitions. 34th Parliament, 1st Session. http://www.ontla.on.ca/web/house-proceedings/house_detail.do?Date=1988-04-14&Parl=34&Sess=1&locale=en.

Ford, D. 2018a, 30 July. Municipal Elections. 42nd Parliament, 1st Session. https://www.ola.org/en/legislative-business/house-documents/parliament-42/session-1/2018-07-30/hansard.

– 2018b, 2 August. Municipal Government. 42nd Parliament, 1st Session. https://www.ola.org/en/legislative-business/house-documents/parliament-42/session-1/2018-08-02/hansard.

– 2018c, 12 September. Municipal Elections. 42nd Parliament, 1st Session. https://www.ola.org/en/legislative-business/house-documents/parliament-42/session-1/2018-09-12/hansard.

– 2018d, 13 September. Municipal Elections. 42nd Parliament, 1st Session. https://www.ola.org/en/legislative-business/house-documents/parliament-42/session-1/2018-09-13/hansard.

– 2018e, 27 September. Oral Questions. 42nd Parliament, 1st Session. http://hansardindex.ontla.on.ca/hansardespeaker/42-1/l029-3_2.html.

– 2018f, 15 October. Employment Standards. 42nd Parliament, 1st Session. https://www.ola.org/en/legislative-business/house-documents/parliament-42/session-1/2018-10-15/hansard.

– 2019a, 20 March. Hunting and Fishing. 42nd Parliament, 1st Session. https://www.ola.org/en/legislative-business/house-documents/parliament-42/session-1/2019-03-20/hansard.

– 2019b, 4 April. Government Accountability. 42nd Parliament, 1st Session. https://www.ola.org/en/legislative-business/house-documents/parliament-42/session-1/2019-04-04/hansard.

Foulds, J. 1982, 23 September. Inflation Restraint Act. 32nd Parliament, 2nd Session. http://hansardindex.ontla.on.ca/hansardeissue/32-2/l101.htm.

Gilchrist, S. 1996, 10 October. Fewer Politicians Act. 36th Parliament, 1st Session. https://www.ola.org/en/legislative-business/house-documents/parliament-36/session-1/1996-10-10/hansard.

Gillies, P. 1986, 19 June. Time Allocation. 33rd Parliament, 2nd Session. http://www.olip.ontla.on.ca/hansardespeaker/33-2/l035-116.html.

Grandmaître, B. 1994, 2 November. Planning and Municipal Statute Law Amendment Act. 35th Parliament, 3rd Session. http://hansardindex.ontla.on.ca/hansardecat/35-3/l152-7.htm.

Grier, R. 1993, 26 July. Expenditure Control Plan Statute Law Amendment Act. 35th Parliament, 3rd Session. http://hansardindex.ontla.on.ca/hansardecat/35-3/l054a-5.htm.

Grossman, L. 1986, 19 June. Time Allocation. 33rd Parliament, 2nd Session. http://hansardindex.ontla.on.ca/hansardetitle/33-2/l035-111.html.

Harris, M. 1989, 24 January. Time Allocation. 34th Parliament, 1st Session. http://hansardindex.ontla.on.ca/hansardeissue/34-1/l134.htm.

– 1991, 6 May. House Business. 35th Parliament, 1st Session. http://www.ontla.on.ca/web/house-proceedings/house_detail.do?Date=1991-05- 06&Parl=35&Sess=1&locale=en.

Hillier, R. 2013, 29 May. Order of Business. 40th Parliament, 2nd Session. http://hansardindex.ontla.on.ca/hansardeissue/40-2/l046.htm.

Johnson, D. 1996, 9 October. Fewer Politicians Act. 36th Parliament, 1st Session. http://hansardindex.ontla.on.ca/hansardETITLE/36-1/L106-81.html.

– 1997a, 2 April 1997, 2 April. City of Toronto Act. 36th Parliament, 1st Session. http://hansardindex.ontla.on.ca/hansardeissue/36-1/l176b.htm.

– 1997b, 22 April. Time Allocation. 36th Parliament, 1st Session. http://www.ontla.on.ca/web/house-proceedings/house_detail.do?Date=1997-04-22&Parl=36&Sess=1&locale=en.

– 1997c, 16 June. Standing Orders Reform. 36th Parliament, 1st Session. http://www.ontla.on.ca/web/house-proceedings/house_detail.do?Date=1997-06-16&Parl=36&Sess=1&locale=en#P347_94941.

Johnston, R.F. 1989, 20 December. Committee Business. 34th Parliament, 2nd Session. http://www.ontla.on.ca/web/house-proceedings/house_detail.do?Date=1989-12-20&Parl=34&Sess=2&locale=en.

Kormos, P. 1989, 29 May. Executive Council Amendment Act. 34th Parliament, 2nd Session. https://www.ola.org/en/legislative-business/house-documents/parliament-34/session-2/1989-05-29/hansard.

– 1990a, 4 April. Orders of the Day. 34th Parliament, 2nd Session. https://www.ola.org/en/legislative-business/house-documents/parliament-34/session-2/1990-04-04/hansard.

– 1990b, 27 April. Time Allocation. 34th Parliament, 2nd Session. http://www.ontla.on.ca/web/house-proceedings/house_detail.do?Date=1990-04-27&Parl=35&Sess=1&locale=en.

– 1992, 25 June. Parliamentary Procedure. 35th Parliament, 2nd Session. http://www.ontla.on.ca/web/house-proceedings/house_detail.do?Date=1992-06-25&Parl=35&Sess=2&locale=en.

– 1997, 3 April. City of Toronto Act. 36th Parliament, 1st Session. http://hansardindex.ontla.on.ca/hansardeissue/36-1/l176e.htm.

– 2003a, 26 June. Time Allocation. 37th Parliament, 4th Session. http://www.ontla.on.ca/web/house-proceedings/house_detail.do?Date=2003-6-26&Parl=37&Sess=4&locale=en.

– 2003b, 2 December. Business of the House. 38th Parliament, 1st Session. http://www.ontla.on.ca/web/house-proceedings/house_detail.do?locale=en&Date=2003

-12-02&Parl=38&Sess=1&detailPage=/house-proceedings/transcripts/files _html/2003-12-02_L008B.htm - tidyout.

– 2004, 22 June. Ministry of Consumer and Business Services Statute Law Amendment Act. 38th Parliament, 1st Session. https://www.ola.org/en/legislative -business/house-documents/parliament-38/session-1/2004-06-22 /hansard-1.

– 2006, 4 April. Emergency Management Amendment Act. 38th Parliament, 2nd Session. http://www.ontla.on.ca/house-proceedings/transcripts/files_html /2006-04-06_L056.htm#PARA745.

Lankin, F. 1997, 2 April. Time Allocation. 39th Parliament, 1st Session. http://www .ontla.on.ca/web/house-proceedings/house_detail.do?Date=1997-04-02&Parl=36 &Sess=1&locale=en#P6_605.

Laughren, F. 1991, 29 April. Budget Speech. 35th Parliament, 1st Session. http:// www.ontla.on.ca/web/house-proceedings/house_detail.do?Date=1991-04-29 &Parl=35&Sess=1&locale=en.

– 1992, 30 April. Budget Speech, 35th Parliament, 2nd Session. http://www.ontla .on.ca/web/house-proceedings/house_detail.do?Date=1992-04-30&Parl=35 &Sess=2&locale=en.

– 1993, 19 May. Budget Speech. 35th Parliament, 1st Session. http:// www.ontla.on.ca/web/house-proceedings/house_detail.do?Date=1993-05-19&Parl =35&Sess=3&locale=en#P460_98736.

Leach, A. 1997a, 14 January. City of Toronto Act. 36th Parliament, 1st Session. http://hansardindex.ontla.on.ca/hansardecat/36-1/l144-6.htm.

– 1997b, 15 January. City of Toronto Act. 36th Parliament, 1st Session. http:// hansardindex.ontla.on.ca/hansardecat/36-1/l145-6.htm.

Leone, R. 2012a, 16 May. Ministry of Energy. Standing Committee on Estimates. 40th Parliament, 1st Session. http://www.ontla.on.ca/web/committee -proceedings/committee_transcripts_details.do?locale=en&Date=2012-05-16 &ParlCommID=8956&BillID=&Business=Ministry+of+Energy&DocumentID =26345#P56_3019.

– 2012b, 27 August. Members' Privileges. 40th Parliament, 1st Session. http:// www.ontla.on.ca/web/house-proceedings/house_detail.do?Date=2012-08-27&Parl =40&Sess=1&locale=en#P414_112575.

Levac, D. 2012, 13 September. Members' Privileges. 40th Parliament, 1st Session. http://www.ontla.on.ca/web/house-proceedings/house_detail.do?Date=2012-09 -13&Parl=40&Sess=1&locale=en#P164_62149.

Mackenzie, B. 1989, 18 July. Time Allocation. 34th Parliament, 2nd Session. http:// www.ontla.on.ca/web/house-proceedings/house_detail.do?Date=1989-07-18 &Parl=34&Sess=2&locale=en#P303_75522.

Mahoney, S. 1992, 25 June. Parliamentary Procedure. 35th Parliament, 2nd Session. http://www.ontla.on.ca/web/house-proceedings/house_detail.do?Date=1992-06-25 &Parl=35&Sess=2&locale=en.

Marchese, R. 2004, 29 March. Education Funding. 38th Parliament, 1st Session. http://www.olip.ontla.on.ca/hansardeissue/38-1/l022.htm.

Martel, E. 1983, 15 February. Consideration of Bill 127. 32nd Parliament, 2nd Session. http://hansardindex.ontla.on.ca/hansardeissue/32-2/l213.htm.

Martel, S. 1991a, 10 April. Time Allocation. 35th Parliament, 1st Session. http://www.ontla.on.ca/web/house-proceedings/house_detail.do?Date=1991-04-10&Parl=35&Sess=1&locale=en.

– 1991b, 13 May. Parliamentary Process. 35th Parliament, 1st Session. http://hansardindex.ontla.on.ca/hansardespeaker/35-1/l032-36.html.

– 1992, 16 April. Waste Management Act. 35th Parliament, 2nd Session. http://www.ontla.on.ca/web/house-proceedings/house_detail.do?Date=1992-04-16&Parl=35&Sess=2&locale=en.

Martin, T. 2002, 16 October. Government Efficiency Act. 37th Parliament, 2nd Session. http://www.ontla.on.ca/house-proceedings/transcripts/files_html/2002-10-16_L043B.htm#PARA29.

McGuinty, D. 1997, 23 January. Government Advertising. 36th Parliament, 1st Session. http://hansardindex.ontla.on.ca/hansardespeaker/36-1/l150-156.html.

– 1999, 6 December. Municipal Restructuring. 37th Parliament, 1st Session. https://www.ola.org/en/legislative-business/house-documents/parliament-37/session-1/1999-12-06/hansard.

– 2012, 2 October. Members' Privileges. 40th Parliament, 1st Session. http://www.ontla.on.ca/web/house-proceedings/house_detail.do?Date=2012-10-02&Parl=40&Sess=1&locale=en#P308_88930.

McLean, A. 1995a, 5 December. Parliamentary Procedure. 36th Parliament, 1st Session. https://www.ola.org/en/legislative-business/house-documents/parliament-36/session-1/1995-12-05/hansard.

– 1995b, 6 December. Orders of Business. 36th Parliament, 1st Session. http://www.ontla.on.ca/web/house-proceedings/house_detail.do?Date=1995-12-06&Parl=36&Sess=1&locale=en.

McLeod, L. 1995, 30 November. Parliamentary Procedure. 36th Parliament, 1st Session. http://www.ontla.on.ca/web/house-proceedings/house_detail.do?Date=1995-11-30&Parl=36&Sess=1&locale=en.

– 1999, 7 December. Safe Streets Act. 37th Parliament, 1st Session. http://hansardindex.ontla.on.ca/hansardeissue/37-1/l024b.htm.

Miller, F. 1982, 23 September. Inflation Restraint Act. 32nd Parliament, 2nd Session. http://hansardindex.ontla.on.ca/hansardeissue/32-2/l101.htm.

– 1985, 18 June. Speech from the Throne. 33rd Parliament, 1st Session. http://www.ontla.on.ca/web/house-proceedings/house_detail.do?Date=1985-06-18&Parl=33&Sess=1&locale=en.

Milloy, J. 2012, 4 September. Time Allocation. 40th Parliament, 1st Session. http://www.ontla.on.ca/web/house-proceedings/house_detail.do?Date=2012-09-04&Parl=40&Sess=1&locale=en#P687_180127.

Morin, G. 1992, 6 May. Gasoline Tax Amendment Act. 35th Parliament, 2nd Session. http://www.ontla.on.ca/web/house-proceedings/house_detail.do?Date=1992-05-06&Parl=35&Sess=2&locale=en.

– 1997, 5 April. City of Toronto Act. 36th Parliament, 1st Session. http://hansardindex.ontla.on.ca/hansardeissue/36-1/1176h.htm.

Nixon, B. 1983, 17 February. Consideration of Bill 127. 32nd Parliament, 2nd Session. http://www.olip.ontla.on.ca/hansardespeaker/32-2/1215-315.html.

– 1984, 25 June. Time Allocation. 32nd Parliament, 4th Session. http://hansardindex.ontla.on.ca/hansardeissue/32-4/1081.htm.

– 1985, 18 June. Speech from the Throne. 33rd Parliament, 1st Session. http://www.ontla.on.ca/web/house-proceedings/house_detail.do?Date=1985-06-18&Parl=33&Sess=1&locale=en.

O'Neill, Y. 1991, 10 April. Time Allocation. 35th Parliament, 1st Session. http://www.ontla.on.ca/web/house-proceedings/house_detail.do?Date=1991-04-10&Parl=35&Sess=1&locale=en.

Peterson, D. 1985, 2 July. Legislative Program. 33rd Parliament, 1st Session. http://www.ontla.on.ca/web/house-proceedings/house_detail.do?Date=1985-07-02&Parl=33&Sess=1&locale=en.

Phillip, E. 1992, 6 May. Gasoline Tax Amendment Act. 35th Parliament, 2nd Session. http://www.ontla.on.ca/web/house-proceedings/house_detail.do?Date=1992-05-06&Parl=35&Sess=2&locale=en.

Prue, M. 2004, 7 December. Time Allocation. 38th Parliament, 1st Session. http://www.ontla.on.ca/web/house-proceedings/house_detail.do?Date=2004-12-07&Parl=38&Sess=1&locale=en#P425_96892.

– 2012, 7 May. Strong Action for Ontario Act. 40th Parliament, 1st Session. https://www.ola.org/en/legislative-business/house-documents/parliament-40/session-1/2012-05-07/hansard.

Rae, B. 1982a, 30 November. Inflation Restraint Act. 32nd Parliament, 2nd Session. http://hansardindex.ontla.on.ca/hansardeissue/32-2/1158.htm.

– 1982b, 8 December. Consideration of Bill 179. 32nd Parliament, 2nd Session. http://hansardindex.ontla.on.ca/hansardeissue/32-2/1167.htm.

– 1982c, 9 December. Inflation Restraint Act. 32nd Parliament, 2nd Session. http://hansardindex.ontla.on.ca/hansardespeaker/32-2/1168-77.html.

– 1986, 19 June. Time Allocation. 33rd Parliament, 2nd Session. http://hansardindex.ontla.on.ca/hansardetitle/33-2/1035-111.html.

– 1989a, 10 January. Report by Committee: Standing Committee on Administration of Justice. 34th Parliament, 1st Session. http://hansardindex.ontla.on.ca/hansardeissue/34-1/1127.htm.

– 1989b, 30 January. Time Allocation. 34th Parliament, 1st Session. http://hansardindex.ontla.on.ca/hansardeissue/34-1/1137.htm.

Runciman, B. 1994, 29 November. Time Allocation. 35th Parliament, 3rd Session. http://hansardindex.ontla.on.ca/hansardespeaker/35-3/1163-611.html.

Silipo, T. 1997, 2 April. City of Toronto Act. 36th Parliament, 1st Session. https://www.ola.org/en/legislative-business/house-documents/parliament-36/session-1/1997-04-02/hansard-1.

– 1981a, 19 November. Ontario Energy Investment. 32nd Parliament, 1st Session. http://hansardindex.ontla.on.ca/hansardeissue/32-1/l103.htm.

– 1981b, 30 November. Ontario Energy Investment. 32nd Parliament, 1st Session. http://hansardindex.ontla.on.ca/hansardeissue/32-1/l084.htm.

Smith, T. 2018a, 13 September. Standing Orders. 42nd Parliament, 1st Session. https://www.ola.org/en/legislative-business/house-documents/parliament-42/session-1/2018-09-13/hansard.

– 2018b, 17 September. Efficient Local Government Act. 42nd Parliament, 1st Session. https://www.ola.org/en/legislative-business/house-documents/parliament-42/session-1/2018-09-17/hansard.

– 2019a, 3 April. Health Care. 42nd Parliament, 1st Session. https://www.ola.org/en/legislative-business/house-documents/parliament-42/session-1/2019-04-03/hansard.

– 2019b, 4 April. Government Accountability. 42nd Parliament, 1st Session. https://www.ola.org/en/legislative-business/house-documents/parliament-42/session-1/2019-04-04/hansard.

Snobelen, J. 1997, 21 January. Fewer School Boards Act. 36th Parliament, 1st Session. http://hansardindex.ontla.on.ca/hansardecat/36-1/l148-7.htm.

Sorbara, G. 1992a, 25 June. Parliamentary Procedure. 35th Parliament, 2nd Session. http://www.ontla.on.ca/web/house-proceedings/house_detail.do?Date=1992-06-25&Parl=35&Sess=2&locale=en.

– 1992b, 20 July. Time Allocation. 35th Parliament, 2nd Session. http://www.ontla.on.ca/web/house-proceedings/house_detail.do?Date=1992-07-20&Parl=35&Sess=2&locale=en.

– 1993, 17 June. Social Contract Act. 35th Parliament, 3rd Session. http://hansardindex.ontla.on.ca/hansardecat/35-3/l034a-8.htm.

Stephenson, B. 1982, 5 October. Inflation Restraint Act. 32nd Parliament, 2nd Session. Retrieved: http://hansardindex.ontla.on.ca/hansardeissue/32-2/l112.htm.

– 1983, 15 February. Consideration of Bill 127. 32nd Parliament, 2nd Session. http://www.olip.ontla.on.ca/hansardeissue/32-2/l212.htm.

Sterling, N. 1991, 6 May. House Business. 35th Parliament, 1st Session. http://www.ontla.on.ca/web/house-proceedings/house_detail.do?Date=1991-05-06&Parl=35&Sess=1&locale=en.

Stockwell, C. 1997a. 2 April. City of Toronto Act. 36th Parliament, 1st Session. https://www.ola.org/en/legislative-business/house-documents/parliament-36/session-1/1997-04-02/hansard-1.

– 1997b, 22 April. Time Allocation. 36th Parliament, 1st Session. http://www.ontla.on.ca/web/house-proceedings/house_detail.do?Date=1997-04-22&Parl=36&Sess=1&locale=en.

Sullivan, B. 1993, 26 July. Expenditure Control Plan Statute Law Amendment Act. 35th Parliament, 3rd Session. http://hansardindex.ontla.on.ca/hansardecat/35-3/1054a-5.htm.

Tabuns, P. 2018, 2 August. Better Local Government Act. 42nd Parliament, 1st Session. https://www.ola.org/en/legislative-business/house-documents/parliament-42/session-1/2018-08-02/hansard.

Tilson, D. 1994, 31 October. Statute Law Amendment Act. 35th Parliament, 3rd Session. http://hansardindex.ontla.on.ca/hansardecat/35-3/1150-8.htm.

Turner, J. 1982, 8 December. "Consideration of Bill 179." 32nd Parliament, 2nd Session. http://hansardindex.ontla.on.ca/hansardeissue/32-2/1167.htm.

Ward, C. 1989, 20 December. Committee Business. 34th Parliament, 2nd Session. https://www.ola.org/en/legislative-business/house-documents/parliament-34/session-2/1989-12-20/hansard#P7_163.

– 1990, 3 April. Time Allocation. 34th Parliament, 2nd Session. http://www.ontla.on.ca/web/houseproceedings/house_current.do?locale=en&Month=4&Year=1990.

Warner, D. 1991, 27 May. Parliamentary Procedure. 35th Parliament, 1st Session. http://www.ontla.on.ca/web/house-proceedings/house_detail.do?Date=1991-05-27&Parl=35&Sess=1&locale=en.

– 1992, 21 July. Time Allocation. 35th Session, 2nd Session. http://www.ontla.on.ca/web/house-proceedings/house_detail.do?Date=1992-07-21&Parl=35&Sess=2&locale=en.

Welch, B. 1981, 3 November. Interim Supply. 32nd Parliament, 1st Session. http://hansardindex.ontla.on.ca/hansardeissue/32-1/1088.htm.

Wells, T. 1982, 8 December. Consideration of Bill 179. 32nd Parliament, 2nd Session. http://hansardindex.ontla.on.ca/hansardeissue/32-2/1167.htm.

– 1983, 16 February. Consideration of Bill 127. 32nd Parliament, 2nd Session. http://www.olip.ontla.on.ca/hansardespeaker/32-2/1214-4170.html.

– 1984, 25 June. Time Allocation. 32nd Parliament, 4th Session. http://hansardindex.ontla.on.ca/hansardeissue/32-4/1081.htm.

Wildman, B. 1997a, 22 April. Time Allocation. 36th Parliament, 1st Session. http://www.ontla.on.ca/web/house-proceedings/house_detail.do?Date=1997-04-22&Parl=36&Sess=1&locale=en.

– 1997b, 17 June. Standing Orders Reform. 36th Parliament, 1st Session. http://www.ontla.on.ca/web/house-proceedings/house_detail.do?Date=1997-06-17&Parl=36&Sess=1&locale=en#P361_87207.

– 1997c, 11 September. Orders of the Day. Standing Orders Reform. 36th Parliament, 1st Session. http://www.olip.ontla.on.ca/hansardespeaker/36-1/1228-6141.html.

– 1997d, 16 December. Time Allocation. 36th Parliament, 1st Session. http://www.ontla.on.ca/web/house-proceedings/house_detail.do?locale=en&Date=1997-12-16&Parl=36&Sess=1&detailPage=/house-proceedings/transcripts/files_html/1997-12-16_L262b.htm#tidyout.

Wilson, J. 1993, 8 December. Ontario Drug Benefit Plan. 35th Parliament, 3rd Session. http://hansardindex.ontla.on.ca/hansardeissue/35-3/1095a.htm.

– 2013, 28 May. Order of Business. 40th Parliament, 2nd Session. http://www.ontla.on.ca/web/house-proceedings/house_detail.do?Date=2013-05-28&Parl=40&Sess=2&locale=en.

Wynne, K. 2013, 25 April. Power Plants. 40th Parliament, 2nd Session. http://hansardindex.ontla.on.ca/hansardespeaker/40-2/l031-310.html.

Zimmer, D. 2006, 4 April. Good Government Act. 38th Parliament, 2nd Session. http://www.ontla.on.ca/house-proceedings/transcripts/files_html/2006-04-04_L054.htm#PARA992.

Bills Passed by the Legislative Assembly

Bill 2: Fiscal Transparency and Accountability Act. 2004. 1st Reading 10 December 2003, 37th Parliament, 4th session. https://www.ontario.ca/laws/statute/04f27.

Bill 2: Urgent Priorities Act. 2018. Royal assent 25 July 2018, 42nd Parliament, 1st session. https://www.ola.org/en/legislative-business/bills/parliament-42/session-1/bill-2.

Bill 5: Better Local Government Act. 2018. Royal assent 14 August 2018, 42nd Parliament, 1st session. https://www.ola.org/en/legislative-business/bills/parliament-42/session-1/bill-5.

Bill 17: Capital Investment Plan Act. 1993. 1st Reading 17 May 1993, 35th Parliament, 3rd session. https://archive.org/stream/v1ontariobills199394ontauoft.

Bill 17: Executive Council Amendment Act. 2004. 1st Reading 1 December 2003, 37th Parliament, 4th session. https://www.ontario.ca/laws/statute/s04025.

Bill 25: Fewer Municipal Politicians Act. 2000. 1st Reading 6 December 1999, 37th Parliament, 1st session. http://www.ontla.on.ca/web/bills/bills_detail.do?locale=en&BillID=732&isCurrent=false&ParlSessionID=37:1.

Bill 26: Savings and Restructuring Act. 1996. 1st Reading 29 November 1995, 36th Parliament, 1st session. http://www.ontla.on.ca/web/bills/bills_detail.do?locale=en&BillID=585&isCurrent=false&ParlSessionID=37%3A1.

Bill 31: Efficient Local Government Act. 2018. 1st Reading 12 September 2018, 42nd Parliament, 1st session. https://www.ola.org/en/legislative-business/bills/parliament-42/session-1/bill-31.

Bill 40: Labour Relations Amendment Act. 1992. 1st Reading 4 June 1992, 35th Parliament, 2nd session. https://archive.org/details/v1ontariobills1992ontauoft.

Bill 48: Social Contract Act. 1993. 1st Reading 14 June 1993, 35th Parliament, 3rd session. https://archive.org/details/v2ontariobills199394ontauoft.

Bill 50: Expenditure Control Plan Statute Law Amendment Act. 1993. 1st Reading 14 June 1993, 35th Parliament, 3rd session. https://archive.org/stream/v2ontariobills199394ontauoft.

Bill 55: Strong Action for Ontario Act. 2012. 1st Reading 27 March 2012, 40th Parliament, 1st session. http://www.ontla.on.ca/web/bills/bills_detail.do?locale=en&BillID=2600&detailPage=bills_detail_the_bill.

Bill 57: Restoring Trust, Transparency and Accountability Act. 2018. Royal assent 6 December 2018, 42nd Parliament, 1st session. https://www.ola.org/en/legislative-business/bills/parliament-42/session-1/bill-57.

Bill 66: Restoring Ontario's Competitiveness Act. 2018. Royal assent 3 April 2019, 42nd Parliament, 1st session. https://www.ola.org/en/legislative-business/bills/parliament-42/session-1/bill-66.

Bill 68: Open for Business Act. 2010. First Reading 17 May2010, 39th Parliament, 2nd session. http://www.ontla.on.ca/web/bills/bills_detail.do?locale=en&BillID=2358&isCurrent=false&ParlSessionID=39%3A2.

Bill 74: Education Accountability Act. 2000. 1st Reading 10 May 2000, 37th Parliament, 1st session. http://www.ontla.on.ca/web/bills/bills_detail.do?locale=en&BillID=585&isCurrent=false.

Bill 74: People's Health Care Act. 2019. Royal assent 18 April 2019, 42nd Parliament, 1st session. https://www.ola.org/en/legislative-business/bills/parliament-42/session-1/bill-74#Sched141.

Bill 81: Expenditure Reduction and Non-Tax Revenues Statute Law Amendment Act. 1993. 1st Reading 27 June 1993, 35th Parliament, 3rd session. https://archive.org/stream/v3ontariobills199394ontauoft.

Bill 81: Fewer Politicians Act. 1996. 1st Reading 1 October 1996. 36th Parliament, 1st Session. https://www.ola.org/en/legislative-business/bills/parliament-36/session-1/bill-81.

Bill 99: Balanced Budget and Taxpayer Protection Act. 1998. 1st Reading 14 December 1998. 36th Parliament, 2nd Session. https://www.ola.org/en/legislative-business/bills/parliament-36/session-2/bill-99.

Bill 103: City of Toronto Act. 1997. 1st Reading 16 December 1996, 36th Parliament, 1st Session. http://www.ontla.on.ca/web/bills/bills_detail.do?locale=en&BillID=1489&ParlSessionID=36:1&isCurrent=false.

Bill 104: Fewer School Boards Act. 1997. 1st Reading 13 January 1997, 36th Parliament, 1st session. http://www.ontla.on.ca/web/bills/bills_detail.do?locale=en&BillID=1490&isCurrent=false&ParlSessionID=36%3A1.

Bill 115: Putting Students First Act. 2012. 1st Reading 27 August 2012, 40th Parliament, 1st session. http://www.ontla.on.ca/web/bills/bills_detail.do?BillID=2665.

Bill 127: Municipality of Metropolitan Toronto Amendment Act. 1982. 1st Reading 20 May 1982, 32nd Parliament, 2nd session.

Bill 142: Barrie-Vespra Annexation Act. 1984. 1st Reading 20 March 1984, 32nd Parliament, 4th session. https://archive.org/details/v4ontariobills1984ontauoft.

Bill 143: Credit Unions and Caisses Populaires Act. 1994. 1st Reading 22 March 1994, 35th Parliament, 3rd session. https://www.canlii.org/en/on/laws/stat/so-1994-c-11/latest/so-1994-c-11.html.

Bill 160: Budget Measures Act. 1994. 1st Reading 18 May 1994, 35th Parliament, 3rd session. https://archive.org/stream/v5ontariobills199394ontauoft.

Bill 160: Education Quality Improvement Act. 1997. 1st Reading 22 September 1997, 35th Parliament, 3rd session. https://www.ola.org/en/legislative-business/bills/parliament-36/session-1/bill-160.

Bill 162: Workers' Compensation Amendment Act. 1988. 1st Reading 20 June 1988, 34th Parliament, 1st session. https://archive.org/details/v5ontariobills198789ontauoft.

Bill 175: Statute Law Amendment Act (Government Management and Services). 1994. 1st Reading 6 June 1994, 35th Parliament, 3rd session. https://archive.org/stream/v6ontariobills199394ontauoft.

Bill 179: Inflation Restraint Act. 1982. 1st Reading 21 September 1982, 32nd Parliament, 2nd session. http://booksnow1.scholarsportal.info/ebooks/oca4/42/v4ontariobills198283ontauoft/v4ontariobills198283ontauoft.pdf.

Bill 179: Government Efficiency Act. 2002. 1st Reading 25 September 2002, 37th Parliament, 3rd session. http://www.ontla.on.ca/web/bills/bills_detail.do?locale=en&BillID=1047&isCurrent=false&ParlSessionID=37%3A3.

Bill 213: Act to Amend the Ministry of Colleges and Universities Act. 1982. 1st Reading 21 December 1982, 32nd Parliament, 2nd session.

Index

www.ingramcontent.com/pod-product-compliance
Lightning Source LLC
LaVergne TN
LVHW090156080826
844660LV00013B/832/J

* 9 7 8 1 4 8 7 5 2 8 0 9 6 *